AN ECONOMETRIC MODEL
OF THE INCOME DISTRIBUTION

AN ECONOMETRIC MODEL OF THE INCOME DISTRIBUTION

CHARLES E. METCALF

University of Wisconsin

**Institute for Research
on Poverty Monograph Series**

MARKHAM PUBLISHING COMPANY / CHICAGO

This book is one of a series sponsored by the Institute for Research on Poverty of the University of Wisconsin pursuant to the provisions of the Economic Opportunity Act of 1964.

The Institute for Research on Poverty is a national center for research established at the University of Wisconsin in 1966 by a grant from the Office of Economic Opportunity. Its primary objective is to foster basic, multidisciplinary research into the nature and causes of poverty and means to combat it.

In addition to increasing the basic knowledge from which policies aimed at the elimination of poverty can be shaped, the Institute strives to carry analysis beyond the formulation and testing of fundamental generalizations to the development and assessment of relevant policy alternatives.

The Institute endeavors to bring together scholars of the highest caliber whose primary research efforts are focused on the problem of poverty, the distribution of income, and the analysis and evaluation of social policy, offering staff members wide opportunity for interchange of ideas, maximum freedom for research into basic questions about poverty and social policy, and dissemination of their findings.

To Loretta and Evan

ACKNOWLEDGMENTS

The initial research underlying this monograph was developed for and incorporated into my dissertation, submitted to the Massachusetts Institute of Technology in 1968. The subsequent work has been done while I have been a member of the senior research staff of the Institute for Research on Poverty at the University of Wisconsin. During this time, I have incurred numerous debts of gratitude.

Joseph A. Kershaw and Robert Levine were instrumental in stimulating my initial interest in topics relating to the distribution of income. Edwin Kuh, Robert M. Solow, and E. Cary Brown provided me with encouragement and valuable criticism as members of my dissertation committee. At various stages of this study, extremely helpful comments were also provided by William Branson, Donald Hester, Robinson Hollister, William Niskanen, Guy Orcutt, Lester Thurow, and Harold Watts.

The T. S. P. regression package written by Robert A. Hall, as well as related subroutines written by J. Phillip Cooper, were used during the equation estimation phases of this study. The efforts of Mark Eisner and his Project TROLL staff at M.I.T. and of the programming and consulting staff of the Data and Computation Center at the University of Wisconsin were essential to the success of the simulation phase of the study. The simulations reported in this study were done with a modified form of PROGRAM SIMULATE, written by Charles Holt and others for the Social Systems Research Institute at the University of Wisconsin. Research assistance was provided at various times by Lynn Curtis, Jerry Liboff, Glenn Hueckel, Mark Keaton, and Ken White.

Financial assistance was provided by a National Science Foundation Graduate Fellowship during the early stages of this study. Subsequent support was provided in part by funds granted to the Institute for Research on Poverty by the Office of Economic Opportunity, pursuant to the Economic Opportunity Act of 1964. The opinions expressed in this monograph are the sole responsibility of the author.

Ann Jacobs and Marjean Jondrow provided valuable editorial assistance, while Margaret Witte typed the manuscript in its final form. Permission to use materials initially reported in my doctoral dissertation and developed into articles published in the *American Economic Review* (Copyright © 1969 American Economic Association) and *Public Policy* (Copyright © 1969 by the President and Fellows of Harvard College) is gratefully acknowledged.

FOREWORD

During much of the postwar period, attainment of the aggregate goals of rapid economic growth, full employment, and stable prices has dominated the economic policy agenda. Efforts of both economists and policy makers have focused on the development of monetary and fiscal policy instruments to simultaneously achieve these three goals. As a result of this work, much is now understood regarding how changes in macroeconomic policy instruments alter the rate of economic growth and levels of unemployment and prices.

Curiously, another important effect of changes in macroeconomic policies was neglected in these research and policy efforts. While policy makers and economists all had their own hunches regarding the relationship of aggregate economic performance to the distribution of income, little systematic research was undertaken to identify the relationship. Indeed, although the major econometric models, such as the Brookings and FRB-MIT models, have produced sophisticated insights into the structure of the U.S. economy, none of them have systematically related changes in aggregate levels of output, income, and employment to changes in the size distribution of income. As a result, monetary and fiscal measures have been and are being undertaken with little understanding of their effects on the absolute size of the poverty population and the relative status of the rich and the poor.

In this volume, Charles E. Metcalf summarizes his efforts to identify the systematic relationship between the distribution of income and aggregate economic performance. Because his analysis is based on an econometric model of the United States, it permits the prediction of the effect of fiscal and monetary policies on the distribution of income — specifically on the poverty population. As a result, his study fills in a major gap in our understanding of how policy changes effect the welfare of the people, especially the poor.

This study began in 1967, when Professor Metcalf was a graduate student at the Massachusetts Institute of Technology. An early version of it served as his Ph.D. dissertation at that institution. Further development of the model and analysis took place at the University of Wisconsin, where Professor Metcalf is a member of the department of economics and a staff member of the Institute for Research on Poverty.

Since its inception in 1966, the Institute for Research on Poverty has placed high priority on investigations of the impacts of economic policies on the distribution of income and the poverty population. This study is the second major Institute publication dealing with the issue of macroeconomic policies. The first study, by Robinson G. Hollister and John L. Palmer, "The Impact of Inflation on the Poor," (Discussion Paper #40–69, Institute for Research on Poverty, University of Wisconsin, 1969) focused on the effect of inflation on low income people. Work in this area is continuing at the Institute with attempts to refine and update models of the income distribution similar to that presented in this volume. One of the Institute's objectives is the development of a running, current model for use in the evaluation of the distributive impact of alternative policy proposals.

Robert H. Haveman, Director
Institute for Research on Poverty

CONTENTS

LIST OF TABLES

Chapter 1

INTRODUCTION

As econometric models have grown in size and complexity in an attempt to mirror the structure of the American economy, a determination of the size distribution of personal income has never been included. The Brookings model, for instance, limited its consideration of the income distribution to a determination of factor shares.[1] Issues relating directly to how families or income units are distributed by size of income were never raised.

Two reasons can be cited for this omission. First, data relating to the distribution of income lag far behind other economic data in accuracy and detail, and are not consistent with the national income account data which pervade most econometric models. Second, it is generally presumed that the relative shape of the income distribution has been roughly constant since World War II.[2] A recent study by Schultz failed to estab-

---

[1] See James S. Duesenberry et al. (eds.), *The Brookings Quarterly Econometric Model of the United States* (Chicago: Rand McNally, 1965), chapter 8.

[2] See U.S. Bureau of the Census, *Income Distribution in the United States* (1960 Census Monograph, prepared by Herman P. Miller) (Washington, D.C.: U.S. Government Printing Office, 1966), p. 22: "All available evidence presented in this chapter points to stability in the distribution of family income during the fifties, following a period of rather rapid change during World War II." This conclusion was also reached by T. Paul Schultz in "Secular Trends and Cyclical Behavior of Income Distribution in the United States: 1944–1965," in Lee Soltow (ed.), *Six Papers on the Size Distribution of Wealth and Income* (Studies in Income and Wealth No. 33) (New York: National Bureau of Economic Research, 1969).

lish a significant cyclical pattern in the concentration of personal income.[3] Yet whenever the issue of price stability is discussed, the "adverse" effects of inflation on the distribution of income are persistently cited.[4]

This study intends to correct this omission by examining the relationships between short-run changes in the United States size distribution of income and the state of the aggregate economy. An econometric model is constructed to reflect these relationships and to permit the simulation of effects of alternative economic policies on the distribution of income.

PUBLIC POLICY AND THE INCOME DISTRIBUTION

During the past several years, the persistence of poverty, by a variety of definitions, has been a major concern of United States domestic policy. Although it has since been overshadowed by other political and economic issues, the War on Poverty stood at the center of the political forum in the mid-1960s.

The distribution of income and wealth has long been an issue of government policy, especially during periods of recession or depression.[5] Given its appearance during a time of prosperity and growth, however, the War on Poverty of the 1960s reflected a welfare judgment more forceful and more broadly based than in previous periods of our history. Government transfer payments since World War II have been a larger fraction of personal income than at any previous time in United States history.[6] While enacted welfare policy has continued primarily to take the form of categorical transfer payments[7] or the passive form of a progressive income tax structure, the War on Poverty has been waged explicitly

---

[3] Schultz, "Secular Trends," p. 87.

[4] See, for instance, *Economic Report of the President* and *Annual Report of the Council of Economic Advisers* (Washington, D.C.: U.S. Government Printing Office, 1964, 1968, 1969), particularly 1964, pp. 116–17; 1968, pp. 100–2; and 1969, p. 63.

[5] In addition to the long history of welfare programs for the poor, a progressive federal income tax was instituted (although temporarily) as early as 1865. The Great Depression was a prime force in molding the current United States welfare structure.

[6] During the 1930s government transfer payments peaked at 2.2 percent of disposable personal income in 1933–35 and 2.9 percent in 1938. In contrast, 8.2 percent of disposable personal income came in the form of nonveteran transfer payments in 1968, or 3.1 percent excluding Social Security benefits.

[7] E.g., OASDI, Unemployment Insurance benefits, aid for dependent children, veteran's benefits.

on a general population characterized by inadequacy of living standards rather than on a group adhering to more restrictive classificatory requirements. For this reason, much attention and experimentation, if not action, has been focused on various guaranteed income proposals where the ultimate eligibility criterion is defined in income terms and where the specific program objective is the elimination of poverty per se. The formation of a government agency (OEO) endowed with the sole objective of eliminating poverty symbolized this broader welfare judgment of the 1960s.[8]

When the War on Poverty was initiated, there were some generally accepted presumptions about the postwar size distribution of personal income: first, that the degree of income inequality or, alternatively, the relative shape of the income distribution, has remained roughly constant since World War II[9]; second, that as economic growth shifts the entire income distribution upward in absolute terms, the incidence of poverty would continue to fall but at a declining rate. In 1964 the Council of Economic Advisers estimated that if economic growth alone were relied upon to reduce the level of poverty, 10 to 13 percent of all American families would still be in poverty by 1980.[10]

Given the judgment that economic growth which improved the absolute, but not the relative, level of income going to low income households[11] could not be relied upon to eliminate poverty at an acceptable speed, it was argued that actions designed explicitly to change the relative shape of the income distribution would have to be taken as well.

This study will argue that any presumption that the rate of economic growth, or aggregate fiscal or monetary policies affecting the level of economic activity in general, influences only the position and not the shape of the income distribution is unwarranted. In addition to moving absolutely, incomes at the extremes of the size distribution vary relative to the mean level in a systematic way with fluctuations in economic ac-

---

[8] The fact that a Republican President has, at the time of this writing, endorsed a limited form of the negative income tax (the Family Assistance Plan) is strong evidence of the current force of this welfare judgment.

[9] See footnote 2, p. 1.

[10] See *Economic Report of the President* and *Annual Report of the Council of Economic Advisers*, 1964, p. 60. The Council's projection was disputed by L. Gallaway, "The Foundations of the 'War on Poverty,'" *American Economic Review* 55 (March 1965), 122–31. Also see W. H. Locke Anderson, "Trickling Down: The Relationship between Economic Growth and the Extent of Poverty among American Families," *Quarterly Journal of Economics* 78 (November 1964), 511–24.

[11] Of course, economic growth which leaves the relative shape of the income distribution unchanged will increase the *absolute* difference between low income households and the mean.

tivity. While the precise nature of the relationship of the income distribution to the business cycle varies for different population groups, the following conclusion will be drawn about the size distribution in aggregate terms: during a recession, the incidence of poverty will rise (as a deviation from trend) not only because of a slowdown in the growth of aggregate income but also because incomes in the lower tail of the distribution will tend to fall relative to the mean. That is, in addition to fluctuations in the size of the pie, the *share* of the pie going to low-income households fluctuates with the level of economic activity. Furthermore, fiscal and monetary actions taken in response to periods of inflation or unemployment have predictable effects on the shape of the income distribution. These effects should be accounted for in the evaluation and proposal of public policies concerning the poor.

Using the presumption that the relative shape of the income distribution or the degree of income inequality has been approximately constant since World War II as a working hypothesis for the design of public policy can be particularly misleading. The simplistic appeal of such a hypothesis is that we need only be concerned about the distributional implications of those programs designed specifically to deal with the distribution of income, and that we may ignore the distributional effects of fiscal actions designed to affect the aggregate level of economic activity. Such a presumption implies either that everyone shares proportionally the benefits of sustained economic growth, the costs of inflation in an overheated economy, and the burdens of high unemployment during a recession; or that the distributional effects of the above phenomena somehow offset each other in an approximate manner. I shall contend that such implications are without merit. Virtually every governmental action has distributional implications,[12] often of a substantial magnitude which cannot be ignored, and which should not be concealed behind some rule of thumb about the relative constancy of the degree of income inequality.

We cannot, therefore, measure the distributional effects of government policies simply by observing explicit actions taken in the realm of welfare payments and taxation. Furthermore, just as the need for explicit welfare programs, given a distributional goal, depends upon the effects of other government actions within the overall economic climate, the absence of such explicit programs constitutes neither the absence of a distributional policy nor a decision to leave the distribution of income unchanged. It is, implicitly or explicitly, a decision to accept the distri-

---

[12] Both on a direct microeconomic level in the designation of program beneficiaries, providers of goods and services to the government, and taxpayers; and through influence on the aggregate level of economic activity.

butional consequences of actions taken with regard to inflation, to unemployment, or to the war in Indochina.

We are now faced with a war economy in which a number of economic issues and objectives compete for our attention. Fiscal actions taken now and after the war will have significant effects on the distribution of income and particularly upon the poverty population. In evaluating alternative fiscal actions as well as the need for explicit policy responses to distributional changes, we should endeavor to determine what these effects are.

OBJECTIVES OF THE STUDY

Three objectives will be pursued in this study, in sequence. First, a convenient mechanism will be sought for describing the size distribution of income with a reasonable degree of accuracy. The possibility of incorporating a micro-income distribution into a macroeconomic model would be enhanced if the desired information about the distribution could be condensed into a limited number of descriptive indicators. Measures of income inequality and of the incidence of poverty are competing indicators which have been used in a number of studies. Chapter 2 will point out the inadequacies of such measures and will argue for a functional determination of the entire income distribution.

Second, an attempt is made to characterize a reduced form relationship between the size distribution of personal income and the aggregate level of economic activity. Implicitly, this is done by relating changes in each of six group distributions to fluctuations in alternative sources of personal income. After a review of postwar changes in the United States income distribution in chapter 3, an econometric model of the income distribution is specified and estimated in chapter 4.

Finally, the model of the income distribution is linked to an annual econometric model of the United States economy. The full model is then used in chapter 5 to simulate the impact of some relatively simple aggregate fiscal policies upon the size distribution of income and upon the economy in general. To the extent that the distributional effect of such policies is of concern to society, it would be helpful to observe these effects in a framework consistent with the observation of other economic implications of government action. The policies focused upon will evolve about the war in Indochina, but many of the conclusions will be relevant for stabilization policy in general.

The full model, which appears in the appendix to chapter 5, provides for an endogenous determination of all income components, employment levels, and prices required by the specification of the distributional sector. In addition, the impact of distributional changes upon consumption patterns, tax receipts, and labor force participation is considered; this set of issues has been generally neglected within the conventional framework of econometric models. Ideally this objective could have been achieved by linking a model of the income distribution to a previously existing econometric model of the United States. This alternative turned out to be infeasible.

Given the amount of ground to be covered, the study must be limited in a number of respects. No attempt is made to deal with the inadequacies of the available data. No distributional data exist which are consistent with the national income accounts, either in concept or in totals after accounting for conceptual differences.[13] With income account totals as the norm, data sources dealing with the size distribution yield aggregate income estimates which are biased downward, particularly at the extremes of the distribution.[14] Despite these difficulties, this study utilizes published Current Population Survey data, available annually since 1947.[15] Since the data refer to pretax income, the study will generally

---

[13] A detailed study of sources of United States income distribution data is provided by T. Paul Schultz, *Statistics on the Size Distribution of Personal Income in the United States* (Joint Economic Committee, 1965). Schultz describes the Office of Business Economics (OBE) estimates of the size distribution of personal income, which are consistent with income account totals, as being "probably the most reliable comprehensive aggregate statistics on the size distribution of income in the United States" (p. 50). The April 1964 *Survey of Current Business* gave aggregate data for 1946–61 and preliminary *extrapolated* estimates of the size distribution for 1962–63. The April 1965 *Survey of Current Business* announced that, due to the unreasonableness of continuing to use a 1953 benchmark and due to the lack of funds for revising estimation procedures, distribution series was being discontinued. Furthermore, as Schultz points out, the OBE series was chiefly dependent on tax data and therefore could not be broken down into demographic groupings.

[14] This comment concerns both Current Population Survey and Internal Revenue Service data, the latter of which omits nonreporting units with extremely low incomes, not required to file tax returns. Regarding the Current Population Survey, in 1965 the Department of Commerce conducted a special survey parallel to the CPS for that year, in which interviewers were asked more detailed questions relating to income than they did in the CPS. With the more detailed questioning, the reported incomes in the two tails of the distribution increased by a greater proportion than they did at the median, which was about 3 percent higher than in the Current Population Survey.

[15] U.S. Bureau of the Census, *Current Population Reports*, Ser. P-60, Nos. 1–53, "Consumer Income" (Washington, D.C.: U.S. Government Printing Office, 1948–67).

stay clear of the relationship between the before- and after-tax income distributions.[16]

Specifications for behavioral equations outside the distributional sector of the model will be drawn from other studies whenever possible. In fact, less borrowing of specifications was engaged in than anticipated. Certain other limitations of the model should be acknowledged. Since the monetary sector and the foreign sector are both exogenous to the model, the range of policy simulations which can be attempted is limited. The fact that an annual (rather than quarterly) model was estimated, to coincide with the availability of distributional data, further restricts the flexibility of the model.

Finally, while a variety of policy simulations are reported in the final chapter, no attempt is made to test the robustness of the full model; no random shocks are applied to the model. Only an informal attempt is made to assess the accuracy and reliability of the model.

---

[16]The impact of federal taxes on the distribution has been considered in a dissertation by Benjamin A. Okner (*Income Distribution and the Federal Income Tax,* Institute of Public Administration, University of Michigan, 1966). My omission of this subject results in some inconsistencies in relating distributional changes to consumption functions, since my distribution parameters relate to gross, not *disposable* income.

Chapter 2

CHARACTERIZING THE SIZE DISTRIBUTION OF INCOME

If the size distribution of personal income is to be analyzed within the context of an econometric model based on aggregative data, a convenient mechanism must be found to describe the size distribution. Such a mechanism may reflect a particular feature of the distribution, or it may approximate the entire distribution by a functional form.

Traditionally, the important feature of the size distribution of personal income has been the degree of income inequality. Various measures of income inequality have been developed and discussed in the literature.[1] More recently, attention has been directed specifically to the lower tail of the income distribution; measures of income inequality have been replaced by measures of the portion of the cumulative distribution lying below some absolute income level or conforming to some definition of poverty.[2]

If the distribution is described by a functional form, measures may

---

[1] See T. Paul Schultz, "The Distribution of Personal Income: Case Study of the Netherlands" (Ph.D. diss., Massachusetts Institute of Technology, 1965), pp. 167–96.

[2] See L. Gallaway, "The Foundations of the 'War on Poverty,'" *American Economic Review* 55 (March 1965), 122–31, and communication on the same subject by H. Aaron and L. Gallaway, *American Economic Review* 57 (December 1967), 1229–43; also various articles by M. Orshansky in *Social Security Bulletin* (January and July 1965; April and May 1966).

in general be derived to reflect a variety of specific features. Available functional approximations discussed below include Pareto-Lévy distributions, Pearson curves, and a number of normal transformations. The function ultimately chosen for this study is the displaced lognormal distribution, a normal transformation corresponding formally to the three-parameter lognormal distribution.

MEASURES OF INCOME INEQUALITY

In this study, the use of measures of income inequality[3] is dismissed for two reasons. First, more information is desired about the distribution of income than can be condensed into a single inequality measure. A general index of inequality describes the shape of the complete distribution only under very specialized assumptions. Second, a single measure of inequality, as traditionally defined, may provide an inadequate or misleading picture to persons interested in income inequality itself.

The most commonly used measure of income inequality is the Gini concentration ratio (or Lorenz measure).[4] If the logarithm of income is normally distributed, the Lorenz measure is monotonically related to the variance of the logarithm of income.[5] In this case, the distribution can be defined as easily by the mean and the Lorenz measure as by the mean and the variance; conversely, the variance of the logarithm of income can stand as a measure of income inequality. Once the hypothesis of lognormality is rejected, this strict relationship disappears. A given change in the Lorenz measure can have different and often ambiguous implications for different functional forms.

The Lorenz measure can also be a misleading indicator of income

[3] See Schultz, "Distribution of Personal Income."

[4] See Schultz, "Distribution of Personal Income"; J. Aitchison and J. A. C. Brown, *The Lognormal Distribution* (Cambridge: At the University Press, 1957), esp. pp. 12–13 and 111–15; U.S. Bureau of the Census, *Income Distribution in the United States* (1960 Census Monograph, prepared by Herman P. Miller) (Washington, D.C.: U.S. Government Printing Office, 1966), pp. 220–21. Miller's use of the Gini Index of Concentration, based upon James Morgan, "The Anatomy of Income Distribution," *Review of Economics and Statistics* 44 (August 1962), 270–83, is the same as the Lorenz measure of Aitchison and Brown, but differs from what Aitchison and Brown define to be the Gini coefficient of mean difference, which is not scale free (Aitchison and Brown, *Lognormal Distribution*, p. 113).

[5] See Aitchison and Brown, The *Lognormal Distribution*. The relationship between the Lorenz measure and the variance is discussed in detail in section 11.5 and calibrated in appendix A-1.

inequality itself. Let Figures 1 and 2 depict an assumed frequency distribution for the logarithm of income, where μ is the mean of the logarithms (which equals the log of the median under the assumption of lognormality) and x_1 and x_2 are any two symmetrically defined quantile measures, such as the logarithms of the 10 percent and 90 percent income cutoffs of the distribution. If the log distribution is normal, the frequency curves should be symmetric, as represented. Any change in the shape of the distribution, i.e., a change in the variance or the Lorenz measure of inequality, must retain the symmetry of the logarithmic distribution if relationship is, in fact, lognormal. With the Lorenz measure denoted by L, the following relationships must hold:

$$\begin{aligned}
\partial L / \partial(\sigma^2) &> 0, \\
\partial x_1 / \partial(\sigma^2) &< 0, \\
\partial x_2 / \partial(\sigma^2) &> 0, \\
\partial x_1 / \partial x_2 &= -1.
\end{aligned} \qquad (2.1)$$

Movements in x_1 and x_2 are symmetric, and a decline in the variance and in the Lorenz measure is unambiguously defined as a contraction of both tails of the distribution toward the mean.

If, instead of obeying strict lognormality, the logarithmic distribution has nonzero and changing skewness, the situation depicted in Figure 2, where both x_1 and x_2 rise relative to the median, is conceivable. Because these movements would have an offsetting effect on the Lorenz measure, such an index would indicate in this case that not much has happened to the distribution. The indication would be entirely misleading to anyone interested in either tail of the distribution separately.

Since the Lorenz measure of inequality is monotonically related to the variance of a lognormal distribution, the above arguments also have implications concerning the appropriateness of using the lognormal distribution to approximate the size distribution of income. This issue will be discussed below.

FIGURE 2.1   FIGURE 2.2

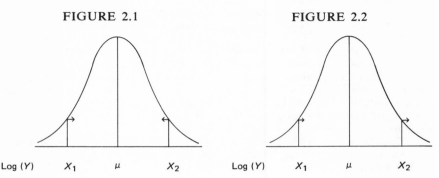

Log (Y) X_1 μ X_2 Log (Y) X_1 μ X_2

DIRECT ESTIMATION OF THE POPULATION IN ABSOLUTE INCOME CELLS

As interest in the War on Poverty increased, the percentage of families earning less than $3000 or conforming to some other measure of poverty commonly appeared as an endogenous variable in regressions explaining changes in the poverty population over time or across states.[6] Such a procedure could be included within a class of approaches in which numbers or proportions of the population are allocated directly to income cells measured in (current or deflated) dollars. While in the usual case the population is divided into two cells (i.e., the poor and nonpoor), one could in a similar way estimate directly the population in any number of income cells for which data are available.

The use of such direct estimation procedures, particularly given a positive time trend in income levels, is completely unsatisfactory for the purposes of this study. The relationship of a given dollar cell to the complete distribution changes as the distribution shifts over time. For instance, an equation determining the percentage of households lying in the $5000–$6000 cell, estimated at a time when the mode of the distribution is below $5000, may be empirically worthless when the mode is above $6000. Similarly (as emphasized by Anderson),[7] if the relative shape of the distribution is fixed, the relation between changes in the proportion of incomes falling below $3000 and changes in the median income level depends upon how far out on the tail of the distribution the $3000 cutoff lies.

If the relative shape of the distribution is not fixed, an additional problem appears. If the percentage of the distribution lying below $3000 is used as a distributional measure, changes resulting from shifts in the position of the distribution may not be distinguished from those resulting from changes in its shape. These two types of changes could easily result from different economic phenomena.

Matters would be improved if the cell were redefined in some relative manner. For instance, if cells were defined as percentages of the mean or median, the cell allocation would be homogeneous of degree zero in income and prices. Changes in the shape of the distribution then could be readily identified.

---

[6] Examples of this approach are Gallaway, "The Foundations of the 'War on Poverty,'" and Lester C. Thurow, "The Causes of Poverty," *Quarterly Journal of Economics* 81 (February 1967), 39–57.

[7] W. H. Locke Anderson, "Trickling Down: The Relationship between Economic Growth and the Extent of Poverty among American Families," *Quarterly Journal of Economics* 78 (November 1964), 511–24.

Further difficulties would remain. Given an allocation of households into a specified number of cells, further assumptions must be made about the form of the distribution to gain a more detailed calibration of the population. In addition, it would be a cumbersome procedure to allocate families directly into n cells with $n - 1$ equations if the distribution could be approximated by a functional form requiring only two or three parameters. The major issue would be whether a simple functional form is sufficiently accurate in its description of the available information.

CHARACTERIZATION OF THE DISTRIBUTION BY A FUNCTIONAL FORM

Descriptions of the distribution of income usually begin with the empirical observation that "in economic data skew frequency curves are the rule rather than the exception."[8] From this point of departure, examinations of the income distribution tend to follow one of two courses. One approach begins with the empirical inadequacy of the normal distribution for a large body of economic data and works back to the implied inappropriateness of the theory of independently generated errors which leads to the normal distribution. The development of an alternative law of errors, implying a distribution of income more in line with empirical observations, would then be attempted. Empirical verification of the theoretical results might then be sought.

A second approach is the pragmatic process of finding a functional form which "fits" the data, without regard for an underlying theoretical justification. The primary emphasis here is upon empirical applications, such as calibration or projection of data cells, rather than upon verification of an underlying process which may not even be perceived.

While the procedure in this study will have the pragmatic flavor of the latter approach, the theoretical development of the lognormal distribution and the Pareto-Lévy law will be considered briefly.

THE LOGNORMAL DISTRIBUTION

The lognormal distribution[9] is defined to be the distribution of a variate whose logarithm obeys the normal law of probability. If changes in in-

---

[8] See Aitchison and Brown, *Lognormal Distribution,* "Preface."

[9] Heavy use will be made of Aitchison and Brown throughout this section.

come are assumed to be multiplicatively defined rather than additively defined, a lognormal distribution is generated. Specifically, income is assumed to be subject to the "law of proportionate effect," defined as follows:

> A variate subject to a process of change is said to obey the law of proportionate effect if the change in the variate at any step of the process is a random proportion of the previous value of the variate.[10]

As a theorem it can be stated that:

> A variate subject to the law of proportionate effect tends for large n, to be distributed as a two parameter [lognormal variate], provided that the sequence X_0, $1 + e_1$, $1 + e_2$, . . . satisfies the conditions of [a multiplicative form of the central limit theorem].[11]

Given that $\log(y) = N(\mu, \sigma^2)$, the following relationships hold for α (mean), β^2 (variance), and λ^3 (third moment about the mean), respectively:[12]

$$\alpha = e^{\mu + 0.5\sigma^2}$$
$$\beta^2 = e^{2\mu + \sigma^2} \cdot (e^{\sigma^2} - 1) = \alpha^2 \eta^2 \qquad (2.2)$$
$$\lambda^3 = \alpha^3(\eta^6 + 3\eta^4) > 0$$

where

$$\eta^2 = e^{\sigma^2} - 1 > 0.$$

Several properties of the lognormal distribution are worth noting. First, since moments of the normal transformation of the distribution are logarithmically defined, σ^2 is homogeneous of degree zero in income and prices; as stated earlier, it is monotonically related to the Lorenz measure of income inequality.

Second, the assumption of lognormality produces a positively skewed distribution, in accordance with observed income data. In the logarithmic (normal) form, μ is both the mean and the median, making the median of the absolute distribution e^μ, compared to a mean of $e^{\mu + 0.5\sigma^2}$. The proportional divergence of the mean from the median is therefore an increasing function of the variance of the logged distribution.

Third, since $\log(0) = -\infty$, the lognormal distribution is defined only

[10] Aitchison and Brown, *Lognormal Distribution*, p. 22.
[11] *Ibid.*, theorem 3.1.
[12] *Ibid.*, p. 8.

over positive income levels. For a wide variety of income definitions, negative incomes are observed empirically, and zero observations are common, depending upon the unit of observation.

The lognormal distribution is simple to work with and has been used in a number of empirical studies. The usefulness of the lognormal distribution is limited, however, in the following sense. While the absolute data are permitted to have a positive third moment, α, β^2, and λ^3 may *not* be observed independently. All moments of the absolute distribution are strict functions of the first two moments of the logarithmic data, μ and σ^2. In logarithmic form, the curve is constrained to be symmetric with a third moment (about μ) equal to zero.

The simple lognormal distribution is rejected as an empirical tool for this study because it is inadequate in two respects. First, it overcorrects for the positive skewness of the data; after logarithmic transformation, the observed distribution typically exhibits negative skewness. The degree of skewness varies over time. Second, it forces a symmetric treatment of movements in the two tails of the distribution. This property severely restricts the ability of the function to characterize cyclical movements in the observed income distribution. While such symmetric reactions might eventually be observed empirically, it does not appear to be a reasonable initial restriction to require, for instance, that changes in unemployment rates, dividend payments, or exogenous transfers must have a symmetric influence on the distribution.

THE PARETO-LÉVY LAW

Perhaps the most serious contender with the lognormal distribution as an underlying theory generating positively skewed income distributions is the Pareto-Lévy law.[13] The essence of the Pareto law is that

> the upper ranges of the income distribution could be described by a curve of the general type, $Y = AX^{-v}$, where X is the income size and Y is the number of persons having that income or larger. The logarithmic form of this curve . . . is . . . a straight line.[14]

---

[13] See Benoit Mandelbrot, "The Pareto-Lévy Law and the Distribution of Income," *International Economics Review* 1 (May 1960), 79–106; also Mandelbrot, "Stable Paretian Random Functions and the Multiplicative Variation of Income," *Econometrica* 29 (October 1961), 517–43. For a discussion of fitting a Pareto curve to the upper end of the income distribution, see U.S. Bureau of the Census, *Income Distribution*, pp. 213–20.

[14] U.S. Bureau of the Census, *Income Distribution*.

Formally, the strongest form of the Pareto-Lévy law is the "strong Pareto law," which asserts that

$$P(u) = \begin{cases} (u/u_0)^{-\alpha} & \text{when } u > u_0 \\ 1 & \text{when } u < u_0, \end{cases} \qquad (2.3)$$

where $P(u)$ is the percentage of individuals with an income level U exceeding some number u, a continuous variable.[15]

A weak form of the Pareto law[16] is that $P(u)$ "behaves like" $(u/u_0)^{-\alpha}$ as $u \rightarrow \infty$, i.e.,

$$\frac{P(u)}{(u/u_0)^{-\infty}} \rightarrow 1 \text{ as } u \rightarrow \infty. \qquad (2.4)$$

The strong Pareto law is rarely claimed to be strictly applicable, but for large incomes the weak Pareto law serves, at the very minimum, as a good approximation.[17]

Mandelbrot defines "Pareto-Lévy distributions" as the class of stable non-Gaussian laws which satisfy the weak Pareto law with $1 < \alpha < 2$. "Stable" laws are defined to be that class of laws for which, if U' and U'' (e.g., two sources of income) follow a given law, then the sum of the random variables $U' \oplus U''$ follows the same law. Paul Lévy has shown that this family of laws is exhausted by the Gaussian law and by what Mandelbrot now refers to as the Pareto-Lévy laws with $0 < \alpha < 2$.[18] The value of α is further restricted to the range $1 < \alpha < 2$ in order to assure that $E(U) < \infty$.

If, therefore, one believes that the same distribution law should apply despite differences in the way income is defined or in the number of income sources aggregated together and, furthermore, if the distribution is clearly non-Gaussian, then the Pareto-Lévy class of distributions is the only available alternative. The lognormal law, based upon multiplicative variations of income, does not possess these convenient additivity properties.

The Pareto-Lévy law is not used in this study for a number of reasons. First, while there is an expression for the limit of $P(u)$ as $u \rightarrow \infty$, there is not an expression for $P(u)$ of the Pareto-Lévy law in closed algebraic form. The Pareto-Lévy law is therefore quite cumbersome to work with except at upper income levels, where the strong Pareto law

---

[15] Mandelbrot, "The Pareto-Lévy Law," pp. 80–81.

[16] *Ibid.*

[17] *Ibid.;* also U.S. Bureau of the Census, *Income Distribution.*

[18] Mandelbrot, "The Pareto-Lévy Law"; the primary reference is Paul Lévy, *Calcul des probabilités* (Paris: Gauthier-Villais, 1925).

can be used as an approximation. Second, despite the additivity properties of the Pareto-Lévy law, it does not appear to be an adequate description of the total income distribution defined across heterogeneous occupational or socioeconomic groups. The Pareto-Lévy law remains "a theory of high income data."[19]

While the Pareto-Lévy law is not used in this study, its convenient additivity properties and its probable superiority to other distributional forms as both a description and an underlying theory of the shape of the upper tail of the distribution must be acknowledged. The empirical concerns of this study require a distributional form which is both easy to handle and a fairly good description of the income distribution, particularly below the median. Because of these priorities, the characterization of the upper tail of the distribution will be less accurate than what is possible with the Pareto-Lévy law.

PRAGMATIC APPROACHES

The above discussion concerns attempts to specify a stable distributional form toward which the distribution of income approaches in the long run, given assumptions about the nature of random disturbances to income. Short-run changes in the shape of the distribution due either to (random or nonrandom) disturbances or to changes in the parameters of the distribution were not considered. If the distribution of income is to be incorporated into an essentially short-run econometric model of the United States, a distributional form capable of reflecting short-run changes in income distribution must be used. The form of the distribution in the limit and its relationship to an underlying generation process are of lesser importance.

The objective, as stated earlier, is to approximate the size distribution of income by a function requiring relatively few parameters. These parameters, or transformations thereof, must be conducive to treatment as endogenous variables in an econometric model of the United States. The following properties would be desirable in such a function:

1. *Simplicity.* The entire distribution should be described by as few parameters as practicable, given the information to be summarized.

---

[19] Mandelbrot, "The Pareto-Lévy Law," p. 82.

For every income group to be characterized, an additional equation is required in the model for each parameter of the distribution function. Since it is argued above that a two-parameter function is *too* simple to reflect the impact of economic fluctuations on the size distribution, a convenient three- (or possibly four-) parameter function will be sought.

2. *The distribution should have known properties.* For instance, if the distribution is a normal transformation, one could proceed from the known properties of normal distributions to the characteristics of the actual distribution. This property is lost in a piecemeal approach, such as fitting a Pareto curve to the upper tail and a lognormal distribution to the remainder.

3. *The parameters of the distribution should be transformable into measures which have direct economic relevance.* For example, if incomes were normally distributed, the variance would be homogeneous of degree two in income and prices. Therefore, a doubling of all prices and money income, having no welfare implications for the distribution, would quadruple the variance measure. Given the resulting positive collinearity in the variance measure, a scale-free transformation of the variance would be more easily manageable and interpretable. If, on the other hand, the logarithm of income were normally distributed (as discussed above), a proportional change in income or prices would affect the position but not the shape of the distribution. Any change in the variance of the distribution would have direct welfare implications.

4. *The error of description should be "small."* The chosen distribution not only should approximate the shape of the observed distribution but also should be flexible enough to characterize changes in the shape of the distribution through changes in parameter values. For a simple example of the lack of such flexibility, suppose that in a given year the income distribution of a population subgroup has zero skewness and that the distribution can be approximated by a normal curve. If the distribution changes the next year in a way that retains the zero skewness, it may be possible to reflect the change by an appropriate shift in the mean and the variance of the normal curve. If the distribution changes such that the data become skewed, the change *cannot* be portrayed by shifting the first two moments of the normal curve. While the normal curve may have provided a good initial fit, it would not have been capable of reflecting relevant changes in the shape of the distribution.

Two pragmatic approaches to curve fitting will be considered below. The first is the Pearson system of four moment distributions. The second is the class of normal transformations of which the lognormal distribution is one example.

PEARSON DISTRIBUTIONS

Pearson distributions[20] are defined as that family of frequency functions [$f(x)$] for which

$$\frac{df}{dx} = \frac{(x - a)f}{b_0 + b_1 x + b_2 x^2}.$$ (2.5)

A member of the Pearson family of distributions is uniquely defined by the first four moments of the distribution. Conversely, a curve form from this family can be found which is consistent with any set of data as measured by its first four moments. On the surface it appears that such a curve system offers great flexibility in characterizing observed income data.[21]

While there are twelve curve forms in the Pearson family, most of these are special cases (including the normal distribution) in which higher moments either vanish or have special configurations relative to each other. Barring such borderline configurations, any given distribution of observations falls into one of three basic curve classifications; two of these are forms of the beta distribution.

For several reasons, the Pearson family is not a particularly useful empirical tool to work with, despite its apparent flexibility.

1. Estimation of the parameters for any given distribution is cumbersome, involving the evaluation of high valued, noninteger gamma functions. The parameters of the distribution must be reestimated for each period of observation.

2. As the observed distribution changes over time, not only the parameters of the distribution but also the curve classification may vary. Instability of the functional form of the assumed distribution would appear to be a prohibitive inconvenience.

3. The classification and the parameter estimation of Pearson curves depend critically on the third and fourth moments of the observed distribution, which are highly unstable when calculated from grouped data. Even a direct estimate of the variance tends to be unreliable. While the classification and the calibration of Pearson curves is based upon knowing the first four moments of the population, Kendall acknowledges the

---

[20] For a detailed discussion of Pearson distributions see M. G. Kendall, *The Advanced Theory of Statistics,* 5th ed. (New York: Hafner, 1952), 1:137–45, 2:43–44. See also W. Palin Elderton, *Frequency Curves and Correlation,* 3d ed. (Cambridge: At the University Press, 1938).

[21] One obvious case to the contrary would be if the upper tail of the distribution does in fact obey the Pareto law, thereby having an infinite variance for an infinite population. While we might be able to approximate the curve for a finite group, the underlying population would not lie within this class.

inefficiency of estimating these moments directly from sample data,[22] even without the further confounding factor of the available data being grouped and having open-ended cells.

NORMAL TRANSFORMATIONS

Given the positive skewness of the observed data, one alternative is to find a transformation of the data which is approximately normal. One such transformation produces the lognormal distribution described above. It was argued earlier that the simple logarithmic transformation over-corrects for the positive skewness in the data, and that as a two-parameter distribution, it is not flexible enough to accommodate nonsymmetric distributional changes.

The transformation utilized in this study is the displaced lognormal distribution, which corresponds formally to the three-parameter log-normal distribution. Rather than the case where $y = N(\alpha, \beta^2)$ or $\log(y) = N(\mu, \sigma^2)$, the situation where $\log(y + c) = N(\mu, \sigma^2)$ is considered, where $c > 0$ is an unknown constant.

Heretofore the three-parameter lognormal distribution has been specified as $\log(y - \tau) = N(\mu, \sigma^2)$, $\tau > 0$, and $\tau < y < \infty$. The existence of some $\tau > 0$ could be reconciled with an underlying theory of a multiplicative error generation process, whereas $\tau < 0$ (equivalent to our $c > 0$) could not. The first known empirical use of a three-parameter lognormal distribution was made by S. D. Wicksell in 1917.[23]

PROPERTIES OF THE DISPLACED LOGNORMAL DISTRIBUTION

Given the empirical assertion that $f(y)$ is positively skewed and $f[\log(y)]$ is negatively skewed, there clearly exists some value of $c > 0$ such that the transformation $\log(y + c)$ has zero skewness, with the range of y being $-c < y < \infty$. That is, c is opposite in sign from its traditional use in three-parameter distributions.

Consider the "shape" of functions $f(y)$, $f[\log(y)]$, and $f[\log(y + c)]$. As the value of c in $f[\log(y + c)]$ is varied continuously from zero to

---

[22] Kendall, *Advanced Theory*, 2:43–44; also "Bibliography," p. 45.
[23] See Aitchison and Brown, *Lognormal Distribution*, pp. 4, 14–16, 55–63.

$+\infty$, the "shape" of $f[\log(y + c)]$ moves from the "shape" of $f[\log(y)]$ to that of $f(y)$.[24]

The displaced lognormal distribution has at least two favorable properties. First, a transformation of the normal distribution which possesses the desired degree of skewness may be fit to the data, unlike the two-parameter lognormal distribution. Second, the degree of skewness in the distribution may vary over time, independently of changes in the variance of the distribution. Three dimensions are available not only to describe the distribution at a point in time, but also to register its movements over time.

When $\log(y + c)$ is assumed to be normally distributed, the variable $(y + c)$ has all the properties of a two-parameter lognormal distribution. If α and β^2 are the mean and the variance of the absolute distribution respectively, then the $(y + c)$ has mean $(\alpha + c)$ and variance β^2. (β^2 is unaffected by the addition of a constant.) Since $(y + c)$ is a simple lognormal distribution, the following relationships can be posited for the mean and the variance:

---

[24] This can be shown by considering the relative distance between any three points along the frequency distribution, say G, H, and J; that is, the distance between H and J relative to the distance between G and H. This relative distance is expressed as $(H - J)/(G - H)$ for $f(y)$, $[\log(H) - \log(J)]/[\log(G) - \log(H)]$ for $f[\log(y)]$, and $[\log(H + C) - \log(J + C)]/[\log(G + C) - \log(H + C)]$ for $f[\log(y + c)]$. The statement that two distributions approach each other in "shape" (i.e., the same except for scale), means that the relative distances among any three arbitrarily chosen points on the one cumulative distribution equal, in the limit, the relative distances among the same three points in the other distribution. What must be shown is that

$$\lim_{c \to 0} \frac{\log(H + C) - \log(J + C)}{\log(G + C) - \log(H + C)} = \frac{\log(H) - \log(J)}{\log(G) - \log(H)},$$

and

$$\lim_{c \to \infty} \frac{\log(H + C) - \log(J + C)}{\log(G + C) - \log(H + C)} = \frac{H - J}{G - H}.$$

The first limit is true by trivial observation. The second limit requires the application of l'Hôpital's rule, where

$$\lim_{c \to \infty} \frac{\log(H + C) - \log(J + C)}{\log(G + C) - \log(H + C)} = \lim_{c \to \infty} \frac{[(J + C)/(H + C)] \cdot [(J - H)/(J + C)^2]}{[(H + C)/(G + C)] \cdot [(H - G)/(H + C)^2]},$$

$$\lim_{c \to \infty} \frac{(J - H) \cdot (G + C)}{(H - G) \cdot (J + C)} \lim_{c \to \infty} \frac{J - H}{H - G} = \frac{H - J}{G - H}.$$

Since continuous variation of c moves the function from negative to positive skewness, there exists some value of $c > 0$ for which the coefficient of skewness is zero for $f[\log(Y + C)]$, provided that the value of the coefficient moves continuously and monotonically.

$$\alpha + c = e^{\mu + 0.5\sigma^2} \tag{2.6}$$

$$\beta^2 = e^{2\mu + \sigma^2}(e^{\sigma^2} - 1)$$
$$= (\alpha + c)^2 \eta^2 \tag{2.7}$$

where

$$\eta^2 = (e^{\sigma^2} - 1) > 0.$$

Similarly,

$$\lambda^3 = (\alpha + c)^3(\eta^6 + 3\eta^4) > 0. \tag{2.8}$$

As before, μ is the mean and the median of normally distributed log $(y + c)$. Therefore, e^μ is the median of $(y + c)$, or

$$e^\mu = (d + c), \quad d = \text{median value of } y. \tag{2.9}$$

Equations (2.6) and (2.7) may be solved by the independent estimation of any three of the five included parameters.

PARAMETER ESTIMATION, DISPLACED LOGNORMAL DISTRIBUTION

When methods of estimation are considered, elegance and convenience conflict directly with each other. The straight quantile methods chosen for use in this study compare well with other nonmaximum likelihood methods in terms of efficiency, and can also provide exceedingly simple solutions.[25]

Consider choosing the median plus two other quantiles placed symmetrically on the two tails of the distribution, such as the 10 percent and 90 percent deciles. Suppose the median is observed at \$d, and the dollar cutoffs of the lower and upper deciles at \$h \cdot d and \$j \cdot d respectively. From the assumption of normality of the transformed distribution, both log $(hd + c)$ and log $(jd + c)$ should be equidistant from the median (mean) of the transformed distribution, log $(d + c)$. That is, both distances, standardized by σ, should equal the number of standard deviations away from the mean appropriate for the chosen quantiles:

$$\frac{\log[(d + c)/(hd + c)]}{\sigma} = \frac{\log[(jd + c)/(d + c)]}{\sigma} = g. \tag{2.10}$$

---

[25] A discussion of alternative methods of estimation appears in the appendix to chapter 2. Also see Aitchison and Brown, *Lognormal Distribution*, section 6.2, "Estimation of the Parameters of the Three-Parameter Distribution," for a further discussion.

Then

$$(d + c)/(hd + c) = (jd + c)/(d + c); \qquad (2.11)$$

$$c/d = (hj - 1)/(2 - h - j), \quad \text{or} \quad c = d[(hj - 1)/(2 - h - j)]. \quad (2.12)$$

The constant of displacement as a proportion of the median is a simple observable function of the two quantile cutoffs expressed as proportions of the median. Given c, μ and σ can be solved for by substitution, where g is observable from the standard normal table:

$$\mu = \log(d + c) \qquad (2.13)$$

$$\sigma = \frac{\log[(d + c)/(hd + c)]}{g} = \frac{\log[(jd + c)/(d + c)]}{g} \qquad (2.14)$$

A displaced lognormal distribution with parameters estimated in the above manner will be consistent with the observed data, in the sense that the estimated cumulative distribution will have zero error (or, the frequency distribution will have zero cumulative error) at the three chosen quantiles.

Any three quantiles may be chosen as the points at which the estimated distribution has zero cumulative error; the median need not be one of them. A simple solution exists as long as the second of the three points is midway between the other two measured in standard deviation units (under the hypothesis of normality).[26] If the three points are randomly placed, an iterative solution is required.

---

[26] For example, suppose zero cumulative error is desired at the lower decile, with a cutoff at \$$h \cdot d$, and at the upper quartile, \$$j \cdot d$. In a standard normal distribution these points lie -1.282 and $+0.674$ deviations from the mean (median), respectively. To avoid an iterative solution procedure, the third point must be the quantile lying -0.304 deviations from the mean, or the 38.06 percent quantile. If 38.06 percent of the observed distribution lies below \$$k \cdot d$, then

$$\frac{\log[(kd + c)/(hd + c)]}{\sigma} = g = \frac{\log[(jd + c)/(kd + c)]}{\sigma},$$

$$\frac{kd + c}{hd + c} = \frac{jd + c}{kd + c},$$

and

$$\frac{c}{d} = \frac{hj - k^2}{2k - h - j}.$$

In these relations d serves an expository purpose only; the estimated distribution will have zero cumulative error at the h, k, and j quantiles, expressed here as proportions of d, but not at d itself. If h and j are symmetrically placed about the median, then $k = 1$ and the initial relation for c/d holds.

When the displaced lognormal distribution is fitted to sample income data by quantile methods, the goodness of fit is not improved by the choice of nonsymmetric quantiles. This finding is consistent with the Aitchison and Brown results for simple lognormal distribution fitted to group data:

> ... the [quantile] method declines in efficiency if ... it is necessary to choose quantiles distant from the most efficient quantiles or pairs of quantiles that are asymmetrically placed. If this is the case it may be preferable to interpolate for the most efficient quantile pairs.[27]

As a general rule symmetric quantiles will be chosen in addition to the median. It must still be decided how far from the median the quantiles should lie. The closer the quantiles are to the median, the greater is the accuracy around the center of the distribution at the expense of accuracy in the tails. Given the motivation of this study, the accuracy to be gained in the extremes of the distribution by moving the quantiles as far as possible from the median is worth the accuracy lost at other points of the distribution.[28]

There is a cost involved in moving the quantiles far from the median in addition to possible loss of accuracy elsewhere in the distribution. To obtain symmetric quantile measurements from grouped data, it is necessary to use some ad hoc assumptions to interpolate the data, such as rectangularity in the cell distributions or a Pareto distribution in the upper cells: assumptions which violate the ultimate assumption of a displaced lognormal distribution. The further one moves into the tails of the distribution, the more critical is the contradiction in assumptions, and the more sparse are the data on which to base the estimates. Because of this difficulty, the 10 percent and 90 percent quantiles were as far from the median as were seriously considered.

OTHER NORMAL TRANSFORMATIONS

The displaced lognormal distribution is certainly not the only transformation available for approximating a normal distribution. While such transformations are *assumed* to produce a normal distribution, in fact,

---

[27] Aitchison and Brown, *Lognormal Distribution*, pp. 53–54.

[28] On this point Aitchison and Brown recommend the 5 percent and 95 percent quantiles (p. 64). See the appendix to chapter 2 for empirical examples indicating the gains and losses in accuracy implied by various quantile choices.

the data are transformed to conform to a specific symmetry criterion, such as a zero coefficient of skewness or symmetrically defined quantiles lying equidistant from the observed median. Since one vital property of the normal distribution is symmetry, the data are endowed with that heretofore-lacking property. Beyond the physical manipulation, it must be recognized that the application of a normal approximation at this point still involves a strong element of assumption.

A thorough discussion of normal transformations is presented by G. E. P. Box and D. R. Cox in "An Analysis of Transformation."[29] They present two general examples of normal transformations, where y is the initial variable and z is the transformed variable, assumed to be normally distributed:

$$z = \frac{y^{\lambda_1} - 1}{\lambda_1}, \quad \lambda_1 \neq 0,$$
$$= \log(y), \quad \lambda_1 = 0. \tag{2.15a}$$

$$z = \frac{(y + \lambda_2)^{\lambda_1} - 1}{\lambda_1}, \quad \lambda_1 \neq 0,$$
$$= \log(y + \lambda_2), \quad \lambda_1 = 0. \tag{2.15b}$$

In (2.15a), with $\lambda_1 \neq 0$, if $(y^{\lambda_1} - 1)/\lambda_1$ is normally distributed, then y^{λ_1} is also. The former expression is chosen because $\lim_{\lambda_1 \to 0} \left(\frac{y^{\lambda_1} - 1}{\lambda_1} \right) = \log(y)$, while y^{λ_1} degenerates to *one* in the limit. In this regard, (2.15b) parallels (2.15a).

With $\lambda_1 \neq 0$, (2.15a) is a three-parameter exponential distribution defined for $y > 0$. With $\lambda_1 = 0$, the function becomes a conventional two-parameter lognormal distribution. Again, if $\lambda_1 \neq 0$, (2.15b) is a four-parameter distribution defined for $y > -\lambda_2$. If $\lambda_1 = 0$, the three-parameter or displaced lognormal distribution is defined, with λ_2 as the constant of displacement. The distribution advocated for use in this study is therefore a limit case of the Box-Cox transformation.

One choosing to deal more generally with transformations as discussed by Box and Cox would face the same range of estimation procedures discussed earlier. If (2.15a) is chosen as a three-parameter alternative to the displaced lognormal distribution, the goodness of fit is not improved, and the method of derivation from three quantile observations is more difficult. In the case of quantiles symmetrically placed around the median, the value of λ_1 which fulfills the following condition is chosen:

[29] *Journal of the Royal Statistical Society,* Ser. B (1964), No. 2, pp. 211–43.

$$\frac{d^{\lambda_1} - (hd)^{\lambda_1}}{\sigma} = g = \frac{(jd)^{\lambda_1} - d^{\lambda_1}}{\sigma} \qquad (2.16)$$

i.e., $h^{\lambda_1} + j^{\lambda_1} = 2$. The solution involves a relatively simple iteration.

If (2.15b) is chosen, the potential goodness of fit is improved, due to the presence of four independent parameters. Equation (2.15b) can be solved from four quantile observations by a rather complicated iteration, or the complexity can be reduced to that of (2.15a) by assigning a priori a constant of displacement and utilizing only three quantiles. As already stated, the need for iterative solutions in this study has been avoided by constraining λ_1 to zero and using limit (2.15b).

In the appendix to chapter 2, numerical examples of the application of the displaced lognormal distribution to Current Population Survey data are compared to the application of other distributional forms. The spirit of the presentation is one of comparison to viable alternatives, rather than one of formal tests to verify or reject the null hypothesis of displaced lognormality.

Chapter 3

POSTWAR CHANGES IN THE
UNITED STATES INCOME DISTRIBUTION

In chapter 2 the displaced lognormal distribution was proposed as a mechanism to describe the size distribution of income. This chapter examines postwar changes in the United States income distribution as reflected in quantile measures and parameters of the displaced lognormal distribution.

Since families differ substantially in the source and variability of their income, a sharper view of distributional patterns can be obtained by examining different subgroups in the population rather than by observing the aggregate population. The groups considered here are families with a male head and a wife in the paid labor force; families with a male head and a wife not in the labor force; families with a male head, "other" marital status; families with a female head; unrelated individuals who were earners; and unrelated individuals who were not earners. Distribution parameters for each year were calculated by quantile methods discussed in the appendix to chapter 2; the quantile measures were constructed by interpolation from Current Population Survey data.[1] The calculated parameters and data appear in Tables 3.1–3.6.

---

[1] See the appendix to chapter 2. The data appear in U.S. Bureau of the Census, *Current Population Reports,* Ser. P-60, Nos. 1–53, "Consumer Income" (Washington, D.C.: U.S. Government Printing Office, 1948–67).

FAMILIES, MALE HEAD

Tables 3.1 and 3.2 report data for families with male head, wife present, by labor force status of the wife in March of the following year. Data are available in this form from 1949 to the present. The 10 percent and 90 percent deciles are used as the quantile measures for both groups.

The labor force orientation of families with a male head has changed substantially during the postward period. The number of such families with the wife in the labor force grew from 7.3 million in 1949 to 14.2 million in 1965, while the number of families with the wife not in the labor force has remained roughly constant at 28 million.

This increase in the proportion of families with a wife in the labor force has an important impact on the aggregate size distribution for two reasons. First, since the two group distributions are shaped differently, a change in their relative proportions will appear as a change in the aggregate distribution even if the shapes of the individual distributions do not change. Second, the two groups appear to show different responses to cyclical movements in the economy. Families at the lower decile cutoff for the wife-in-labor-force (MWL) group have incomes in the vicinity of 40 percent (36.3–44.4) of the group median, while the corresponding level for the wife-not-in-labor-force (MWN) group is about 30 percent (28.2–33.0) of the respective median. The lower decile statistic for the MWL group shows a fairly systematic cyclical pattern with peak values observed in 1951, 1953, 1956, and 1959, and an upward trend since a 1960 trough. While there appears to be a positive time trend both in the proportion of families in this group and in the value of H, deviations from trend for the two variables are negatively correlated with each other. The corresponding statistic for the MWN group follows a different pattern; it rises substantially in 1951, falls sharply in 1953, builds to a peak in 1958, and then reaches a trough in 1960.

The upper tail parameter J has a range of 1.68–1.82 for the MWL group and 1.90–2.10 for the MWN group. The MWN group has a lower median than the MWL group, but it has an upper distributional tail which is considerably more extended. This pattern suggests that high income families in the MWL group derive their position largely from the presence of multiple labor force participants, while the wives in families having large concentrations of nonwage income or a head with a relatively high salary tend to stay out of the labor force. The value of J for both groups shows a mild countercyclical tendency, rising in recession years. This implies that family incomes are more sharply affected by the business cycle at the median than above the median.

TABLE 3.1. DISTRIBUTIONAL DATA FOR FAMILIES, MALE HEAD, WIFE IN PAID LABOR FORCE, 1949–65

Year	Families (1000)	Quantiles ($)			H	J	C/D	σ	A($)
		Median	10%	90%					
1965	14183	8597	3820	15000	0.4443	1.7448	1.1888	0.2285	9095
1964	13647	8170	3603	14091	0.4410	1.7247	1.4448	0.2338	8723
1963	13398	7789	3273	13645	0.4202	1.7518	1.5343	0.2026	8198
1962	13028	7461	3172	13158	0.4251	1.7636	1.3236	0.2218	7893
1961	12366	7188	2946	12675	0.4098	1.7634	1.6016	0.2007	7568
1960	12007	6900	2796	12106	0.4052	1.7545	1.8103	0.1855	7234
1959	11265	6705	2788	11520	0.4158	1.7181	2.1329	0.1610	6979
1958	11014	6214	2557	10871	0.4115	1.7494	1.7408	0.1886	6574
1957	10696	6141	2529	10520	0.4118	1.7131	2.3579	0.1503	6376
1956	10266	5957	2485	10092	0.4172	1.6941	2.6343	0.1364	6161
1955	9786	5622	2329	9440	0.4143	1.6791	3.2580	0.1155	5782
1954	9005	5336	2186	9120	0.4097	1.7091	2.5236	0.1430	5529
1953	8630e	5401	2214	9164	0.4099	1.6967	2.8565	0.1296	5576
1952	9154	4900	1779	8540	0.3631	1.7429	3.4642	0.1201	5058
1951	8044	4631	1925	8153	0.4157	1.7605	1.5221	0.2056	4881
1950	7855e	4020	1498	7228	0.3726	1.7979	1.9361	0.1876	4230
1949	7256e	3869	1418	7037	0.3664	1.8187	1.8023	0.2000	4008

Primary data source: U.S. Bureau of the Census, *Current Population Surveys*, Ser. P-60, Nos. 1–51 (Washington, D.C.: U.S. Government Printing Office, 1948–69). Quantiles derived by rectangular interpolation except at upper tail, where a Pareto approximation was used (see appendix to chapter 2). Current dollars.

H = Lower quantile/median

C = Constant of displacement

A = Assumed mean under assumption of displaced lognormality

σ = Assumed standard error of transformed distribution

e denotes indirect estimate; supplementary use was made of Herman P. Miller, Census Technical Paper No. 8, for data relating to 1953 and years prior to 1951. Data drawn from Miller were derived in constant dollars and then adjusted to a current dollar basis.

$A = (D + C)e^{0.5\sigma^2} - C$

$C/D = (HJ - 1)/(2 - H - J)$

D = Median

J = Upper quantile/median

TABLE 3.2. DISTRIBUTIONAL DATA FOR FAMILIES, MALE HEAD, WIFE NOT IN PAID LABOR FORCE, 1949–65

| Year | Families (1000) | Quantiles ($) | | | H | J | C/D | σ | $A(\$)$ |
		Median	10%	90%					
1965	27925	6592	2125	13442	0.3224	2.0391	0.9477	0.33358	7326
1964	28000	6338	2058	12761	0.3247	2.0134	1.0240	0.31671	6998
1963	27913	6039	1974	12281	0.3269	2.0336	0.9298	0.33465	6711
1962	27895	5764	1900	11761	0.3296	2.0404	0.8851	0.34289	6422
1961	28039	5592	1732	11640	0.3097	2.0815	0.9085	0.34975	6265
1960	27617	5520	1707	10995	0.3092	1.9918	1.2761	0.28222	6031
1959	28070	5317	1690	10571	0.3178	1.9882	1.2033	0.28909	5817
1958	27571	4983	1633	9798	0.3277	1.9663	1.2095	0.28309	5433
1957	27416	4833	1488	9197	0.3097	1.9030	1.9635	0.20751	5145
1956	27583	4645	1427	9160	0.3072	1.9720	1.4119	0.26419	5043
1955	27414	4236	1276	8469	0.2950	1.9577	1.6719	0.23899	4661
1954	27390	4051	1143	8181	0.2822	2.0195	1.4256	0.27375	4426
1953	27411e	4118	1176	8084	0.2856	1.9630	1.7675	0.23299	4431
1952	26628	3812	1250	7468	0.3279	1.9591	1.2460	0.27742	4148
1951	27152	3634	1185	7032	0.3261	1.9351	1.4127	0.25558	3925
1950	26701e	3325	943	6932	0.2836	2.0851	1.1085	0.32391	3703
1949	27035e	3057	853	6413	0.2790	2.0978	1.1006	0.32802	3406

See Table 3.1 for explanation of source and terms. Current dollars.

Since H and J for a given distribution are directly observable as quantile observations expressed as proportions of the observed median, their movements may be discussed without reference to an underlying distributional form. Given the relationships specified in chapter 2, on the other hand, H and J can be converted into parameters of an assumed displaced lognormal distribution. Included in Tables 3.1–3.6 are derived values for C/D, σ, and A, where C is the constant of displacement, D is the observed median of the distribution in question, σ is the implied standard error of the transformed distribution, i.e., of log $(Y + C)$, and A is the mean of the absolute distribution as implied by the displaced lognormal assumption. While the mean and median may be defined in either current or real dollars, C/D and σ are invariant to price transformation so long as a uniform deflator is used across the entire distribution.

Returning to the MWL and MWN groups, we find that the estimated constant of displacement is positive for every observation for both groups; this finding corresponds to the claimed properties of the shape of the income distribution described in chapter 2. For every year the value of the constant of displacement relative to the median is larger for the MWL group than it is for the MWN group. This indicates a larger displacement from simple lognormality for the MWL group than for the MWN group, or conversely, a smaller displacement from normality.

The cyclical pattern of C/D is ambiguous for the two groups. For the MWL group, C/D troughs in 1951 and peaks in 1952 before drifting into a procyclical pattern from 1954 through 1960; through the 1960s C/D assumes a declining trend. In contrast, the constant of displacement for the MWN group peaked in 1951 and 1953 before assuming a pattern parallel to the one displayed by the MWL parameter. The lower constant of displacement for both groups during the 1960s implies that the distribution of income has been more highly skewed during the current decade than it was in the 1950s. One factor contributing to this increased skewness has been the improved relative position of the lower tail of both groups, as indicated by the values of H.

Both decile measures of the MWL distribution are relatively closer to the median than is the case for the MWN distribution. In conventional terms, therefore, the male head, wife-in-labor-force group distribution has a smaller proportional variance than the wife-not-in-labor-force group distribution. While this smaller variance does appear in the estimated standard errors of the transformed distributions (σ), direct comparisons of values of σ cannot be made either across groups or across time within one group. The reason for this lack of comparability is that the standard error of log $(Y + C)$ is being observed for a given sample: for a given array of values of Y, the value of σ will be a decreasing function of the value of C which is chosen. While the standard error of a two-parameter lognormal transformation has directly interpretable correspondences (such as its monotonic relationship to a Lorenz measure), the standard error in the three-parameter case relates to a different transformation in each year and therefore loses its direct relationship to the absolute distribution. If a fixed value of C/D were specified over time (such as zero in the simple lognormal case), this direct relationship could be retained.

For the two groups now being observed, changes in the value of C/D are negatively correlated with changes in σ. Relatively small changes in the values of H and J correspond to large, offsetting changes in the values of C/D and σ. While a direct economic interpretation is possible for independent changes in the values of H and J, C/D and σ must be observed together in order to derive meaningful implications.

Table 3.3 provides distributional data for families having a male head but no wife present, for the years 1947–65. Again the data are based upon the 10 percent and 90 percent deciles. This group has the lowest median of the three groups having male heads, and the most unequal income distribution according to Lorenz criteria. Families at the lower decile cutoff had incomes of only about 25 percent (17.3–29.7) of the median group income, while incomes at the upper decile cutoff were about 225 percent (208.5–251.5) of the median. Because of the large sampling error associated with this small group, it is hard to discern a clear cyclical pattern in the data.

FAMILIES, FEMALE HEAD

Table 3.4 presents data for families with a female head. The two quantiles used in addition to the median are the 15.87 and 84.13 percent points, corresponding to a single standard deviation on either side of the mean under a null hypothesis of normality. For families with a female head, the value of H fell during the postwar years through 1951 before assuming an upward trend for the remaining years. The value of J showed no discernible trend. The constant of displacement for this group is smaller than that of any other family group. The value of C/D jumped abruptly during the Korean war years; it has shown a declining trend since 1956. This declining trend in C/D is attributable to the increasing value of H in the presence of a trendless pattern in J.

TABLE 3.3. DISTRIBUTIONAL DATA FOR FAMILIES, MALE HEAD, OTHER MARITAL STATUS, 1947–65

Year	Families (1000)	Quantiles ($) Median	10%	90%	H	J	C/D	σ	A($)
1965	1179	6148	1824	12967	0.2967	2.1091	0.9221	0.35540	6918
1964	1182	5792	1387	12738	0.2395	2.1992	1.0789	0.35531	6577
1963	1243	5710	1573	12881	0.2755	2.2559	0.7123	0.42918	6653
1962	1334	5711	1457	11932	0.2551	2.0893	1.3560	0.29654	6316
1961	1293	5069	1244	12522	0.2454	2.4703	0.5502	0.52045	6209
1960	1202	4860	1306	10706	0.2687	2.2029	0.8654	0.38825	5570
1959	1233	4613	1255	10396	0.2721	2.2536	0.7358	0.42412	5367
1958	1285	4260	1078	9640	0.2531	2.2629	0.8281	0.40977	4942
1957	1292	4581	1065	9641	0.2325	2.1046	1.5150	0.28407	5055
1956	1230	4167	1020	8965	0.2448	2.1214	1.1946	0.32909	4676
1955	1404	4190	891	8738	0.2126	2.0854	1.8678	0.25045	4573
1954	1314	4014	899	8483	0.2240	2.1134	1.5608	0.28168	4430
1953	1336e	4114	866	8969	0.2104	2.1803	1.3855	0.31364	4608
1952	1396	3615	821	8217	0.2271	2.2730	0.9674	0.38930	4175
1951	1216	3452	737	7642	0.2135	2.2138	1.2343	0.33851	3907
1950	1226	3115	693	7242	0.2225	2.3247	0.8823	0.41570	3645
1949	1265	2825	489	7105	0.1732	2.5150	0.8201	0.47252	3432
1948	1287	3304	879	7730	0.2662	2.3396	0.6226	0.46962	3929
1947	1234	2944	716	6854	0.2433	2.3284	0.7583	0.43907	3468

See Table 3.1 for explanation of source and terms. Current dollars.

TABLE 3.4. DISTRIBUTIONAL DATA FOR FAMILIES, FEMALE HEAD, 1947–65

Year	Families (1000)	Quantiles ($)			H	J	C/D	σ	A($)
		Median	15.87%	84.13%					
1965	4992	3532	1323	7591	0.3746	2.1492	0.3721	0.60846	4517
1964	5006	3458	1273	7581	0.3681	2.1923	0.3444	0.63494	4496
1963	4882	3211	1035	7126	0.3223	2.2192	0.5259	0.58723	4125
1962	4741	3131	1009	6860	0.3223	2.1910	0.5724	0.56389	3980
1961	4643	2993	948	6581	0.3167	2.1988	0.5889	0.56218	3807
1960	4609	2968	992	6561	0.3342	2.2106	0.4794	0.59790	3827
1959	4494	2764	903	6270	0.3267	2.2685	0.4350	0.63334	3645
1958	4332	2741	861	6044	0.3141	2.2050	0.5922	0.56349	3492
1957	4310	2763	818	5915	0.2961	2.1408	0.8379	0.48286	3391
1956	4366	2754	746	5894	0.2709	2.1402	1.0221	0.44718	3339
1955	4239	2471	734	5497	0.2970	2.2246	0.6506	0.55503	3150
1954	4225	2294	610	5281	0.2659	2.3021	0.6829	0.57307	2983
1953	3825e	2484	671	5773	0.2701	2.3241	0.6266	0.59553	3268
1952	3842	2235	609	4712	0.2725	2.1083	1.1174	0.42094	2674
1951	4030	2220	521	4826	0.2347	2.1739	1.1987	0.42781	2688
1950	4040	1918	528	4285	0.2753	2.2340	0.7559	0.53227	2430
1949	3637	2107	636	4642	0.3017	2.2032	0.6641	0.54407	2666
1948	3713	2065	652	4627	0.3156	2.2409	0.5261	0.59504	2675
1947	3757	2182	755	4627	0.3461	2.1200	0.5713	0.53813	2716

See Table 3.1 for explanation of source and terms. Current dollars.

UNRELATED INDIVIDUALS

Tables 3.5 and 3.6 report distributional data for the two groups of un-related individuals. Both groups present unique problems. Data for un-related individuals who were earners (UIE) are based upon quartile observations. The degree of displacement from lognormality in the UIE case was quite large and unstable. Chapter 2 states that the shape of the transformed distribution passes from the shape of the logarithmic dis-tribution to that of the absolute distribution as C moves from zero to $+\infty$. Given the usual case of a negatively skewed logarithmic distribution and a positively skewed absolute distribution, there exists a positive value of C which fulfills some nonskewness criterion applied to the trans-formed distribution. If both the logarithmic and the absolute forms are positively skewed, the displacement constant must assume a negative value to fulfill the nonskewness criterion. In the rare case where both forms of the distribution are *negatively* skewed, however, the value of C reaches infinity before a point of zero skewness in the transformed dis-tribution can be reached. Beyond that point the computational formula for C yields negative values. When quartile observations from the UIE group are observed for the years 1951 and 1953, the formula for C/D yields a negative value because of such negative skewness.[2] Therefore, the displaced lognormal distribution is not defined for the UIE group in these two years, and the computational formulas do not apply. While uninterrupted time series cannot be observed for C/D and σ, movements in the median and in H and J can still be observed. Furthermore, while the complete time series for the mean no longer exists, it is possible to proceed by making special assumptions about the mean for years in which the displaced lognormal distribution breaks down. In such years, it will be assumed that the mean equals the observed median.

The value of H for the UIE group has moved in a cyclical manner since 1954, with a trough in 1954, a steady rise through 1957, troughs in 1958 and 1960, and an upward trend since 1963. The behavior of J appears to be less conventional. Through the 1955 boom, the value of J for the UIE group behaves countercyclically much like the MWL and MWN groups, with trough values in 1951, 1953, and 1955. The pattern

---

[2]While the absolute distribution appears to have negative skewness for 1951 and 1953 when 25 percent quantiles are used, this property would probably disappear with the use of quantiles further out of the tails, because of the rela-tively "bounded" nature of the lower income tail.

TABLE 3.5. DISTRIBUTIONAL DATA FOR UNRELATED INDIVIDUALS, EARNERS, 1947–65

Year	Persons (1000)	Quantiles ($)			H	J	C/D	σ	A($)
		Median	25%	75%					
1965	7336	3657	1868	5852	0.5108	1.6002	1.6450	0.30317	4112
1964	7421	3384	1646	5556	0.4864	1.6418	1.5710	0.33035	3872
1963	6986	3098	1464	5264	0.4726	1.6992	1.1467	0.41800	3705
1962	6723	3036	1438	5152	0.4736	1.6970	1.1506	0.41620	3627
1961	6988	2973	1435	4875	0.4827	1.6398	1.7020	0.31509	3382
1960	6863	2897	1349	4627	0.4657	1.5972	4.0731	0.16497	3098
1959	6518	2654	1313	4389	0.4947	1.6537	1.2257	0.38178	3101
1958	6768	2604	1236	4212	0.4747	1.6175	2.5184	0.23972	2871
1957	6800	2380	1162	4000	0.4882	1.6807	1.0628	0.42280	2839
1956	6095	2341	1112	3852	0.4750	1.6455	1.8124	0.30632	2657
1955	6206	2174	1030	3438	0.4738	1.5814	4.5417	0.14789	2307
1954	6170	2020	925	3297	0.4579	1.6322	2.8036	0.22795	2223
1953	6450e	2245	1081	3302	0.4818	1.4712	x	x	x
1952	6426	2172	1147	3348	0.5283	1.5421	2.6321	0.20630	2341
1951	5961	2082	956	3170	0.4592	1.5226	x	x	x
1950	6154	1779	803	2831	0.4513	1.5914	6.5995	0.11107	1862
1949	6055	1697	831	2650	0.4896	1.5619	4.5689	0.14252	1793
1948	5189	1618	834	2596	0.5156	1.6048	1.4336	0.32904	1837
1947	5353	1423	626	2383	0.4397	1.6744	2.3120	0.27475	1605

x denotes displaced lognormal distribution not defined due to negative skewness of absolute distribution. See Table 3.1 for explanation of source and other terms. Current dollars.

TABLE 3.6. DISTRIBUTIONAL DATA FOR UNRELATED INDIVIDUALS, NONEARNERS, 1947–65

Year	Persons (1000)	Median	79.46%	95%	K	J	C/D	σ	A($)
1965	4796	1155	1930	4219	1.6710	3.6528	−0.6565	1.31651	1702
1964	4636	1067	1811	4402	1.6973	4.1256	−0.7191	1.51680	1714
1963	4196	1025	1695	3450	1.6537	3.3659	−0.5963	1.17057	1432
1962	4290	1013	1705	3417	1.6831	3.3731	−0.5366	1.10124	1404
1961	4175	892	1592	3156	1.7848	3.5381	−0.3641	0.97724	1239
1960	4037	839	1460	3231	1.7402	3.8510	−0.6002	1.27378	1258
1959	4184	784	1429	2885	1.8227	3.6798	−0.3457	0.98980	1108
1958	3983	735	1331	2533	1.8109	3.4463	−0.2024	0.85274	992
1957	3513	713	1291	2531	1.8107	3.5498	−0.2921	0.92783	985
1956	3563	715	1229	2240	1.7189	3.1329	−0.2565	0.82234	929
1955	3560	659	1195	2413	1.8134	3.6616	−0.3603	1.26724	1178
1954	3453	628	1066	2466	1.6975	3.9268	−0.6824	1.41255	969
1953	3064e	599	1090	2265	1.8206	3.7837	−0.4106	1.06037	865
1952	3348	614	1107	2411	1.8029	3.9267	−0.5120	1.18257	917
1951	3054	494	931	1950	1.8846	3.9474	−0.3359	1.02934	723
1950	3040	512	967	2128	1.8873	4.1546	−0.4295	1.14049	780
1949	2780	493	927	1691	1.8791	3.4272	0.1552	0.68792	645
1948	2947	508	979	1946	1.9269	3.8295	−0.1195	0.87425	716
1947	2703	585	1223	2856	2.0903	4.8796	−0.3003	1.14187	961

K = intermediate quantile/median
C/D = (J − K²)/(2K − J − 1).
See Table 3.1 for explanation of source and other terms. Current dollars.

reverses in the latter half of the time period, however, with J moving with the cycle beginning in 1957.

In the appendix to chapter 2 unrelated individuals who were non-earners (the UIN group) are specially treated because of the extremely low value of the median. Both quantiles are observed above the median, although in an absolute sense both are at fairly low income levels. For this group, the negative constant of displacement indicates the presence of extremely skewed data with the logarithmic data also being positively skewed. The lower of the two upper-tail quantiles (K) displays a mild procyclical movement, while the uppermost quantile J reverses its cyclical pattern much like the behavior of J in the UIE case.

CORRELATIONS AMONG DISTRIBUTIONAL VARIABLES

In the discussion of the rejection of a simple lognormal distribution, two questions were distinguished: whether the "constant" of displacement was in fact constant over time, and whether it was centered about the value zero. For five of the six groups, the displacement factor is consistently positive; for the sixth group, it is consistently negative. It is quite unlikely, therefore, that the displacements are random variations about a zero mean.

The displacement factor is also highly variable for all groups. Since much of the variation in C/D for a given group may be purely random or due to instability in the calculation procedure, we should consider the relationship between H and J directly before rejecting the restriction that the two tails of the distribution move symmetrically.

There is a negative zero order correlation between H and J for each of the five groups which have H and J placed symmetrically about the upper and lower tails of the distribution. In four of the five groups, however, the square of the zero order correlation coefficient is not significant according to a 90 percent F test (the correlations appear in Part A of Table 3.7).

The values of H and J for the MWL group have a zero order correlation of $-.47$ ($R^2 = .22$). In this case, R^2 is significantly greater than zero at a 90 percent test level but fails a 95 percent test. This statistical significance disappears whenever either H or J is regressed against the other in the presence of economic variables such as the ones specified in chapter 4. The correlation coefficients for the MWN, MOT, FEM, and UIE groups are $-.28$, $-.25$, $-.19$, and $-.20$, respectively. The $+.62$ value of

TABLE 3.7.   CORRELATION MATRICES OF DISTRIBUTIONAL VARIABLES

Prefixes:	H	= Lower quantile income/median income
	J	= Upper quantile income/median income
	K	= Intermediate quantile income/median income, UIN group
Suffixes:	MWL	= Families male head, wife in labor force
	MWN	= Families male head, wife not in labor force
	MOT	= Families male head, other marital status
	FEM	= Families female head
	UIE	= Unrelated individuals, earners
	UIN	= Unrelated individuals, nonearners

A. Correlation of H variable with J variable within each group

Variables Correlated	Time Period	Correlation Coefficient (R)
HMWL, JMWL	1949–65	−.4725
HMWN, JMWN	1949–65	−.2763
HMOT, JMOT	1947–65	−.2547
HFEM, JFEM	1947–65	−.1891
HUIE, JUIE	1947–65	−.2002
KUIN, JUIN	1947–65	+.6209

B. Correlation of H variables, 1949–65

HMWL	HMWN	HMOT	HFEM	HUIE	KUIN
1.000	.449	.603	.514	−.078	−.636
	1.000	.633	.379	.345	−.386
		1.000	.637	.171	−.660
			1.000	.342	−.546
				1.000	−.094
					1.000

C. Correlation of J variables, 1949–65

JMWL	JMWN	JMOT	JFEM	JUIE	JUIN
1.000	.668	.700	−.172	−.031	.062
	1.000	.584	.184	.172	−.020
		1.000	.009	−.171	−.026
			1.000	−.182	.229
				1.000	−.432
					1.000

the UIN group is not surprising in light of the fact that both H and J lie above the median for that group. The general weakness of the negative correlations is consistent with the decision to reject curve-fitting methods which restrict both tails of a distribution to respond symmetrically to a given stimulus.

Parts B and C of Table 3.7 report zero order correlation coefficients among the lower tail variables for all six groups and, similarly, among the upper tail variables. To the extent that group distributions behave similarly, we would expect to observe positive correlation coefficients.

The relationships among values of H for the four family groups are all positive, with correlation coefficients as high as +.64. There are also substantial differences in the lower tail responses, however, as the estimated model will indicate. The lower tail responses of the two largest groups, MWL and MWN, have a correlation of only +.45.

The correlations among upper tail responses for family groups with male heads reach as high as +.7, but like variables for unrelated individuals and for families with female heads are not significantly correlated. In short, it appears that the various group distributions do not respond uniformly to economic changes.

In chapter 4, variations in the distributional parameters for each of the above groups will be implicitly related to fluctuations in alternative sources of personal income. We shall find that the response of group size distributions to economic phenomena will indeed be heterogeneous; this heterogeneity will be predictable to a significant extent by differences in sources of income.

Chapter 4

AN ECONOMETRIC MODEL OF THE INCOME DISTRIBUTION

An attempt is made here to estimate a reduced form relationship between the size distribution of personal income and the macroeconomy. Implicitly, this will be done by relating changes in each group distribution to fluctuations in alternative sources of personal income received by that group.

For each of the six groups discussed in chapter 3, a three-equation system will be estimated to determine the levels of the group mean, of H, and of J. While these equations will be directly interpretable without reference to an underlying distributional form,[1] transformations corresponding to the functional form development of chapter 2 will be added to express the estimates in terms of the three-parameter lognormal distribution and to provide density estimates of the poverty population.

THE RELATION OF DISTRIBUTIONAL PARAMETERS TO THE MODEL

Chapters 2 and 3 argue that a displaced lognormal distribution can be used to obtain a fairly close-fitting and flexible description of the size distribution of income for a number of family groups. The distribution

---

[1] While all three equations will be directly interpretable, distributional assumptions *are* involved in the construction of the group mean data.

can be specified by three parameters; these parameters can be quantiles or moments relating to the absolute data, or they may be parameters of the transformed distribution, i.e., μ, σ, or the constant of displacement.

Having been chosen to specify a given distribution at a point in time, the three parameters can then be treated as endogenous variables over time, to be predicted as a function of economic variables. The procedure must be repeated for each group distribution to be estimated. In addition, households must be allocated into the groups by some (endogenous or exogenous) mechanism.

Once the distributional model has been constructed, it can be embedded in a model of the general economy. The distributional sector can receive inputs from other sectors of the model; simultaneously, it can provide outputs which may be useful in structuring the remainder of the model. For instance, the effects of distributional variables on consumption expenditures, tax receipts, and labor force participation can be investigated.

What three parameters should be chosen for treatment as directly estimated endogenous variables? Given the decision to use quantile methods of curve fitting, we may choose among the median, H, J, the mean, the standard error of the transformed distribution (σ), and the constant of displacement (c). The first three are directly observable quantiles and can be used without commitment to the displaced lognormal distribution. The latter three are derivable from the assumption of displaced lognormality, given the quantile observations. Once three variables are chosen for endogenous treatment in stochastic equations, the remaining ones can be determined by nonlinear identities specified from the formulas in chapter 2.

A natural first choice would be to relate mean or the median household income to mean levels of personal income components for the entire United States. For the remaining two equations we can either relate the transformation variance and the constant of displacement directly to the model, or estimate the lower and upper tail variables, H and J, leaving σ and c to be constructed through the identities.

Dealing with H and J would be the preferable procedure for a number of reasons. First, H and J have clearly identifiable relationships with the tails of the distribution. Success in constructing empirical relationships for H and J, therefore, depends upon whether the economic determinants of the relative positions of the tails of the distribution can be found. While the task may not be easy, it is well defined. On the other hand, relatively small changes in the tails of the distribution tend to result in large, offsetting movements in the variance and the constant of displacement. It would be extremely difficult to construct directly interpretable relationships between these variables and the economy which could also be estimated with reasonable simplicity. Furthermore, if limited information methods were used to estimate the two equations, the likelihood of negative covariance between the two error terms would be ignored. If the equations did not fully reflect the offsetting movements in c and σ, the predictive power of the model would be seriously impaired. Finally, stochastic equations based on c and σ suffer relative to equations based on H and J due to their lack of direct interpretability and to their heavy reliance upon the validity of the displaced lognormal distribution for even an indirect economic interpretation of the model. H and J provide the information necessary to make full use of the displaced lognormal distribution and yet retain some meaning even if the distributional assumption is later rejected.

We must still choose between estimating a group mean and a group median in the first stochastic equation. Consider initially the case where a displaced lognormal distribution is to be fitted to aggregate data for all income units. If the distributional data and the income account data had been drawn from a consistent source, the mean of the distribution could have been expressed as a nonstochastic sum of mean income components drawn from the national accounts. Furthermore, if the displaced lognormal distribution were assumed to apply, an estimate of the median could be derived from the following transformation of equation (2.6):

$$N = B(e^{-0.5\sigma^2}) + c(e^{-0.5\sigma^2} - 1), \tag{4.1}$$

where now N and B refer to *real* values of the median and the mean, respectively. Given the complication that the distributional data are inconsistent with income account data due to differences both in definition of income and in the method of data collection, the observed mean of the distribution is not an identical sum of components from the income accounts. If we assume, however, that there is a linear stochastic relationship between the two mean estimates, the further assumption of displaced lognormality provides us with an observed median which is a nonlinear function of the national income account data. Not only is the median relationship distinctly nonlinear, but no simple transformation can make it linear. If we had assumed a simple lognormal distribution with $c = 0$, the remaining relationship, $N = B(e^{-0.5\sigma^2})$, could have been logarithmically transformed to specify a linear relationship between $\log(N)$ and $\log(B)$. With $c \neq 0$, the transformation cannot be made.

This argument suggests that a stochastic relationship between the mean of the distributional data and national income account variables (per capita or per income unit) would be a reasonable specification, while efforts to state a linear relationship between the distribution median and income account means would lead to serious specification errors.

Further complications reduce the weight of the above argument. First, the median of the distribution has been directly observed, while the "observed" mean is constructed through identities which assume the displaced lognormal distribution to hold. By using such a construction, we introduce the possibility of specification error in the event that the distributional assumption is not appropriate. Second, we are dealing not with an aggregate income distribution but with six disaggregated distributions. There can be no general presumption that the mean of a population subgroup is linearly related to the global mean.

Despite these problems, group means were chosen for treatment rather than group medians. As an additional check on the displaced lognormality assumption, mean income specifications were reestimated with the observed median appearing as the left-hand variable. In most cases, equations based upon the mean produced far better empirical results than similar equations based upon the median.

GROUP MEAN INCOME EQUATIONS

The construction of a mean income specification for group i begins with an identity such as

$$
\begin{aligned}
B_i = {} & [(\text{annual wage rate})_i \cdot (\text{employment rate})_i \cdot (\text{labor force} \\
& \text{participation rate})_i] + [(\text{unemployment benefit rate})_i \cdot \\
& (\text{unemployment rate})_i \cdot (\text{labor force participation rate})_i] \\
& + (\text{other transfer benefits})_i + (\text{other personal income})_i,
\end{aligned}
\tag{4.2}
$$

where the subscripted components are mean levels for the group in question.[2] Since detailed data about the sources of group income are not available, it is necessary to specify assumed relationships between the above components and corresponding aggregate data reported in the national income accounts or by the Bureau of Labor Statistics.

The equation to be estimated is then a relationship between a constructed group mean and aggregate personal income and employment data. Coefficients on individual components are interpretable as implicit weights determining the sources of the group's income; the weights need not add to one because the group may have a different mean income than the population at large, and because of the inconsistency of the data sources.

---

[2] The definition includes all personal income sources covered in the Current Population Survey. Generally, imputed income sources are omitted.

SPECIFICATION OF EQUATIONS

When specification (4.2) is applied to the MWL (male head, wife in labor force) group, we can note that wives are in the labor force by definition; it is further assumed that the proportion of group family heads in the labor force is also constant[3] and that other secondary participants are not of quantitative significance. Because the structure of the MWL group may change as it becomes a larger proportion of total families, the relationship between the group and the aggregate wage rates is permitted to vary as a function of time and the proportion of wives in the labor force.[4] All other components in specification (4.2) are assumed to be proportional to the comparable global variables.[5] When these assumed relationships are substituted into (4.2) the specification for $BMWL$ becomes

$$BMWL = (a_1 + a_2T + a_3PAR1) \cdot W \cdot E + a_4UBR \cdot U + a_5Y_{TR} \\ + a_6(Y_{ID} + Y_O) + u_1, \tag{4.3}$$

the variables being defined in real terms in Table 4.1.[6]

The MWN (male head, wife not in labor force) group is the largest of the six considered, although its size is declining relative to the MWL group. Again defining the mean level of real income as a sum of income components, we have a specification of the form

$$BMWN = (a_1 + a_2T + a_3PAR1) \cdot W \cdot E \cdot L + a_4UBR \cdot U \cdot L \\ + a_5Y_{TR} + a_6(Y_{ID} + Y_O) + u_2. \tag{4.4}$$

Specification (4.4) differs from (4.3) in that the group labor force participation rate is no longer assumed to be constant.[7]

---

[3] This is assumed, despite the fact that the participation rate for all males has been declining over time due to changes in age composition and retirement age. The justification is that husbands with wives in the labor force are likely to be of working age themselves and, therefore, not affected by the aggregate trend. The assumption is also justified ex post because it provides superior empirical results.

[4] That is, the proportion of families with male head, wife present, which constitutes the MWL group.

[5] Strictly speaking, it is possible for both the employment and unemployment rates to be proportional to corresponding global rates only if the factor of proportionality is one. More complex specifications, which relaxed the proportionality restrictions at the expense of greater losses in degrees of freedom, were tested and rejected.

[6] While specification (4.3) and the ones to follow involve a number of multiplicative variables, linearity in the coefficients is strictly maintained throughout the model.

[7] The argument used to justify the constancy assumption for specification (4.3), stated in footnote 3, no longer applies.

TABLE 4.1. VARIABLES INCLUDED IN DISTRIBUTION EQUATIONS

A. DISTRIBUTION BLOCK

Primary data source: U.S. Bureau of the Census, *Current Population Reports*, Ser. P-60, Nos. 1–53, *Consumer Income*.

Quantile variables obtained by interpolation procedures discussed in appendix to chapter 2. Mean income variables derived from quantiles under assumption of displaced lognormality. The constant of displacement (c_i), the standard deviation of the transformed distribution (σ_i), and the poverty threshold variables (GPV_i, YPV_i) are defined in equations (4.30), (4.31), and (4.34) and are omitted from this list. All variables are in real terms (1958 dollars, $PGNP$ deflator). Sample mean values for 1949–65 appear in parentheses. (Many regressions extend back to 1947, but mean values are reported on a uniform basis here for comparative purposes.)

MWL Group: Families, Male Head, Wife in Paid Labor Force

1. BMWL   (6638)   Mean income
2. HMWL   (0.4090)   Income below which 10 percent of families lie, divided by group median
3. JMWL   (1.7401)   Income above which 10 percent of families lie, divided by group median
4. NMWL   (6338)   Median income

MWN Group: Families, Male Head, Wife Present but Not in Paid Labor Force

5. BMWN   (5431)
6. HMWN   (0.3096)
7. JMWN   (2.0027)   } Definitions parallel those of MWL group
8. NMWN   (4948)

FEM Group: Families, Female Head

9. BFEM   (3550)   Mean income
10. HFEM   (0.3037)   Income below which 15.87 percent of families lie, divided by group median
11. JFEM   (2.2051)   Income above which 15.87 percent of families lie, divided by group median
12. NFEM   (2798)   Median income

MOT Group: Families, Male Head, Other Marital Status

13. BMOT   (5269)
14. HMOT   (0.2392)
15. JMOT   (2.2238)   } Definitions parallel those of MWL group
16. NMOT   (4614)

TABLE 4.1 (cont.)

UIE Group: Unrelated Individuals, Earners

17. BUIE	(2900)	Mean income
18. HUIE	(0.4804)	Income below which 25 percent of individuals lie, divided by group median
19. JUIE	(1.6103)	Income above which 25 percent of individuals lie, divided by group median
20. NUIE	(2613)	Median income

UIN Group: Unrelated Individuals, Nonearners

21. BUIN	(1135)	Mean income
22. HUIN	(1.7752)	Income above which 79.46 percent of individuals lie, divided by group median
23. JUIN	(3.6790)	Income above which 95 percent of individuals lie, divided by group median
24. NUIN	(779)	Median income

Allocation Variables

25. PAR1	(0.277)	Number of families in MWL group as proportion of number of families in MWL and MWN groups combined
26. PAR3	(0.6392)	Number of individuals in UIE group as proportion of total number of unrelated individuals

B. OTHER VARIABLES

Primary data source: National income account data from Office of Business Economics, as reported in the *Annual Report of the Council of Economic Advisers*, 1967 and 1968. Employment data from the Bureau of Labor Statistics, as reported in the above and also in the *Manpower Report of the President*, 1965 and 1966.

Mean values for 1949–65 appear in parentheses. Per capita figures deflated by the noninstitutional population aged 14 or over; dollar figures in real terms, deflated by the GNP implicit price deflator.

1. CWEN	(1.037)	$(W_t/W_{t-1}) \cdot (PGNP_t/PGNP_{t-1})$; rate of change of annual wage rate, current dollars
2. E	(0.949)	$1 - U$; employment rate
3. L	(0.560)	Civilian labor force as fraction of population aged 14+
4. E*	(0.531)	$E \cdot L$; employment as fraction of population aged 14+
5. PAR2	(0.3955)	Labor force participation rate, females other marital status, March of year following income period, BLS data
6. PGNP	(0.962)	Implicit price deflator for gross national product, 1958 = 1.000

TABLE 4.1 (cont.)

7. $PROF^{**}$ (0.173) Corporate profits and capital consumption allowances as a share of gross private product

8. T (11) Time trend; 1947 = 1, 1948 = 2, etc.

9. U (0.051) Unemployment rate

10. UBR (639) Unemployment benefits per unemployed person, 1958 dollars per year

11. W (4369) Private wage and salary disbursements per private wage and salary employee (including agricultural wage and salary employees), 1958 dollars per year

12. Y (2919) Personal income per capita, 1958 dollars, excluding rental income of persons

13. Y_{ID} (270) Interest and dividend income per capita, 1958 dollars

14. Y_{TR} (169) Government transfer payments per capita, 1958 dollars, excluding unemployment benefits

15. Y_{UB} (18) Unemployment benefits per capita, 1958 dollars

16. Y_w (2064) Wage disbursements per capita, 1958 dollars

17. Y_O (398) $Y - Y_w - Y_{TR} - Y_{UB} - Y_{ID}$; other personal income per capita, 1958 dollars

18. $Y_{ID}^{**} + Y_O^{**}$ (0.269) Interest, dividend, "other," and rental personal income as a share of *total* personal income, including rental income

19. Y_{TR}^{**} (0.0537) Government transfer payments, excluding unemployment benefits, as a share of *total* personal income.

Estimating the mean for families with a female head is considerably more difficult, both because of the smaller sample size underlying the data source and because of substantial fluctuations in the group mean during the early post-World War II and Korean war periods. With the simplifying restriction that wage income and unemployment compensation go entirely to group members with a participant in the labor force and that other income goes exclusively to the remaining members, specification (4.5) is obtained:

$$BFEM = (a_1 W \cdot E + a_2 UBR \cdot U) \cdot PAR2 + [a_3 Y_{TR} + a_4(Y_{ID} + Y_O)] \cdot (1 - PAR2) + u_3. \quad (4.5)$$

Specifications for the remaining three groups appear as follows:

$$BMOT = a_1 W \cdot E \cdot L + a_2 UBR \cdot U \cdot L + a_3 Y_{TR} + a_4(Y_{ID} + Y_O) + u_4 \quad (4.6)$$

$$BUIE = a_1 W \cdot E + a_2 UBR \cdot U + a_3 Y_{TR}$$
$$+ a_4(Y_{ID} + Y_O) + u_5 \tag{4.7}$$

$$NUIN = a_1 Y_{TR} + a_2(Y_{ID} + Y_O) + a_3 U + u_6. \tag{4.8}$$

Specifications (4.6) and (4.7) are similar to previous expressions with a male head, with two exceptions. First, a time trend and the labor force participation rate of wives were included in the wage rate terms for the MWL and the MWN groups to account for secular and cyclical movements between the two groups; these variables are excluded here. Second, the labor force participation rate of unrelated individuals who are earners is assumed to be constant.[8]

Specification (4.8), for unrelated individuals who are not earners, is based on the group median rather than the mean. With a median in the vicinity of $1000 and with both quantile measures above the median, the mean income estimate for the UIN group is less stable than for the preceding five groups.[9] By definition, the UIN group receives no wage income. Since the composition of the nonearner group changes with labor market conditions, the unemployment rate is included in the specification to reflect the influence of these changes on median income.

GROUP MEAN INCOME SPECIFICATIONS: ESTIMATED EQUATIONS

We can now proceed with a discussion of empirical estimates of the group mean income equations specified above. Estimates were obtained by a two-stage least squares estimation procedure described in the appendix to chapter 4. Corresponding to the specifications, the equations were estimated without an intercept term, unless the inclusion of a free intercept reduced the standard error of estimate.[10]

Equations (4.9)–(4.13) and (4.15) correspond to specifications (4.3)–(4.8) above, with several alterations. Given the severe lack of degrees of freedom at our disposal, income sources were combined whenever their individual coefficients were not significantly different from each other; an income source was excluded entirely if such action improved

---

[8] This is not definitionally true, since earners need not be in the labor force at the time the survey is taken.

[9] See Table 3.6. Estimates for both the median and the mean will be presented below.

[10] See the appendix to chapter 4 for a discussion of the implications of this procedure.

the goodness of fit more than combining it with another source. In addition, the assumption of a constant group labor force participation rate yielded systematically better empirical results than the assumption of proportionality of the group rate with the aggregate rate (L). The aggregate labor force participation rate was therefore omitted from the wage income variable.

For the mean income of families in the MWL group, coefficients associated with nonwage income sources were not statistically significant.[11] This result is not entirely surprising since the MWL group presumably receives most of its income from wage sources. The wage coefficient is highly significant; it is increasing over time but decreasing as the labor force participation rate of wives rises.[12] Since the participation rate of wives has been increasing over time, we can interpret the negative coefficient as applying to deviations of the participation rate from its trend.[13]

This interpretation suggests that marginal entrants into this classification, exclusive of trend, are receiving lower average wages than the remainder of the group: this would occur if such entrants are more likely

---

[11] If specification (4.3) is estimated by ordinary least squares, we obtain the following:

$$BMWL = (1.789 + 0.036T - 2.256PAR1) \cdot W \cdot E + 3.211UBR \cdot U$$
$$\quad\;\; (0.169)\;\; (0.005)\quad (0.619)\qquad\qquad\qquad (1.543)$$
$$\quad -2.977Y_{TR} + 0.86(Y_{ID} + Y_O)$$
$$\quad\;\; (1.654)\qquad (0.88)$$

$$R^2 = .997 \qquad F(5, 11) = 870$$
$$D\text{-}W = 1.14 \qquad \text{s.e.} = 53.8$$
$$1949\text{-}65$$

The coefficient on transfer income is negative, contrary to its representation as an income component, and insignificant. The coefficient on "other" personal income is exceeded in value by its standard error. The coefficient on unemployment benefits is significant, but larger than expected. The Durbin-Watson statistic has a disreputably low value.

The deletion of the coefficient on "other" personal income has little effect on the structure of the equation, except that it increases the significance of the unemployment variable and decreases the absolute value of the transfer coefficient. The deletion of the transfer variable removes the significance of the unemployment variable and inflates the Durbin-Watson statistic to a respectable level.

[12] That is, as the proportion of families with male heads falling into the MWL classification rises.

[13] We have $PAR1 = \alpha T + e$, $\alpha > 0$. Then the expression $(0.0313T - 2.170PAR1)$ can be written as $(0.0313 - 2.17\alpha)T - 2.17e$, where the net time coefficient is still positive.

to be part-time participants, have generally lower skill levels, or if the wives are providing a substitute income source for husbands with temporarily low income levels. The positive time trend in the wage coefficient[14] suggests that the average compensation of working wives is rising relative to the male wage rate: either because the long-run tendency is toward a higher proportion of wives (of those in the labor force) working full time, or because female wage rates are rising on the average relative to male wage rates.

The mean value of the wage coefficient[15] is about 1.6; this result is quite reasonable given the typical presence of two labor force participants, and the presumption that the average working wife receives less than the full-time equivalent annual wage.[16] The coefficient on unemployment benefits is not significant, although it assumes a reasonable value.

The mean income estimate for the MWN group appears as equation (4.10). Unlike the case in equation (4.9), transfer income played a significant role in determining the mean, but complications in the wage rate specification did not. The transfer coefficient is surprisingly large, but it is offset by a significantly negative intercept. Nonwage, nontransfer sources of income do not have a significant effect on the estimate of BMWN; whether this is so because interest and dividend income is more likely to be underreported in the CPS data than other types of income or because it is too collinear with other income sources is unclear.

Equation (4.11) provides a mean income estimate for families with a female head.[17] Given the importance to this group of transfer payments as an income component, we would expect to observe a heavy weight placed upon the transfer variable. Given the approximation that families with the head in the labor force receive only wage income and that other families receive only transfer income, we find that the marginal wage-receiving family receives 88 percent of the average annual wage, and that the marginal transfer receiving family receives six times the average transfer level (excluding unemployment benefits) per person over fourteen. As in the two previous groups, other sources of personal income played no significant role in predicting the mean level of income. In addition, there is a significantly positive intercept of approximately $1500; the intercept may be reflecting other sources of group income

---

[14] Net of the negative sign on the trend in the $PAR1$ variable.

[15] That is, of $(1.855 + 0.0313T - 2.170PAR1)$.

[16] The above comments about wives in the labor force are meant to be suggestive only; a careful investigation of the labor force behavior of wives is beyond the scope of this study.

[17] Specifications using observations from 1947 or using the median provided an even poorer fit.

EQUATIONS (4.9)–(4.15). ESTIMATED MEAN INCOME
SPECIFICATIONS

$BMWL = (1.855 + 0.0313T - 2.170PAR1) \cdot W \cdot E + 1.343UBR \cdot U$
(0.139) (0.0054)   (0.705)   (1.374)

$R^2 = .997$ $F(3, 13) = 1296$ (4.9)
$D\text{-}W = 1.86$ s.e. $= 56.9$
1949–65

$BMWN = -712.6 + 1.222W \cdot E + 6.225(Y_{TR} + Y_{UB})$
(231.5) (0.078)   (0.639)

$R^2 = .994$ $F(2, 14) = 1101$ (4.10)
$D\text{-}W = 2.25$ s.e. $= 58.9$
1949–65

$BFEM = 1533 + 0.879W \cdot E \cdot PAR2 + 6.007Y_{TR} \cdot (1 - PAR2)$
(566) (0.473)   (2.928)

$R^2 = .742$ $F(2, 14) = 20.1$ (4.11)
$D\text{-}W = 2.25$ s.e. $= 170.5$
1949–65

$BMOT = 0.543W \cdot E + 3.578(Y_{TR} + Y_{UB} + Y_{ID} + Y_O)$
(0.270)   (1.289)

$R^2 = .874$ $F(1, 17) = 117.4$ (4.12)
$D\text{-}W = 1.29$ s.e. $= 216.7$
1947–65

$BUIE = -1658 + 0.591W \cdot E + 3.008(Y_{TR} + Y_{UB}) + 2.346(Y_{ID} + Y_O)$
(519) (0.128)   (1.181)   (1.184)

$R^2 = .966$ $F(3, 15) = 143.8$ (4.13)
$D\text{-}W = 2.01$ s.e. $= 95.9$
1947–65

$BUIN = 630 + 5.214Y_{TR} - 6583U$
(140) (0.870)   (3087)

$R^2 = .703$ $F(2, 16) = 18.9$ (4.14)
$D\text{-}W = 1.63$ s.e. $= 125.7$
Ordinary least squares
1947–65

$NUIN = 401 + 3.538Y_{TR} - 3829U$
(56) (0.342)   (1304)

$R^2 = .880$ $F(2, 16) = 58.9$ (4.15)
$D\text{-}W = 1.93$ s.e. $= 48.3$
1947–65

Coefficient standard errors are reported in parentheses. With the exception of (4.14), which is not included in the final model, all equations were estimated by the two-stage least squares procedure described in the appendix to chapter 4. Estimation by ordinary least squares produced similar results. Variables are defined in Table 4.1.

better than attempts to relate these sources to their aggregate counter-parts.

If a more complex relationship is constructed to account for the effects of labor force participation changes, price changes, and the size of the armed forces, the goodness of fit improves considerably. Such relationships involve the presence of a number of highly collinear variables bearing nonsensical coefficients; the transfer coefficient is typically negative.[18] Only extremely simple specifications produced results capable of meaningful interpretation.

The MOT (families, male head, "other" marital status) group is the smallest of the six.[19] Correspondingly, its data are drawn from a smaller sample and have a larger sampling variance. The specification of significant distributional relationships was correspondingly more difficult, especially in the H and J equations discussed below. Equation (4.12) combines all sources of nonwage income into a single variable; an alternative specification separated transfer income from other nonwage income, with the resulting coefficients being significantly different from zero but not from each other.

A major characteristic of the MOT group and of the unrelated individual groups is the relatively heavy dependence upon nonwage income sources. Both families in the MOT group and unrelated individuals who were earners (UIE) had implicit wage receipts in the range of 54–60 percent of the average annual wage payment (per person in the labor force). Factors contributing to this low coefficient value could include the possibility that labor force participants in these groups face lower wage rates, that their unemployment rate is higher, or that their effective labor force participation rate (after adjusting the part-time participants) is lower than comparable aggregate levels.[20] The implicit weight on transfer payments is 3.0–3.6 times the average level per person over fourteen. The

---

[18]Consider, for example, the following least squares regression, where the transfer coefficient is -9.2:

$$BFEM = 1.585W - 9.168Y_{TR} - 0.0020PAR2 - 0.038ARMY$$
$$(0.320) \quad (3.309) \quad (0.0016) \quad (0.014)$$

$$R^2 = .866 \quad F(3, 13) = 28.0$$
$$D\text{-}W = 2.32 \quad \text{s.e.} = 127.6$$
$$1949\text{-}65$$

Such results in the presence of highly collinear variables typically lead one to suspect rounding error as a major contributor to the goodness of fit.

[19]In 1965, only 1.2 million out of 43.3 million families were in this category.

[20]It should be recalled that the UIE group includes all unrelated individuals who were earners *at any time* during the previous year; it therefore includes a larger proportion of unrelated individuals.

MOT group is the only one in which nontransfer sources of nonwage income had a significantly positive effect on the mean income estimate.

As stated above, median income had a much stronger empirical relationship with the aggregate data than mean income for unrelated individuals who were nonearners. Both the median and the mean vary positively with the level of transfer payments[21] and negatively with the unemployment rate.

H AND *J* EQUATION ESTIMATES

Obtaining empirical estimates for the *H* and *J* variables involves a more complex procedure. While a group mean is a linear sum of mean income components, quantile distributional variables are nonlinearly related to the group mean. A quantile income total equals the sum of component incomes at that quantile, each of which is at best nonlinearly related to the mean level of that income source. Since it is not possible to aggregate displaced lognormal functions, income components will not be distributed according to the same functional form as the distribution of total group income. As a result, some approximation must be utilized.

When group decile income $Y10_i$ is expressed as a sum of components in a manner parallel to the construction of equation (4.2) for the mean, such as

$$Y10_i = \text{(decile wage income)}_i + \text{(decile transfer income)}_i + \text{(decile ``other'' personal income)}_i, \quad (4.16)$$

a critical problem is immediately encountered: no order statistics of the required sort are available. The decile income components must be approximated by functions of mean levels of the appropriate aggregate variables. One approximation of equation (4.16) which can be estimated from available data is

$$Y10_i \cong [b_1\text{(mean wage income)}_i + b_2\text{(mean transfer income)}_i + b_3\text{(mean ``other'' personal income)}_i] \cdot (N_i/B_i), \quad (4.17)$$

where quantile components are replaced by linear functions of group mean income components deflated by the ratio of the median to the mean. The deflation is assumed to linearize the relationship, although such an assumption is true only in the limit as the quantile being observed on

---

[21] Again, other sources of nonwage income had no significant impact on the equation. This is particularly surprising for a group which by definition receives no wage income.

the left-hand side approaches the median. At that point, equation (4.17) degenerates into a trivial identity.

If both sides of equation (4.17) are divided by N_i, the value of H_i is specified to be a linear function of group income shares with the sum of the shares theoretically adding to one. The inclusion of an intercept would be redundant under such circumstances.[22] In fact, however, variables such as (mean wage income)$_i$ are approximated as functions of global income data, while B_i is derived from the CPS distributional data. The implicit shares in the specification will therefore not add to one, and an intercept could be included. As before, all equations of this type were tried both with and without intercept terms; where the intercept was not significant it was deleted.[23]

While equation (4.17) serves as a stylistic model for the H and J specifications, the statement that H or J is estimated as a linear function of group income shares is not strictly true. Before estimation, the linear components in equation (4.17) are further broken down in the manner shown by equation (4.2). Assumed relationships between individual components and their global counterparts are not necessarily the same in different equations.

Consider the specification for the lower tail of the MWL group:

$$HMWL = [(b_1 + b_2 U) \cdot UBR + (b_3 + b_4 T + b_5 PAR1) \cdot W \cdot$$
$$(b_6 + b_7 E) + b_8 Y_{TR} + b_9 (Y_{ID} + Y_O)]/BMWL + u_7. \qquad (4.18)$$

Since unemployment is presumably a more important factor in determining income levels at the lower tail of the distribution than elsewhere, it was decided to test for nonproportionality of group employment and unemployment rates with their global counterparts; the numerator of (4.18) therefore differs in form from the specification of the mean [equation (4.3)].[24] The form of the wage rate is the same as in equation (4.3), but the coefficients are permitted to take on different values.

An unrestricted estimation procedure for equation (4.18) would require ten degrees of freedom. Because the MWL group is primarily dependent upon wage income, however, coefficients b_8 and b_9 were not significant. Furthermore, because of paucity of degrees of freedom and because of collinearity among the multiplicative terms involving b_3

---

[22] Or any other circumstance where the sum of estimated factor shares is constant, regardless of whether they sum to one.

[23] Similarly, an intercept could be included in numerator specification (4.16) prior to deflation by (N_i/B_i) and division by N_i. In the estimation form such as (4.17), the result would be not a free intercept, but a term such as (b_0/B_i).

[24] Since $U = 1 - E$, a strict specification would require that $b_6 = (1 - b_1 - b_2)$ and $b_2 = b_7$.

through b_6, the equation was modified by the omission of the cross-product terms involving $b_4 \cdot b_6$ and $b_5 \cdot b_6$.

Two alternatives to specification (4.17) and the form represented by (4.18) were examined. One alternative was to eliminate the (N_i/B_i) deflation term in (4.17), or equivalently to substitute the group median (NMWL) for the mean (BMWL) in the denominator of (4.18). Empirically, removal of the (N_i/B_i) deflator reduces substantially the goodness of fit in most H and J equations. Furthermore, removal of the deflator destroys certain homogeneity properties of a specification such as (4.18): both sides of (4.18) are scale-free numbers in that HMWL is a ratio of two quantile levels of dollars per year, while the right-hand side is implicitly a linear combination of mean income components divided by a group mean. If the (N_i/B_i) deflator were removed, the revised specification for (4.18) would relate a scale-free quantile ratio to a "mixed" ratio of mean income variables to a quantile measure.

The remaining alternative is to abandon the attempt to find implicit group income shares and to relate the H_i and J_i variables directly to aggregate personal income shares, such as the ratio of total wage and salary income to personal income. Such a specification would lose some sensitivity to characteristics unique to a given group, but it is worth considering for some of the smaller sample groups with a lot of "noise" in the distributional data.

This procedure brings to the surface the collinearity problem involved in including intercept terms in the previous specifications: here the shares add precisely to one, and either the intercept or one of the income components *must* be omitted for estimation to proceed. Variables such as T and $PAR1$, which appear multiplicatively in specification (4.18), can be attached in the same manner to the income shares of this latter procedure.[25]

In most cases, for the reasons stated, the two alternatives discussed above were discarded in favor of the specification initially proposed. While the particular specification considered above dealt with the bottom decile income level, a parallel approach was taken to variables relating to the upper tail of the distribution.

Estimated equations for specification (4.18) and for similar relationships for the upper tail of the distribution for the six groups appear below.[26] The coefficients in equations (4.20) through (4.30) do not indicate

---

[25] Due to the relationship among the income shares, inclusion of a *linear* time trend in the specification would be equivalent to attaching it multiplicatively to *every* share variable and constraining all the coefficients to be the same.

[26] It was not possible to find a specification which could significantly determine the upper tail of the FEM group.

the total effect of global variables on the tails of the group distributions because the same variables often enter the mean income equation as well; the mean, in turn, is an argument of the H and J equations. Total elasticities of estimated variables with respect to all global variables appear in Table 4.2. The elasticity of an H (or J) equation with respect to any argument X is defined as follows.

$$\frac{E(H)}{E(X)} = \left[\frac{\partial H}{\partial X} + \left(\frac{\partial H}{\partial B} \cdot \frac{\partial B}{\partial X}\right)\right] \cdot \left(\frac{X}{H}\right) \tag{4.19}$$

According to equation (4.20), the lower tail of the MWL group distribution responds positively to increases both in the real wage rate and in the employment rate. There is a positive time trend, while the sign on *PAR1*, the wife labor force participation rate, is negative. Since *PAR1* has increased over time these effects are largely offsetting. An increase in unemployment benefits per unemployed person improves the lower tail relative to the median at unemployment rates in excess of 5.8 percent.

EQUATIONS (4.20)–(4.30). ESTIMATED DISTRIBUTIONAL VARIABLE SPECIFICATIONS

$HMWL = \{(-3.755 + 64.86U) \cdot UBR + W \cdot [-9.682 + (11.43 + 0.0379T$
$\qquad$ (1.300) (22.70) $\qquad\qquad$ (3.098) $\quad$ (3.26) (0.0047)

$\qquad -3.365PAR1) \cdot E]\}/BMWL$
$\qquad$ (0.601)

$$\tag{4.20}$$

$\qquad\qquad R^2 = .928 \qquad F(5, 11) = 28.4$
$\qquad\qquad D\text{-}W = 2.08 \qquad\quad \text{s.e.} = 0.00728$
$\qquad\qquad 1949\text{–}65$

$JMWL = 2.618 - 2.383PROF^{**} + [(-3.010 - 0.0531T + 1.172CWEN$
$\qquad$ (0.596) (0.639) $\qquad\qquad$ (1.169) (0.0226) $\quad$ (0.302)

$\qquad + 1.943PAR1) \cdot W \cdot E + 7.746Y_{TR} + 12.604Y_{ID}]/BMWL$
$\qquad$ (1.886) $\qquad\qquad$ (2.151) $\qquad$ (3.141)

$$\tag{4.21}$$

$\qquad\qquad R^2 = .952 \qquad F(7, 9) = 25.0$
$\qquad\qquad D\text{-}W = 2.19 \qquad\quad \text{s.e.} = 0.0108$
$\qquad\qquad 1949\text{–}65$

$HMWN = [829.6 + (-0.9230 + 0.7151CWEN + 1.327PAR1) \cdot W \cdot E$
$\qquad$ (590.1) $\quad$ (0.2249) $\quad$ (0.1588) $\qquad$ (0.343)

$\qquad + 2.450UBR \cdot U]/BMWN$
$\qquad$ (1.652)

$$\tag{4.22}$$

$\qquad\qquad R^2 = .845 \qquad F(4, 12) = 16.4$
$\qquad\qquad D\text{-}W = 2.59 \qquad\quad \text{s.e.} = 0.00824$
$\qquad\qquad 1949\text{–}65$

$$JMWN = 4.500 + [-7452.6 + (-0.0979T - 4.3715CWEN) \cdot W \cdot E^*$$
$$(0.530) \quad (2239.2) \quad\quad (0.0261) \quad\quad (0.4813)$$

$$+ 10.186(Y_{ID} + Y_O)]/BMWN$$
$$(1.816)$$

$$(4.23)$$

$$R^2 = .882 \quad\quad F(4, 12) = 22.4$$
$$D\text{-}W = 2.33 \quad\quad \text{s.e.} = 0.0219$$
$$1949\text{--}65$$

$$HFEM = 0.3384 + \{-1087.8 + [-0.5263 + (3.0402 - 2.325CWEN)$$
$$(0.2115) \quad (524.5) \quad\quad (0.3290) \quad (1.1988) \quad (1.048)$$

$$\cdot E \cdot PAR2] \cdot W + 2.997Y_{TR} \cdot (1 - PAR2) + 2.858(Y_{ID} + Y_O)\}/BFEM$$
$$(2.369) \quad\quad\quad\quad\quad\quad (1.481)$$

$$(4.24)$$

$$R^2 = .842 \quad\quad F(6, 10) = 8.88$$
$$D\text{-}W = 2.46 \quad\quad \text{s.e.} = 0.0186$$
$$1949\text{--}65$$

$$HMOT = 0.3587 + [-911.8 + (-0.519 + 0.913CWEN \cdot E^*) \cdot W$$
$$(0.1196) \quad (451.4) \quad\quad (0.233) \quad (0.495)$$

$$+ 2.293Y_{TR}]/BMOT$$
$$(1.566)$$

$$(4.25)$$

$$R^2 = .610 \quad\quad F(4, 14) = 5.47$$
$$D\text{-}W = 2.50 \quad\quad \text{s.e.} = 0.0205$$
$$1947\text{--}65$$

$$JMOT = 1.210W \cdot E^*/NMOT + 9.803Y_{TR}^{**} + 7.863(Y_{ID}^{**} + Y_O^{**}) - 6.056PROF^{**}$$
$$(0.643) \quad\quad\quad\quad\quad\quad (2.436) \quad\quad (1.343) \quad\quad\quad (2.078)$$

$$(4.26)$$

$$R^2 = .643 \quad\quad F(3, 15) = 9.01$$
$$D\text{-}W = 2.58 \quad\quad \text{s.e.} = 0.0799$$
$$1947\text{--}65$$

$$HUIE = 0.6823 + [(-3.267 + 3.790E) \cdot W + (-2.685PAR3 - 0.6196CWEN)$$
$$(0.0904) \quad (0.823) \quad (1.038) \quad\quad\quad (0.3255) \quad\quad (0.1346)$$

$$\cdot W \cdot E + 9.343UBR \cdot U + 1.522(Y_{ID} + Y_O)]/BUIE$$
$$(3.455) \quad\quad\quad (0.472)$$

$$(4.27)$$

$$R^2 = .812 \quad\quad F(6, 12) = 8.66$$
$$D\text{-}W = 3.28 \quad\quad \text{s.e.} = 0.0117$$
$$1947\text{--}65$$

$$JUIE = 2.086 + [(0.888 - 0.0152T - 1.129PAR3) \cdot W \cdot E$$
$$(0.368) \quad (0.506) \quad (0.0069) \quad (0.551)$$

$$+ 7.030Y_{TR} - 3.655(Y_{ID} + Y_O)]/BUIE$$
$$(2.469) \quad\quad (1.970)$$

$$(4.28)$$

$$R^2 = .606 \quad\quad F(5, 13) = 4.01$$
$$D\text{-}W = 1.49 \quad\quad \text{s.e.} = 0.0445$$
$$\text{Ordinary least squares}$$
$$1947\text{--}65$$

$$H\text{UIN} = [845.4 + 2.753Y_{TR} - 1.915(Y_{ID} + Y_O)]/B\text{UIN} + 1.881C\text{WEN} - 0.0151T$$
$$\phantom{H\text{UIN} = [}(500.2)\ (0.865)\quad (0.920)\phantom{]/B\text{UIN} }\quad\quad (0.103)\quad\quad (0.0048)$$

$$
\begin{aligned}
&R^2 = .884 \qquad F(4,\ 14) = 26.7 \\
&D\text{-}W = 2.40 \qquad \text{s.e.} = 0.0413 \\
&1949\text{–}65
\end{aligned}
\qquad\qquad (4.29)
$$

$$J\text{UIN} = -1556.8/B\text{UIN} + 5.440C\text{WEN} - 0.0501T$$
$$\phantom{J\text{UIN} = }(446.4)\phantom{/B\text{UIN} }\quad\quad (0.478)\quad\quad\ \ (0.0121)$$

$$
\begin{aligned}
&R^2 = .709 \qquad F(2,\ 16) = 19.5 \\
&D\text{-}W = 1.87 \qquad \text{s.e.} = 0.2206 \\
&1947\text{–}65
\end{aligned}
\qquad\qquad (4.30)
$$

When the effects of these same variables on the mean are also accounted for, an increase in the real wage rate has a negligible effect ($E < 0.1$) on the *relative* position of the lower tail of the distribution. Roughly speaking, a 1 percent increase in real wages shifts the entire MWL distribution upward by 1 percent. A change in the employment rate has a substantial effect on both the position and the shape of the distribution, with the elasticities of the mean (BMWL), HMWL, and JMWL with respect to the employment rate being 0.9, 1.3, and -0.4, respectively. An increase in the employment rate raises the lower tail of the distribution relative to the median by a substantial amount, while the relative (but not the absolute) position of the upper tail of the distribution tends to fall.

Changes in the participation rate of wives have a noticeable effect on the shape of the MWL distribution. Abstracting from trend, marginal entrants into the group have the effect of lowering the mean of the distribution ($E = -1.0$). Although *PAR1* enters the *J*MWL equation directly with a positive sign, the total effect of that variable is negligible.

A number of factors tend to affect the upper tail of the MWL distribution exclusively. Both transfer payments (excluding unemployment benefits) and interest and dividend payments have a positive effect on the upper tail of the distribution, with the elasticity with respect to interest and dividend payments being 0.3.

At the same time, the relative position of the upper tail of the distribution is negatively correlated with corporate profits (including depreciation allowances) as a share of gross private product (GPP). This phenomenon reappears in the distribution for families with a male head, "other" marital status. The corporate share of GPP tends to rise as the economy moves out of a recession into a boom. During such periods, the share of measured personal income going to the upper tail of the distribution declines; this cyclical movement is apparently *not* adequately reflected by changes in levels of aggregate *mean* income components.

Finally, the upper tail of the MWL group improves relative to the remainder of the distribution when current dollar wage rates are changing rapidly, given the real level of all income components (including wage income). Since an increase in nominal wages, given the *real* wage rate, is equivalent to a change in prices, there is an implicit positive elasticity of response to the GNP price deflator of 0.4.[27] This finding is unique for the upper tail of a group distribution; it is probably attributable to the labor-force-oriented character of the group.

The response of families with a male head and a wife not in the labor force differs substantially from the group just observed. The MWN-group family typically has one earner rather than two and is considerably more dependent upon nonwage income sources than is the MWL-group family.

The specifications for equations (4.22) and (4.23) are similar to the corresponding structures for the MWL group. The implicit wage rate relevant for the lower tail of the MWN group is a higher proportion of the aggregate wage rate when wages are changing rapidly; the allocation of families between the MWL and MWN groups is also an important factor. The upper tail specification provided better empirical results when employment was defined as a fraction of the adult population (E^*) rather than as a fraction of the civilian labor force.

The mean of the MWN group has an elasticity of 0.93 with respect to W and 0.54 with respect to E, compared to corresponding elasticities of 1.00 and 0.88 for the MWL group. An increase in real wages has a positive effect on the lower tail of the distribution ($E = 1.35$) and a negative effect on the upper tail ($E = -1.0$). An increase in the employment rate affects both tails of the distribution negatively, but the opposite signs on W and E in the lower-tail equation may be due to a collinearity problem. Given that W and E tend to move together during the business cycle, the net effect appears to be that the lower tail of the distribution rises and the upper tail falls during a period of tight employment. This conclusion is reinforced by the elasticity of response to a change in prices. A 1.0 percent increase in the GNP price deflator would bring about a 1.8 percent increase in HMWN and a 1.0 percent decline in JMWN. It should be kept in mind, however, that real, not nominal, levels of income sources are held fixed when these elasticities are calculated.

Nonwage income sources have a significantly positive effect on the

---

[27] It should be noted that if the rate of change in nominal wages is interpreted as consisting of a real wage change and a price change, the major source of variation is the price component. The explicit use of a price change variable produces virtually equivalent empirical results.

TABLE 4.2. PARTIAL ELASTICITIES OF DISTRIBUTIONAL VARIABLES WITH RESPECT TO GLOBAL VARIABLES

	Elasticity of							
With respect to:	BMWL	HMWL	JMWL	BMWN	HMWN	JMWN	BFEM	HFEM
W	0.998	0.089	0.042	0.933	1.354	−1.000	0.406	−4.794
E	0.875	1.305	−0.427	0.544	−0.969	−0.518	0.406	1.005
$PAR1$	−0.376	−1.0485	0.093	—	0.907	—	—	—
$PAR2$	—	—	—	—	—	—	0.293	0.806
$PAR3$	—	—	—	—	—	—	—	—
T^{a}	130.0	—	—	—	—	—	—	—
UBR	0.066	0.0157	−0.0240	0.021	0.217	−0.0418	—	—
Y_{TR}	—	−0.112	0.002	0.194	−0.194	0.026	—	—
Y_{TR}^{**}	—	—	0.113	—	—	0.242	0.173	0.304
Y_{ID}	—	—	0.294	—	—	0.626	—	—
$(Y_{ID} + Y_{0})$	—	—	—	—	—	—	—	1.771
$(Y_{ID}^{**} + Y_{0}^{**})$	—	—	—	—	—	—	—	—
$PGNP$	—	—	0.436	—	1.828	−0.967	—	−3.665
$PROF^{**}$	—	—	−0.237	—	—	—	—	—

TABLE 4.2 (cont.)

	Elasticity of									
	BMOT	HMOT	JMOT	BUIE	HUIE	JUIE	BUIN	NUIN	HUIN	JUIN
W	0.427	2.490	0.157	0.845	-2.947	0.249	–	–	1.098	1.533
E	0.427	1.258	0.157	0.845	2.605	0.249	5.504	4.665	-0.0861	2.053
PAR1	–	–	–	–	–	–	–	–	–	–
PAR2	–	–	–	–	–	–	–	–	–	–
PAR3	–	–	–	–	-0.511	-0.641	–	–	–	–
T^a	–	–	–	–	–	-0.217	–	–	–	–
UBR	0.013	0.006	-0.004	0.020	0.227	0.006	–	–	0.0151	0.0501
Y_{TR}	0.115	0.313	–	0.175	0.074	0.306	0.776	0.768	0.219	0.290
Y^{**}_{TR}	–	–	0.237	–	–	–	–	–	–	–
Y_{ID}	–	–	–	–	–	–	–	–	–	–
$(Y_{ID} + Y_O)$	0.454	0.227	0.952	0.297	0.957	-0.363	–	–	-0.635	–
$(Y^{**}_{ID} + Y^{**}_O)$	–	–	–	–	–	–	–	–	–	–
PGNP	–	1.741	–	–	-1.912	–	–	–	1.098	1.533
PROF**	–	–	-0.471	–	–	–	–	–	–	–

Source: Equations (4.9)–(4.15) and (4.20)–(4.30). If $B = F(\ldots X, \ldots)$ then $E(B)/E(X) = (\partial B/\partial X) \cdot (X/B)$. If H or $J = F(\ldots X, \ldots B)$, then $E(H)/E(X) = \{(\partial H/\partial X) + [(\partial H/\partial B) \cdot (\partial B/\partial X)]\} \cdot (X/H)$.

[a] Partial derivative, not elasticity.

level of $JMWN$, a much stronger effect than what is observed for $JMWL$. This finding is consistent with the presumption that the MWN group is the more dependent of the two upon nonwage income sources. What is surprising is that, except for unemployment benefits, nonwage income sources have no significant impact on the lower tail of the MWN distribution.

The specification for the bottom of the distribution of families with a female head utilizes the simplifying restriction introduced in the mean income equation for the same group: wage income is assumed to go entirely to families with the head in the labor force, while transfer income is assumed to go only to families with the head *not* in the labor force. It was not possible to obtain a reasonable estimated relationship determining the upper tail of the female head distribution. The upper-tail statistic has no perceptible time trend[28] and has a small variance relative to its expected variance from sampling error alone.

Taken as a group, families with a female head respond positively to an increase in real wages or employment, with the elasticities of 0.4 being close to the labor force participation rate of these heads. The elasticity of response to an increase in real transfer levels (excluding unemployment benefits) is positive but rather small. As one might expect, an increase in the labor force participation rate (of females, "other marital status") has a positive effect on the mean of the distribution and an even stronger effect ($E = 0.8$) on the lower tail of the distribution.

Families at the bottom end of the female head income distribution respond in a radically different way from other low income families. While an increase in the employment rate does have a positive effect ($E = 1.0$), increases in W and $PGNP$ have an overwhelmingly negative effect on the level of HFEM, with elasticities of -4.8 and -3.7, respectively. The dependence of such families upon nonwage income sources is apparent, with an elasticity with respect to real transfer levels of 0.3 and with respect to other nonwage income sources of almost 1.8.

Because of the large sampling variability in the MOT group data, standards of selection for the equation specifications were more lax than for the previous groups. Equation (4.25) is a simplification of a more complex expression, from which a number of collinear terms were deleted.[29] The best results obtainable for the upper tail of the distribution were generated by a combined form [equation (4.26)] using a median deflator

---

[28] $JFEM = 2.206 - 0.0003TIME;$ $R^2 = .001;$ 1947–65. In the simulations to be reported below, $JFEM$ is assumed to remain fixed in value.

[29] Equation (4.25) is derived from an initial specification of the form

$$HMOT = a_0 + (a_1 + \hat{W} \cdot \hat{E} + a_6 Y_{TR})/BMOT$$

on the wage income variable and "share" variables for other income sources.

The final results are not unreasonable in light of the responses of the groups already examined. The position of the lower tail responds positively to the level of transfer payments ($E = 0.31$) and to "other" personal income ($E = 0.23$), as well as to conditions of tight employment. While the point estimates of the partial elasticities of HMOT with respect to the real wage rate (2.49), employment per capita (1.26), and the price level (1.74) are *individually* sensitive to the choice of equation specification, the pattern of the response to the three variables taken together is not.

The response of the upper tail of the MOT distribution to increases in wage income is small but positive ($E = 0.16$), while the shares of personal income derived from transfers ($E = 0.24$) and "other" personal income ($E = 0.95$) play a more important role. The negative relationship between the corporate profit share and the upper tail of the distribution, which appeared for the MWL group, occurs again for the MOT group.

Unrelated individuals who were earners were similar to families with a female head in the positive response of the lower tail of the distribution to the employment rate ($E = 2.6$) and the negative response to wage ($E = -0.295$) and price ($E = -1.91$) changes. Given the labor force orientation of the group, HUIE responded positively to unemployment benefits but only indirectly to other transfers.

The upper tail of the UIE distribution is positively related to wage and employment levels ($E = 0.25$) and exhibits a negative time trend. Increases in "other" personal income pinch both tails of the distribution toward the median. Increases in the proportion of unrelated individuals belonging to the UIE group depress both tails relative to the median, suggesting that marginal entrants are concentrated at the center of the distribution.

---

where

$$\hat{W} = (a_2 + a_3 CWEN) \cdot W$$

and

$$\hat{E} = (a_4 + a_5 E^*).$$

The terms involving cross-product coefficients $a_2 \cdot a_4$, $a_2 \cdot a_5$, $a_3 \cdot a_4$, and $a_3 \cdot a_5$ are highly collinear with each other, and a similar goodness of fit can be obtained by excluding virtually any two of the four terms. The specific elasticities of response to W, E^*, and $CWEN$ are sensitive to the choice of specification, although the pattern of the three variables taken together is always similar. The chosen equation omits cross-product terms $a_2 \cdot a_5$ and $a_3 \cdot a_4$, provides the best fit of the competing simplified specifications, and is an intermediate choice in terms of the range of elasticities of response to changes in W, E^*, and $CWEN$.

As stated in chapter 3, both distributional variables for the UIN group lie on the upper tail of the distribution. Increases in transfer payments improve not only the group median ($E = 0.77$) but also both distributional variables relative to the median ($E = 0.22$ for HUIN and 0.29 for JUIN). Both equations reflect a tendency for the upper tail of the distribution to contract over time. There is a negative response to "other" personal income in the HUIN equation. A rather surprising positive response to tight labor market conditions is evident;[30] this phenomenon presumably reflects not so much the effect of a tight economy on a fixed group of individuals but the effect of compositional shifts between the UIE and UIN groups during such periods.

IDENTITIES

Each distribution block contains four nonlinear identities in addition to the three stochastic specifications. Two of the identities define the constant of displacement (C_i) and the standard deviation (σ_i) of the transformed distribution; the third relates the group mean to the group median, while the fourth identity provides a density estimate of the poverty population.

Given the quantile measures H_i and J_i defined relative to the group median, we have

$$C_i = N_i \cdot \left(\frac{H_i \cdot J_i - 1}{2 - H_i - J_i} \right), \quad \text{all } i \text{ except UIN,} \qquad (4.31a)$$

$$CUIN = NUIN \cdot \left[\frac{JUIN - (HUIN)^2}{2 \cdot HUIN - JUIN - 1} \right], \qquad (4.31b)$$

$$\sigma_i = \left[\log_e \left(\frac{N_i + C_i}{H_i \cdot N_i + C_i} \right) \right] / G_i, \text{ all } i \text{ except UIN,} \qquad (4.32a)$$

where G_i is the distance of the quantile levels from the transformation mean in standard deviation units under the hypothesis of normality;[31]

$$\sigma_{\text{UIN}} = \left[\log_e \left(\frac{HUIN \cdot NUIN + CUIN}{NUIN + CUIN} \right) \right] / G_{\text{UIN}}, \qquad (4.32b)$$

$$N_i = (B_i + C_i) \cdot \exp[-0.5(\sigma_i)^2] - C_i, \text{ all } i \text{ except UIN,} \quad (4.33)$$

---

[30] The possibility that the high significance of $CWEN$ in equations (4.29) and (4.30) was due to the omission of an intercept term was investigated and rejected.
[31] $G_i = 1.2817$ for the MWL, MWN, and MOT groups; 1.0 for the FEM group; 0.6745 for the UIE group; and 0.8226 for the UIN group.

$$BUIN = (NUIN + CUIN) \cdot \exp[0.5(\sigma_{UIN})^2] - CUIN. \quad (4.34)$$

Finally, we can write

$$GPV_i = \left[\log_e\left(\frac{YPV_i + C_i}{N_i + C_i}\right)\right]/\sigma_i, \text{ all } i, \quad (4.35)$$

where YPV_i is any income level and GPV_i is a point on the cumulative distribution measured in deviation units. If YPV_i is a poverty threshold for the group, equation (4.34) will provide a standard deviation measure which defines an estimate of the incidence of poverty in the group.

CONCLUDING OBSERVATIONS

Despite major problems in coordinating Current Population Survey and national income account data, a number of significant and plausible relationships between the size distribution of personal income and changes in aggregate economic activity have been uncovered. With one exception, a set of three significant relationships was estimated for each group.

While the minimum objective was finding significant relationships between the set of distributional variables and aggregate economic variables within a fairly strict specification structure, the sampling variance of the data placed an upper bound on how much of the total variance in the distributional data could be explained. The larger the sampling variance relative to the total variance of the data, the more difficult it was to establish significant economic relationships; this situation was more prevalent when the group observed was represented by a small portion of the sample observations.

Mean income equations were estimated for five of the six groups; a median was estimated for the UIN group. Well-fitting relationships were found for the means of the two largest groups (MWL and MWN) and of unrelated individuals who were earners. All were expressed as a sum of income components. A similar relationship was estimated for families with a male head, "other" marital status, except that the presence of a large sampling error prevented the test statistics from being as impressive. Mean income for the MWL group was found to depend upon wage income, with the implicit group wage rate varying negatively with the participation rate of wives and positively with a time trend. The other three groups were sensitive to the levels of wage and transfer income; the UIE and MOT groups were also sensitive to other sources of personal income.[32]

Families with a female head were harder to characterize, but ultimately the mean was expressed as a weighted sum of wage and transfer income; the elasticity of response to employment and real wage changes was smaller than for families with a male head. For unrelated individuals who were nonearners, the median was a function of transfer income; it varied cyclically with the unemployment rate, presumably due to compositional changes in the group.

Increases in real wages and employment rates tend to improve the relative position of low income families in the male head groups; increases in the price level have a parallel effect.

The lower-tail variables for families with a female head and for unrelated individuals who were earners show a strongly negative response to increases in prices and real wages, although the effect of an increase in employment is positive. The same groups show a strong positive response to increases in nonwage income sources.

Two types of general reactions on the part of low income households were observed. Family groups with a labor force orientation benefit from tight employment and inflationary situations; their incomes improve relative to the median. Among families with a female head and unrelated individuals, inflationary situations may be a genuine threat. Although persons aged sixty-five or over were not observed separately in this study, one might extrapolate this second type of reaction to the aged as well.

While periods of tight employment and inflation appear to be beneficial to low income households as a group, a serious examination of changes in the size distribution must account for the heterogeneity of low income households, as described above.

The position of high income families tends to fall relatively, but not absolutely, in the face of increases in real wages and employment rates and to respond positively to increases in nonwage personal income, including transfers. In addition, two groups (MWL and MOT) respond negatively to increases in corporate profits as a share of gross private product.

We can expect the following distributional response to a movement from recession to tight employment. The mean of the income distribution moves with an increase in output. As the unemployment rate falls and real wages rise, the lower tail of the distribution improves relative

---

[32] Other sources of personal income were conspicuously absent from the mean estimates of all other groups.

to the median.[33] The upper tail of the distribution improves relative to the median when the nonwage share of personal income increases. This is more likely to occur in recessions rather than in the early stages of a boom, however, for the increased profit share found during boom periods is slow in finding its way into the personal income stream. Overall, the upper tail of the distribution tends to be fairly stable, in absolute terms, over the cycle. Equivalently, it improves relative to the median during recessions and declines during periods of tight employment.

Given this general pattern, families and individuals in the lower tail of the distribution who are not "related" to the labor force tend to be harmed during inflationary periods, relative to the median. The extent of this harm, and the harm suffered by labor force oriented groups in a recession, depends upon the level of transfer payments. Not surprisingly, at a given level of wages and employment, the lower tail of the income distribution is improved relative to the median by increased levels of transfer payments.

Despite the crudity of the specifications tested in this chapter, the results are encouraging. The heterogeneity of response of group size distributions to economic phenomena can be predicted to a significant extent by differences in sources of income. Knowledge about the behavior of group distributions can be combined with information about changes in the relative size of the groups to provide a picture of the aggregate size distribution of personal income.

---

[33]The increase in real wages can be expected to lag behind the increase in output. See the wage rate equation presented in the appendix to chapter 5.

Chapter 5

POLICY IMPLICATIONS OF THE MODEL: SIMULATION EXPERIMENTS

In this chapter, the model of the income distribution presented in chapter 4 is linked to an econometric model of the entire economy. The full model is then used to simulate the impact of some relatively simple aggregate fiscal policies upon the size distribution of income and upon the economy in general. Since no attempt is made to test the robustness of the full model, and since large scale econometric models have not distinguished themselves in terms of predictive power, the specific results presented in this chapter are meant only to be suggestive of the distributional effects of fiscal policies.

THE FULL MODEL

The complete model used in the simulation experiments appears in the appendix to chapter 5. It determines all the inputs required by the distribution sector and includes attempts to account for the impact of distributional changes elsewhere in the economy. The primary intention of this study was to construct a model of the income distribution; a wholesale borrowing of specifications from other econometric models for the remaining behavioral equations would have been consistent with this emphasis. An ideal extreme would have been to construct a distributional sector which could be linked to a previously existing econometric model.

Unfortunately, success at borrowing equations from other sources fell short of expectations; even in cases where equation specifications were firmly established in the literature, it was necessary to make revisions to make them compatible with the model. A major difficulty was the paucity of suitable models which were specified on an annual basis.[1]

In addition to the equations specified in chapter 4, the distribution sector includes two allocation functions to determine the proportion of wives who are in the labor force and the proportion of unrelated individuals who are earners, plus estimates of five aggregate distributional measures. It was decided to construct these latter measures rather than to try to account separately for the effects of distributional changes in each of six groups upon economic relationships elsewhere in the model. Given the properties of the displaced lognormal distribution, this aggregation was "illegal" in a strict sense. Despite this formal difficulty, extremely well-fitting approximations of aggregate distributional variables were obtained. The final distribution sector contains twenty-four stochastic equations and twenty-four identities.[2]

The remainder of the model consists of an expenditure sector, an income sector, an employment-labor force sector, and a price sector. An outline of each sector appears below.

Expenditure Sector

The expenditure sector determines real gross national product on the expenditure side. The levels of personal consumption and gross private domestic investment are determined, both in constant dollars. Net exports and government purchases of goods and services are left exogenous to the system.

Initially, a single equation was specified to determine the level of personal consumption expenditures. The specification permitted the marginal propensity to consume to vary with changes in the shape of the income distribution. Preliminary results indicated that increases in the upper tail of the distribution relative to the mean or median have an apparent positive effect on the marginal propensity to consume.

Since the result is contrary to the usual presumption that the marginal propensity to consume is either constant or declines as income rises,

---

[1] An attempt was made to utilize portions of the model developed by Lester C. Thurow in his "Policy Planning Model of the American Economy" mimeographed (Cambridge, Mass., 1967), but this was only partially successful.

[2] In chapter 4, both a mean and a median were estimated for the UIN group. Only the median equation was used.

a further investigation of the consumption sector was warranted. Three equations were specified to determine real levels of durable, nondurable, and service consumption. These specifications included expressions for "permanent" and "transitory" disposable personal income, as well as the stock of durable consumption goods. Crude forms of these three variables were defined by identities.

It was not possible to obtain a satisfactory, single-equation description of gross private domestic investment. Rather, three equations were chosen to determine changes in business inventories, investment in plant and equipment, and investment in residential structures. Identities determined the stock of business inventories and the net private (fixed domestic) capital stock. Distributional variables were not introduced into the investment block.

In addition to the consumption and investment blocks, the expenditure sector includes identities to determine real gross national product and gross private product.[3] In total, the expenditure sector consists of six stochastic equations and seven identities.

Income Sector

The income sector includes each component of personal income, as well as other elements of the income side of GNP, including corporate income and tax receipt blocks. Except for the specification for nonfarm entrepreneurial income, all equations in the income sector are defined in current dollars.

Sources of Personal Income
The following equations determine the sources of personal income.

(a) *Wage disbursements.* An identity determines private wage disbursements as a product of a wage rate and private wage and salary employment. The wage rate equals the level of annual private wage disbursements per wage and salary employee. The stochastic equation determines the percentage change in the wage rate variable. Government wage disbursements and "other labor income"[4] are treated as exogenous variables.

(b) *Proprietors' income.* A single equation determines the level of business and professional proprietors' income. Farm proprietors' income is left as an exogenous variable, like all variables relating to the agricultural sector.

---

[3] Gross government product was assumed to be exogenous.

[4] "Other labor income" has followed a steady time trend.

(c) *Transfer payments.* Separate equations establish the current dollar levels of Old Age and Survivors Insurance benefits and state unemployment insurance. Other government transfers and business transfers to persons are exogenous.

(d) *Other sources of personal income.* Two equations determine consumer interest payments and net federal interest payments to persons; an identity defines total personal interest income, including several exogenous components. An additional equation determines corporate dividend payments. Personal contributions for social insurance are obtained as an identity after separate equations determine total and employer social insurance contributions.

Tax Equations

Five tax functions are included in the model. The two equations determining federal and state-local personal tax receipts make full use of variables obtained from the distribution sector. In addition, there are two indirect business tax equations (federal and state-local) and a corporate income tax equation.

Corporate Profits and Capital Consumption

Three stochastic equations determine the gross flow of corporate funds, corporate capital consumption, and noncorporate capital consumption. The income sector is completed by identities determining current dollar gross national product, personal income, disposable personal income, and total government transfer payments. The statistical discrepancy and net subsidies of government enterprises are assumed to be exogenous. As listed, the income sector includes seventeen stochastic equations and seven identities.[5]

Employment-Labor Force Sector

The employment-labor force sector is the weakest part of the model. The prime reason for this weakness is the difficulty in adapting conventional quarterly employment specifications to annual models. Since disaggregation did not improve matters, a single equation was chosen to determine the level of private nonagricultural wage and salary employment. All other components of employment are exogenous.

---

[5] Net subsidies of government enterprises are assumed to be exogenous. The statistical discrepancy component of the national income accounts is determined as a residual by the model (see the appendix to chapter 5 for a brief discussion of the residual).

Two equations determine the labor force participation rate by sex. The model continues to use labor force and employment data defined for a population aged fourteen and over, although the Department of Labor has recently shifted its data to an age-sixteen-and-over basis. One specialized labor force equation determines the participation rate of females, "other marital status," which is required in the distributional block.

Unemployment is derived by a simple identity, but a stochastic equation estimates the number of persons unemployed in excess of twenty-six weeks. In total, the employment-labor force sector includes five stochastic equations plus three identities.[6]

Price Sector

Six price levels appear among the right-hand variables of the equations listed in the above four sectors of the model: the wholesale price index and implicit price deflators for gross national product, gross private product, total consumption expenditures, durable consumption expenditures, and gross private fixed domestic investment. Consequently, the price sector includes specifications to predict rates of change for each of the six price indices.

PROPERTIES OF THE MODEL

In assessing the experimental results presented below, the reader should be aware of certain properties of the model. The simulation experiments are conducted using point estimates of all coefficients, and without the inclusion of randomly generated error terms. Thus, little if anything is known about the error statistics associated with the predicted economic variables; in the absence of independent supporting evidence, little can be said to defend the robustness of the conclusions postulated below.

No financial sector was estimated for the model; the entire impact of monetary policy is assumed to work through interest rates, which appear exogenously in the model. Thus, the economic effects of the "credit crunch" of the late 1960s are not adequately reflected in the analysis below. The model also contains no export sector, but this does not appear to have created major difficulties.

The weakness of the employment sector of the model was mentioned

---

[6] In addition to total unemployment, the identities state total employment and the total civilian labor force.

above. In addition, the model tends to overestimate the level of employment, as well as the rate of price increase, during periods of high demand. Part of this tendency may reflect the model's oversight in accounting for the tight monetary policy during the period in question. As a result, the simulated magnitude of some of the distributional effects of fiscal policies during a boom is exaggerated.

The equations of the model were estimated using data for the years 1947–65. The contemporary issues of macroeconomic policy, however, revolve about the impact of the Indochinese war upon the domestic economy and the impact of fiscal measures designed to control the economy.[7] The decision was made to conduct simulation experiments over years extending beyond the observation period, rather than to examine historical postwar policy actions. The policy simulations reported below begin with 1968 (reported variables are defined in Table 5.1). The impact of alternative policies was examined by altering the values of exogenous variables for 1968 through 1972.[8]

Initial conditions for the endogenous variables and assumed values for all exogenous variables were required to conduct the experiments. Historical data were used where available for exogenous values through 1968; various assumptions were used to set post-1968 values, depending upon the policy being simulated. Initial conditions for the endogenous variables were specified with actual values for the year preceding the first year of the simulation;[9] in subsequent years of the solution period, *predicted* values of lagged endogenous variables were used where needed.

A set of exogenous variable assumptions was specified to define "no change" from the fiscal policies of the mid-1960s; detailed specifications appear in the appendix to chapter 5. "No change" was defined to mean (1) a continuation of the Indochinese war at the 1968 level of intensity, (2) a permanent imposition of the 1968 tax surcharge, and (3) no restraint on nondefense government expenditures. The nondefense portion of real government expenditures was assumed to continue its historical (1963–68) average growth rate of 6.73 percent per year. Except for variables denoting tax or contribution rates, most exogenous variables were assumed to continue their recent historical trends.

Since economic conditions after 1965 have been drastically dif-

---

[7] At this writing the United States economy has entered a recession, despite continuation of the war and of a rapid rate of inflation.

[8] The initial trial simulations spanned the years 1966–72; since no policy variations were considered for the period 1966–67, it was decided to begin the reported simulations in 1968, based upon 1967 initial conditions.

[9] In some cases, actual values for two and three years back were required by the lag structure of the model.

TABLE 5.1. VARIABLES REPORTED IN SIMULATION RESULTS

C_{58}	Personal consumption expenditures (billions of 1958 dollars)
DPI	Disposable personal income (billions of dollars)
GNP	Gross national product (billions of dollars)
GNP_{58}	Gross national product (billions of 1958 dollars)
$MFAM$	Median family income (current dollars)
MWP	Group of families with male head, wife present (sum of MWL, MWN groups)
$PCON$	Implicit price deflator for personal consumption expenditures (1958 = 1.000)
$PGNP$	Implicit price deflator for gross national product (1958 = 1.000)
PI	Personal income (billions of dollars)
$PROF$	Corporate profits (before taxes) (billions of dollars)
TCP	Corporate profit tax liabilities (billions of dollars)
TFP	Federal personal tax and nontax receipts (billions of dollars)
$TRAG$	Total government transfers to persons (billions of dollars)
U	Unemployment rate
W^*	Private wage and salary disbursements per private wage and salary employee (current dollars)
WP	Private wage disbursements (billions of dollars)
$Y10$	Income below which 10 percent of all families lie (dollars)
$Y90$	Income above which 10 percent of all families lie (dollars)

See Table 4.1 for general data sources and for definitions of group distributional variables.

ferent from those prevailing during the period of observation, one might question the capability of the model to characterize these changed conditions. Table 5.2 reports a trial simulation for the years 1966–69 to illustrate the model's predictive performance. The rate of price increase is overpredicted in 1966–67 and underpredicted in 1968–69; the unemployment rate is persistently underestimated. In general, the model missed the slowdown in 1967 and overpredicted most indicators of economic activity for that year. The maximum error of prediction for real GNP during the four-year period was $7.8 billion; there was a $16.2 billion overestimate of current dollar personal income in 1967, but this error was reduced to $2.0 billion by 1969. The income level at the lower decile is closely predicted for 1966 and 1967 but underpredicted for 1968. Given the absence of a financial sector and the fact that simulations were conducted for economic conditions not observed during the period of

TABLE 5.2. TRIAL SIMULATION, 1966–69

Actual values of exogenous variables through 1968; 1969 values as defined in Table A5.1, appendix to chapter 5, with tax surcharge continued through 1969. P = projected; A = actual. Variables are defined in Table 5.1.

		1966	1967	1968	1969
Aggregate Output, Expenditure, and Price Variables					
GNP_{58}	P	655.7	680.9	700.1	722.9
	A	657.1	673.1	707.6	727.5
C_{58}	P	420.6	436.2	451.3	467.4
	A	417.8	430.5	452.6	466.1
$\Delta PCON/PCON_{t-1}$	P	0.036	0.049	0.029	0.037
	A	0.024	0.026	0.038	0.042
Employment and Income Variables					
PROF	P	83.5	89.4	89.0	97.5
	A	85.6	81.6	91.1	93.7
PI	P	591.7	645.0	693.4	749.2
	A	586.8	628.8	687.9	747.2
DPI	P	515.2	560.1	594.4	637.0
	A	511.6	546.3	590.0	629.7
WP	P	322.6	354.8	378.8	409.9
	A	316.9	337.1	369.0	405.3
U	P	3.3%	2.7%	3.0%	3.0%
	A	3.8%	3.8%	3.6%	3.5%
Distributional Variables					
Y10	P	2338	2575	2701	2972
	A	2338	2537	2940	
MFAM	P	7496	8244	8715	9365
	A	7436	7974	8632	
Y90	P	14910	16000	17080	18060
	A	14603	15894	16805	

estimation, the model tracks the economic conditions of the late 1960s quite adequately.[10]

---

[10] Initial simulations were run at the Massachusetts Institute of Technology on the TROLL system developed under the direction of E. Kuh and M. Eisner. An IBM 7094 computer was used. All the simulations reported in this study were done with PROGRAM SIMULATE, developed under the direction of C. Holt at the Social Systems Research Institute of the University of Wisconsin. A Univac 1108 was used for these latter simulations.

In the following pages, policy alternatives are examined for each of two economic climates. The first set of simulations concerns fiscal actions given a continuation of the war in Indochina. The second set considers fiscal responses to an end of the war.

POLICY SIMULATIONS: THE WAR IN INDOCHINA TO CONTINUE

The Federal Income Tax Surcharge

What has been the fiscal impact of the federal income tax surcharge? Despite the enactment of the surcharge in 1968, the unemployment rate fell from 3.8 percent in 1967 to 3.6 percent in 1968 and 3.5 percent in 1969. The rate of increase of the implicit price deflator for consumption purchases rose from 2.6 percent in 1967 to 3.8 percent in 1968 and 4.2 percent in 1969.

A proper assessment of the impact of the surcharge cannot be made by such comparisons; other things were occurring simultaneously, including a continued expansion of government expenditures. The appropriate comparison is between what happened since the tax increase and what would have happened in its absence, ceteris paribus. While such a comparison is not directly observable, we can gain insight into this type of hypothetical circumstance with appropriately designed simulation experiments.

Table 5.3 reports simulation results for 1968–72 under the assumptions that the tax surcharge is in effect for the entire period, and that consumer response to a change in disposable income is not affected by whether it is due to a change in tax liabilities or to a change in pretax income.[11] Table 5.4 reports the differential impact of not imposing the tax

---

[11] The model, as estimated, implies that the short-run response of nondurable and services consumption to changes in disposable income is smaller than the long-run response. The assumption used in the simulation implies that income changes due to the tax surcharge are in part "transitory" in the short run, regardless of the publicly stated duration of the tax. Since the short-run consumption coefficients are larger than what would be strictly implied for transitory income according to the permanent income hypothesis, the simulation will overstate the effects of the surcharge if the income changes it induces are considered to be *more transitory* than other income changes; it will understate the effects of the surcharge if the induced income changes are believed to be permanent. The surcharge was assumed to begin on 1 April 1968 for federal personal taxes and on 1 January 1968 for corporate taxes.

TABLE 5.3. SELECTED SIMULATION RESULTS: WAR CONTINUES,
PERMANENT TAX SURCHARGE

	1968	1969	1970	1971	1972
gregate Output					
d Price Variables					
GNP_{58}	693.1	726.7	754.6	780.5	801.9
GNP	870.1	968.8	1060	1146	1223
$PGNP$	1.240	1.305	1.380	1.448	1.506
$\Delta PGNP/PGNP_{t-1}$	0.057	0.052	0.057	0.049	0.040
rporate Sector					
$PROF$	91.3	103.4	111.6	117.5	120.3
TCP	40.3	45.4	48.9	51.4	52.6
ployment and					
ome Variables					
I	684.8	750.3	821.4	892.0	958.0
FP	80.0	92.5	105.6	119.5	133.2
PI	587.1	638.4	694.4	748.9	798.9
VP	367.5	408.0	450.9	492.1	527.9
RAG	53.5	57.8	62.3	67.0	72.1
$V*$	6478	6949	7477	7969	8400
$\Delta W*/W*_{t-1}$	0.071	0.073	0.076	0.066	0.054
J	0.032	0.026	0.023	0.023	0.027
tributional					
iables					
10	2692	2936	3244	3515	3771
FAM	8486	9313	10190	10980	11650
90	16870	18080	19340	20540	21610
MWL	0.5095	0.5526	0.5719	0.5707	0.5543
MWN	0.3272	0.3217	0.3253	0.3266	0.3306
MOT	0.3312	0.3410	0.3483	0.3488	0.3475
FEM	0.3720	0.3707	0.3664	0.3818	0.4009
UIE	0.5181	0.5247	0.5249	0.5310	0.5334
cent Poor,					
Group					
WL	2.26	0.74	0.30	0.32	0.61
WN	10.5	10.1	9.55	9.2	8.9
WP	7.65	6.88	6.32	6.03	5.84
OT	11.6	10.6	9.1	9.7	9.65
EM	37.6	36.9	36.5	36.0	35.5
IE	19.9	18.85	18.2	17.3	16.75
IN	56.1	54.3	53.3	53.2	53.3

ariables defined in Table 5.1.

TABLE 5.4. SELECTED SIMULATION RESULTS:
WAR CONTINUES, NO TAX SURCHARGE, AS
DIFFERENCE FROM TABLE 5.3

	1968	1969
Aggregate Output and Price Variables		
GNP_{58}	+10.1	+8.2
GNP	+30.4	+38.2
$PGNP$	+0.024	+0.042
$\Delta PGNP/PGNP_{t-1}$	+0.021	+0.014
Corporate Sector		
$PROF$	+9.8	+6.8
TCP	+0.3	−1.3
Employment and Income Variables		
PI	+17.5	+25.7
TFP	−1.8	−3.1
DPI	+19.2	+28.5
WP	+13.9	+20.6
$TRAG$	−0.6	−0.5
W^*	+156	+268
$\Delta W^*/W^*_{t-1}$	+0.026	+0.015
U	−0.006	−0.006
Distributional Variables		
$Y10$	+112	+127
$MFAM$	+296	+445
$Y90$	+230	+480
$HMWL$	+0.0484	+0.0495
$HMWN$	+0.0038	−0.0013
$HMOT$	+0.0123	+0.0065
$HFEM$	−0.0284	−0.0224
$HUIE$	−0.0084	−0.0026
Percent Poor, by Group		
MWL	−1.62	−0.71
MWN	−0.40	−0.15
MWP	−0.74	−0.23
MOT	−0.90	−0.40
FEM	0.0	+0.20
UIE	−0.10	−0.25
UIN	+0.10	+0.60

surcharge in 1968 and 1969.[12] The assumed values of all exogenous variables were identical in the two simulations except for the federal corporate and personal tax parameters.

Compared to actual values, the simulation reported in Table 5.3 underestimates real gross national product by $14.5 billion in 1968, but only by $0.8 billion in 1969. The rate of inflation was overestimated; the unemployment rate, underestimated. Real GNP is projected to grow at a declining rate, reaching $802 billion in 1972. The projected rate of inflation peaks at 5.7 percent in 1970, while the wage rate reaches a maximum growth of 7.6 percent in the same year. Corporate profits continue to grow throughout the period but are a declining share of GNP.

Table 5.4 indicates that the simulated effect of the tax surcharge was to reduce real GNP by $10 billion and the rate of inflation by 2.1 percentage points in 1968; the resulting impact on current dollar GNP was over $30 billion. Corporate profits absorbed a disproportionate share of the brunt of the surcharge.

Conditional on the assumption that the effect of the surcharge on the general economic climate was approximately as simulated, the predicted impact on the distribution of income corresponds closely with the pattern described in chapter 4. In the absence of the tax surcharge, the simulation indicates that low income families with a male head would have improved their position relative to their group medians; low income families with a female head and unrelated individuals, on the other hand, would have been made relatively worse off. The relative position of high income families would have declined as well.

Estimated poverty incidences are reported at the bottom of Tables 5.3 and 5.4. It will be recalled that the distributional model reported in chapter 4 included an identity to keep count of the proportion of the cumulative distribution lying below a given income level [see equation (4.35)]. By inserting poverty thresholds into the identities, we can examine the impact of our policy simulations upon the size of the poverty population.[13]

---

[12]The model did not converge to a solution beginning in 1970 for the no-surcharge assumption.

[13]The poverty thresholds used by the U.S. government are based on family size, as well as on other factors not treated in this study. It was therefore necessary to derive a single income cutoff for each of the six groups examined here. Using 1966 as a benchmark, the following procedure was used: Orshansky in "The Shape of Poverty in 1966," *Social Security Bulletin* (March 1968), classifies 3.326 million families out of 27.548 million in the MWN group as being poor in 1966. This total was obtained by applying separate poverty thresholds to subgroups of the data. For use in this study, I chose that single income cutoff which, when applied to the aggregate form of the same data, yielded the same poverty

According to Table 5.3, the incidence of poverty is projected to decline in all six population groups. While the incidence of poverty in the MWL group is sharply underestimated during inflationary periods, this factor combines with an underestimate of the proportion of families with a male head, wife present (MWP = MWL + MWN) belonging to the MWL group. When the two groups are combined to obtain a poverty incidence for the MWP group, the two errors systematically offset each other. If all four family groups are weighted together, an estimated 10.8 percent of all families were predicted to be poor in 1968. While the actual incidence reported by the Current Population Survey was only 10.0 percent, it should be noted that a procedural change in allocating non-responding households shifted the "official" incidence of poverty downward by 0.9 percent in 1966. The definitional change is not reflected in the simulated poverty estimates.

Given what has already been said about the distributional effects of increased employment and inflation, we would expect that the imposition of the tax surcharge has been to the detriment of the poor as a whole, but to the benefit of groups which are highly dependent upon fixed income sources. The results in Table 5.4 support this conclusion.

Gains in real personal income for families as a whole would have been relatively minor; the absence of the tax surcharge would have increased median income for all families by 3.5 percent in 1968, compared to the price increment of 2.1 percent. In 1969, however, the additional median income growth would have been exceeded by the inflationary impact. Despite the apparent increasing cost of additional employment in terms of the rate of inflation, however, low income families with a male head would have made substantial gains relative to others in the economy, at least in 1968. Absence of the surcharge would have meant 336,000 fewer poor families with a male head in 1968 and 106,000 fewer in 1969.

In contrast to the gains made by some low income households, families having a female head and unrelated individuals who are non-earners would have suffered additional losses in the absence of the tax

---

estimate for 1966. In other words, 3.326 million families in the MWN group were classified as poor in 1966, according to Orshansky's definition; when the MWN group was ranked by income without regard to family size, 3.326 million families had incomes under $2586. Thus $2586 was chosen as the 1966 current dollar poverty threshold for the MWN group. This procedure was repeated to get thresholds for each of the six groups. All thresholds were then converted into 1958 dollars by the GNP implicit price deflator, and held fixed in real terms throughout the simulation period. In 1958 dollars, the following cutoffs were calculated: for the MWL group, $2657; MWN, $2270; MOT, $2148; FEM, $2510; and for unrelated individuals, $1426. The assumption underlying such a procedure is that the composition of each group remains fixed. To the extent that this is not true the poverty projections will be distorted.

surcharge. An estimated 11,000 families with a female head and 31,000 nonearner unrelated individuals would have been added to the 1969 poverty rolls.

Fiscal Restraint

As an alternative to the above simulations, we could assume that the federal government would exercise fiscal restraint in addition to imposing the tax surcharge. One form of fiscal restraint would be to deduct the well-publicized $6 billion required cut in the federal budget (an amendment attached to the 1968 tax legislation) from the level of government purchases of goods and services. Not only is a reduction in purchases of goods and services not equivalent to a reduction in the administrative budget, but a $6 billion cut in federal nondefense expenditures is probably not feasible. Of the $178.4 billion of government purchases of goods and services in 1967,[14] $72.4 billion were for national defense, $87.8 billion were state and local purchases, and only $18.2 billion were federal nondefense expenditures. We would therefore be talking about a reduction of 33 percent of this latter figure.

The following alternative, more balanced, restrictions on federal nondefense activities were applied to the model, in addition to the tax increase:

(a) Real federal purchases of goods and services for nondefense purposes were reduced by 2 percent each year starting in 1968; real defense purchases continued to be held constant at their 1968 level, while state and local purchases were assumed to continue to rise at a 6.5 percent annual rate.

(b) Federal civilian employment was frozen at 1967 levels; state and local government employment was assumed to grow 6.6 percent per year.

(c) The growth rate of "other" government transfers, i.e., excluding Social Security and unemployment benefits, was cut in half, from 8.7 percent to 4.35 percent per year.

No change was made in gross government product, since it was already growing slower in real terms than was government employment; any restraint in gross government product or in wage disbursements on the part of the federal government was assumed to be offset by increases in the state-local sector, already the dominant source of growth in these categories.

Table 5.5 reports the effects of imposing such a package of fiscal

---

[14] Current dollars, *Economic Report of the President, 1969*, Table B-1.

TABLE 5.5. SELECTED SIMULATION RESULTS: WAR CONTINUES, PERMANENT TAX SURCHARGE PLUS "FISCAL RESTRAINT" (DIFFERENCE FROM TABLE 5.3 IN PARENTHESES)

	1968	1969	1970	1971	1972
Aggregate Output and Price Variables					
GNP_{58}	685.8 (−7.3)	719.0 (−7.7)	746.6 (−8.0)	770.8 (−9.7)	789.1 (−12.8)
GNP	851.8 (−18.3)	941.3 (−27.5)	1017 (−43)	1086 (−60)	1145 (−78)
PGNP	1.228 (−0.012)	1.278 (−0.027)	1.333 (−0.047)	1.381 (−0.067)	1.421 (−0.085)
$\Delta PGNP/PGNP_{t-1}$	0.047 (−0.010)	0.041 (−0.011)	0.043 (−0.014)	0.036 (−0.013)	0.029 (−0.011)
Corporate Sector					
PROF	85.3 (−6.0)	97.7 (−5.7)	103.6 (−8.0)	107.2 (−10.3)	108.0 (−12.3)
TCP	37.8 (−2.5)	43.0 (−2.4)	45.5 (−3.4)	47.05 (−4.35)	47.4 (−5.2)
Employment and Income Variables					
PI	673.6 (−11.2)	730.6 (−19.7)	790.3 (−31.1)	847.9 (−44.1)	900.1 (−57.9)
TFP	78.5 (−1.5)	90.2 (−2.3)	101.8 (−3.8)	113.8 (−5.7)	125.4 (−7.8)
DPI	577.5 (−9.6)	621.4 (−17.0)	667.7 (−26.7)	711.3 (−37.6)	749.9 (−49.0)
WP	359.2 (−8.3)	393.4 (−14.6)	427.9 (−23.0)	459.1 (−33.0)	484.2 (−43.7)

TRAG	52.6 (−0.9)	55.9 (−1.9)	59.3 (−3.0)	62.9 (−4.1)	66.7 (−5.4)
W*	6393 (−85)	6773 (−176)	7176 (−301)	7557 (−432)	7843 (−557)
$\Delta W^*/W^*_{t-1}$	0.057 (−0.014)	0.060 (−0.013)	0.060 (−0.016)	0.050 (−0.016)	0.041 (−0.013)
U	0.037 (+0.005)	0.032 (+0.006)	0.030 (+0.007)	0.032 (+0.009)	0.037 (+0.010)
Distributional Variables					
Y10	2632 (−60)	2851 (−85)	3093 (−151)	3306 (−209)	3506 (−265)
MFAM	8294 (−192)	8966 (−347)	9628 (−562)	10190 (−790)	10630 (−1020)
Y90	16620 (−250)	17560 (−520)	18520 (−820)	19370 (−1170)	20080 (−1530)
HMWL	0.4827 (−0.0268)	0.5126 (−0.0400)	0.5243 (−0.0476)	0.5172 (−0.0535)	0.4974 (−0.0569)
HMWN	0.3282 (+0.0010)	0.3273 (+0.0056)	0.3313 (+0.0060)	0.3353 (+0.0087)	0.3429 (+0.123)
HMOT	0.3212 (−0.0100)	0.3299 (−0.0111)	0.3350 (−0.0133)	0.3345 (−0.0143)	0.3321 (−0.0154)
HFEM	0.3853 (+0.0133)	0.3849 (+0.0142)	0.3880 (+0.0216)	0.4054 (+0.0236)	0.4230 (+0.0221)
HUIE	0.5203 (+0.0022)	0.5245 (−0.0002)	0.5277 (+0.0028)	0.5323 (+0.0013)	0.5296 (+0.0038)
Percent Poor, by Group MWL	3.4 (+1.14)	2.0 (+1.26)	1.5 (+1.20)	1.7 (+1.38)	2.3 (+1.69)

TABLE 5.5. (cont.)

	1968	1969	1970	1971	1972
MWN	10.7 (−0.2)	10.2 (+0.1)	9.6 (+0.05)	9.3 (+0.1)	8.85 (−0.05)
MWP	8.14 (+0.49)	7.33 (+0.45)	6.68 (+0.36)	6.49 (+0.46)	6.36 (+0.52)
MOT	12.3 (+0.7)	11.2 (+0.6)	10.7 (+1.6)	10.5 (+0.8)	10.5 (+0.85)
FEM	37.8 (+0.2)	37.3 (+0.4)	36.9 (+0.4)	36.5 (+0.5)	36.2 (+0.7)
UIE	19.9 (0.0)	18.9 (+0.05)	18.05 (−0.15)	17.25 (−0.05)	17.0 (−0.25)
UIN	59.0 (+2.9)	57.3 (+3.0)	56.9 (+3.6)	57.8 (+4.6)	59.5 (+6.2)

restraint. The cost in real output of the program would be $7.3 billion the first year, rising gradually to $12.8 billion by 1972. The rate of inflation would be substantially reduced, with the GNP price deflator predicted to be 5.6 percent lower in 1972 as a result of the package. At the same time, the nominal wage rate would be 6.6 percent lower and median family income 8.8 percent lower by 1972. The projected unemployment rate would be a half percentage point higher in 1968 and a full percentage point higher by 1972.

Like the tax surcharge, the package of fiscal restraint is predicted to have a detrimental effect on the poverty population; unlike the surcharge, however, restraints which involve restricting the growth of transfer programs affect unrelated individuals and families with a female head, as well as labor force oriented groups. Given a continuation of the tax surcharge, the additional presence of the fiscal restraint package increases the projected number of poor families with a male head by 224,000 in 1968.[15] At the same time, despite an improvement in the lower tail of the distribution of female heads of families (relative to the group mean, *not* to the economy as a whole), poverty among such families rises by 11,000 in 1968 and 39,000 by 1972. Poverty among unrelated individuals who are nonearners is projected to increase by 151,000 in 1968 and 322,000 by 1972, relative to the nonrestraint situation.

Figure 5.1 represents the effects on the aggregate poverty population of the simulations discussed above.[16] Given a continuation of the tax surcharge without a program of fiscal restraint, the poverty population is projected to decline from 27.3 million in 1968 to 24.7 million in 1970; subsequently the rate of decline slows down, with a projected poverty population of 24.0 million in 1972. The official poverty estimate for 1968 is 25.4 million persons;[17] the projection overestimate of 1.9 million is almost entirely accounted for by the 1966 revision in tabulation procedures mentioned above. Absence of the tax surcharge would have reduced the 1968 poverty level by 1.4 million, but after 1968 the beneficial effects of its absence are substantially reduced. The fiscal restraint package adds 1.1 million persons to the poverty rolls in 1968–70, after which the rate of poverty reduction declines more sharply than with the tax surcharge alone. The differential created by the restraint package reaches 1.5 million persons by 1972.

---

[15] The corresponding figure is 240,000 in 1972.

[16] The average family sizes of the 1968 poverty population were used to obtain an aggregate level: 4.16 for families with a male head and 3.98 for families with a female head.

[17] U.S. Bureau of the Census, *Current Population Reports,* Ser. P-60, No. 68, "Poverty in the United States 1959 to 1968" (Washington, D.C.: U.S. Government Printing Office, 1969).

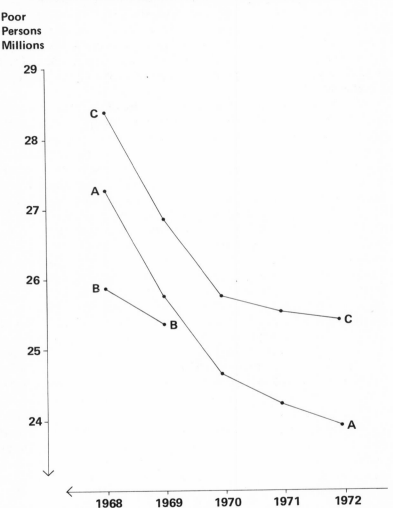

FIGURE 5.1. PROJECTED TOTAL POVERTY
POPULATION, GIVEN CONTINUATION OF WAR

A. War continues, permanent tax surcharge (Table 5.3)
B. War continues, no tax surcharge (Table 5.4)
C. War continues, permanent tax surcharge plus "fiscal restraint"
   (Table 5.5)

Ending the Tax Surcharge

Tables 5.6 and 5.7 report the effects of terminating the tax surcharge, given a continuation of both the war and the fiscal restraint package.[18] Table 5.6 is based on the assumption that the surcharge is terminated at the end of 1969; Table 5.7 assumes that the surcharge is cut in half for 1970 and terminated at the end of 1970. In both cases, there is a short-run stimulating effect during the years of the tax cut, after which the impact of the change diminishes. This pattern is well revealed by the projections of real GNP and the rates of change of prices and wages. When the surcharge is terminated at the end of 1969, the 1970 level of real GNP jumps by $13.2 billion; by 1972, however, real GNP is only $5.4 billion higher than it would have been if the surcharge were to continue. The same action would increase the GNP price deflator by 3.0 percent and the wage rate by 3.8 percent in 1970, after which there would be virtually no differential impact. If the surcharge is cut in half for 1970 and not terminated until the end of 1970, similar effects are spread over 1970 and 1971.

Termination of the tax surcharge has a parallel effect on the poverty population; the number of poor is substantially reduced at first, but in both cases an absolute increase in the incidence of poverty occurs after the initial reduction. Figure 5.2 illustrates the impact on the aggregate poverty population.

POLICY SIMULATIONS: FISCAL POLICY AFTER THE WAR

An entirely new range of problems will face the economy when the war in Indochina ends, and the impact on the distribution of income will depend critically on the nature of the fiscal and monetary response.[19]

When analyzing the aggregative impact of the war on the economy through the use of an econometric model, the manner in which the war affects the economic variables within the model must be specified. Defense activities enter the model in three direct ways: (1) defense purchases of goods and services form a part of the demand for total gross national product; (2) changes in the level of defense expenditures have

---

[18] The model would not converge to a solution beyond 1969 if the same experiment were conducted without the restraint package.

[19] Throughout these simulations, it is assumed that monetary policy is such as to hold interest rates constant.

TABLE 5.6. SELECTED SIMULATION RESULTS: EFFECT OF
TERMINATING SURCHARGE AT END OF 1969, WITH
CONTINUING WAR AND "FISCAL RESTRAINT," AS
DIFFERENCE FROM TABLE 5.5

	1970	1971	1972
Aggregate Output and			
Price Variables			
GNP_{58}	+13.2	+10.6	+5.4
GNP	+49	+41	+33
$PGNP$	+0.038	+0.042	+0.042
$\Delta PGNP/PGNP_{t-1}$	+0.030	+0.002	−0.001
Corporate Sector			
$PROF$	+15.6	+4.8	+1.8
TCP	+2.0	−2.3	−3.5
Employment and			
Income Variables			
PI	+28.4	+29.1	+25.6
TFP	−2.8	−4.3	−5.6
DPI	+31.1	+32.9	+30.6
WP	+22.6	+23.8	+20.8
$TRAG$	−0.75	−0.70	−0.40
$W*$	+258	+278	+268
$\Delta W*/W*_{t-1}$	+0.038	+0.001	−0.003
U	−0.008	−0.008	−0.004
Distributional			
Variables			
$Y10$	+211	+90	+105
$MFAM$	+492	+470	+420
$Y90$	+320	+610	+570
$HMWL$	+0.0600	+0.0444	+0.0187
$HMWN$	+0.0092	−0.0093	−0.0047
$HMOT$	+0.0176	+0.0020	−0.0013
$HFEM$	−0.0466	−0.0034	−0.0013
$HUIE$	−0.0154	+0.0123	+0.0080
Percent Poor,			
by Group			
MWL	−1.34	−1.22	−0.63
MWN	−0.60	+0.15	−0.10
MWP	−0.77	−0.25	−0.15
MOT	−1.2	−0.2	0.0
FEM	+0.2	+0.1	+0.1
UIE	+0.40	−0.94	−0.50
UIN	−0.45	+0.30	+1.10

TABLE 5.7. SELECTED SIMULATION RESULTS: EFFECT OF
CUTTING TAX SURCHARGE IN HALF FOR 1970 AND OF
ELIMINATING IT AT END OF 1970, WITH CONTINUING WAR
AND "FISCAL RESTRAINT," AS DIFFERENCE FROM TABLE 5.5

	1970	1971	1972
Aggregate Output and Price Variables			
GNP_{58}	+6.9	+12.3	+9.7
GNP	+24	+46	+38
$PGNP$	+0.017	+0.040	+0.040
$\Delta PGNP/PGNP_{t-1}$	+0.013	+0.017	−0.001
Corporate Sector			
$PROF$	+7.5	+10.7	+3.8
TCP	+1.0	0.0	−2.7
Employment and Income Variables			
PI	+13.6	+29.3	+28.3
TFP	−1.4	−3.7	−5.2
DPI	+14.9	+32.7	+32.9
WP	+10.8	+23.7	+23.2
$TRAG$	−0.4	−0.8	−0.65
W^*	+120	+267	+267
$\Delta W^*/W^*_{t-1}$	+0.017	+0.020	−0.002
U	−0.004	−0.008	−0.007
Distributional Variables			
$Y10$	+97	+162	+96
$MFAM$	+232	+490	+450
$Y90$	+150	+460	+590
$HMWL$	+0.0280	+0.0478	+0.0315
$HMWN$	+0.0040	+0.0009	−0.0077
$HMOT$	+0.0084	+0.0100	+0.0009
$HFEM$	−0.0211	−0.0254	0.0
$HUIE$	−0.0060	−0.0008	+0.0134
Percent Poor, by Group			
MWL	−0.79	−1.28	−1.04
MWN	−0.30	−0.30	+0.15
MWP	−0.43	−0.57	−0.25
MOT	−0.60	−0.70	−0.10
FEM	+0.10	+0.10	0.0
UIE	+0.10	−0.25	−0.90
UIN	−0.30	−0.30	+0.40

FIGURE 5.2. PROJECTED TOTAL POVERTY POPULATION
GIVEN CONTINUATION OF WAR, TERMINATION OF TAX
SURCHARGE, AND CONTINUATION OF FISCAL RESTRAINT

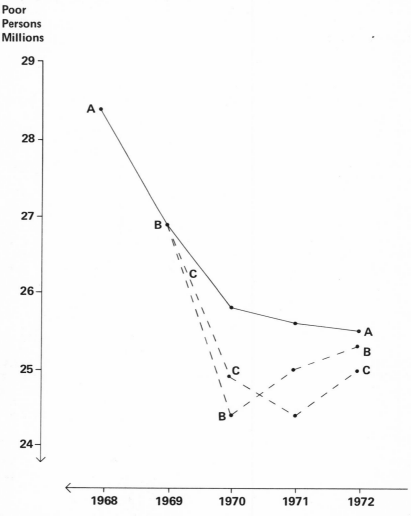

A. War continues, permanent tax surcharge plus "fiscal restraint" (Table 5.5,
   same as Figure 5.1)
B. War continues with fiscal restraint, surcharge terminated end of 1969
   (Table 5.6)
C. Same as B, except surcharge terminated June 30, 1970 (Table 5.7)

an impact on private inventory accumulation; and (3) the personnel level of the armed forces affects the size of the civilian labor force. Operating through these equations, defense activities have a powerful impact throughout the model of the economy.[20]

In terms of the model, the end of the war is defined as a $19.2 billion decline in defense expenditures (1958 dollars) and a decline in armed forces personnel (as reported by the Bureau of Labor Statistics) of 812,-000, restoring both variables to their 1965 levels. The decline in both variables is spread over a two-year period, 1970 and 1971.

Let us first suppose that the war ends and that there is no response in terms of fiscal policy: assume that nondefense spending continues to grow according to its historical trend and that the tax surcharge remains in effect. There would be a decline in the demand for goods and services due both to the drop in defense spending ($9.6 billion decline in each of two years) and to a drop in inventory accumulation in response to the war's end. The unemployment rate would rise not only because of a decline in the demand for labor but also because of an increase in the civilian labor force with the reduction of the armed forces.

Table 5.8 reports simulation results based on the end of the war, as defined. Given these assumptions, the level of real GNP is projected to be $16.5 billion lower in 1970 and $25.6 billion lower in 1971 than it would be if the war were to continue. The inflationary pressure on the economy would be essentially halted, with projected increases in the implicit price deflator for GNP of 1.2 and 2.5 percent in 1970 and 1971, compared to the war projections of 5.7 and 4.9 percent.

Given the substantial effect on the rate of inflation, the impact of the defense cutbacks measured in *current* dollars is quite large. The level of current dollar GNP is projected to be $100 billion lower by the second year of the defense cutback than it would be if the war were to continue.[21] The differential reduction in personal income before taxes is $38 and $62 billion for the two years, and $31 and $51 billion after taxes. Corporate profits would suffer the brunt of the recession, with a projected differential decline of $22 billion ($13.5 billion *absolute* decline) the first year and $20 billion the second.

Although much of the deflationary effect falls outside the realm of

---

[20] Various microeconomic effects of defense activities, such as the concentration of military demand in specific industries or regions, are not meaningfully characterized by the model.

[21] Note that the *absolute* two-year growth in GNP is projected to be $77 billion rather than the war growth of $177 billion. Much of the latter figure is illusory, since prices were projected to rise by over 10.6 percent during the same period.

TABLE 5.8. SELECTED SIMULATION RESULTS: WAR ENDS, 1970–71, TAX SURCHARGE CONTINUES (DIFFERENCE FROM TABLE 5.3 IN PARENTHESES)

	1968	1969	1970	1971	1972
Aggregate Output and Price Variables					
GNP_{58}	693.1	726.7	738.1 (−16.5)	754.9 (−25.6)	798.7 (−3.2)
GNP	870.1	968.8	990.1 (−70)	1046 (−100)	1155 (−68)
$PGNP$	1.240	1.305	1.321 (−0.059)	1.354 (−0.094)	1.406 (−0.100)
$\Delta PGNP/PGNP_{t-1}$	0.057	0.052	0.012 (−0.045)	0.025 (−0.024)	0.039 (−0.001)
Corporate Sector					
$PROF$	91.3	103.4	89.9 (−21.7)	97.5 (−20.0)	119.2 (−1.1)
TCP	40.3	45.4	39.7 (−9.2)	42.9 (−8.5)	52.1 (−0.5)
Employment and Income Variables					
PI	684.8	750.3	783.1 (−38.3)	830.3 (−61.7)	907.6 (−50.4)
TFP	80.0	92.5	98.6 (−7.0)	108.8 (−10.7)	125.1 (−8.1)
DPI	587.1	638.4	662.9 (−31.5)	698.1 (−50.8)	757.0 (−41.9)
WP	367.5	408.0	418.6 (−32.3)	438.6 (−53.5)	484.1 (−43.8)
$TRAG$	53.5	57.8	63.8 (+1.5)	69.6 (+2.6)	73.2 (+1.1)

	6478	6949	7086 (−391)	7344 (−625)	7764 (−636)
W*	6478	6949	7086 (−391)	7344 (−625)	7764 (−636)
ΔW*/W*_{t-1}	0.071	0.073	0.020 (−0.056)	0.036 (−0.030)	0.057 (+0.003)
U	0.032	0.026	0.038 (+0.015)	0.051 (+0.028)	0.041 (+0.014)
Distributional Variables					
Y10	2692	2936	2922 (−322)	3185 (−330)	3513 (−258)
MFAM	8486	9313	9410 (−780)	9756 (−1224)	10580 (−1070)
Y90	16870	18080	18780 (−560)	19250 (−1290)	20250 (−1360)
HMWL	0.5095	0.5526	0.4891 (−0.0828)	0.4567 (−0.1140)	0.4935 (−0.0608)
HMWN	0.3272	0.3217	0.3115 (−0.0138)	0.3362 (+0.0096)	0.3428 (+0.0122)
HMOT	0.3312	0.3410	0.3245 (−0.0238)	0.3340 (−0.0148)	0.3532 (+0.0057)
HFEM	0.3720	0.3707	0.4426 (+0.0762)	0.4292 (+0.0474)	0.4227 (+0.0218)
HUIE	0.5181	0.5247	0.5464 (+0.0215)	0.5117 (−0.0193)	0.5174 (−0.0160)
Percent Poor, by Group					
MWL	2.3	0.7	2.8 (+2.5)	4.0 (+3.7)	2.4 (+1.8)
MWN	10.5	10.1	10.65 (+1.1)	9.4 (+0.2)	8.65 (+0.25)

TABLE 5.8 (cont.)

	1968	1969	1970	1971	1972
MWP	7.65	6.88	7.80 (+1.58)	7.33 (+1.30)	6.25 (+0.41)
MOT	11.6	10.6	11.7 (+2.6)	10.9 (+1.2)	9.3 (−0.35)
FEM	37.6	36.9	36.2 (−0.3)	35.9 (−0.1)	35.1 (−0.4)
UIE	19.9	18.85	17.55 (−0.65)	19.0 (+1.7)	17.7 (+0.95)
UIN	56.1	54.3	54.5 (+1.2)	55.3 (+2.1)	51.7 (−1.6)

personal income, most of the decline within personal income can be attributed to a fall in wage disbursements. There is a substantial negative effect on the nominal wage rate, but most of the real decline in wage disbursements is due to an absolute rise in the unemployment rate. By the second year of the expenditure decline, the unemployment rate is projected to rise to 5.1 percent, with 2.4 million additional people being unemployed compared to the war projection.

It is worth noting that the economy is projected to "turn around" in 1972 after defense expenditures settle at their new level. Real GNP recovers to within $3.2 billion of the 1972 war projection; corporate profits also enjoy a substantial recovery. Personal income and unemployment rate indicators reflect only a partial recovery, however. Since the simulations were carried only through 1972, it is not known for certain whether the projected 1972 recovery is a short term upswing or the beginning of a sustained growth period.[22]

Table 5.9 lists the results of a simulated end of the war in an economy with continued fiscal restraint. While the qualitative characteristic of a two-year decline followed by an upswing is retained, the deflationary impact of the war's end is more severe, and the ensuing recovery is less vigorous. In terms of real GNP, the deflationary impact of the war is $31.7 billion by 1971 with continued fiscal restraint (*in addition* to the $9.7 billion impact of the restraint in Table 5.5), compared to $25.6 billion without restraint. While in the absence of fiscal restraint the 1972 recovery is only $3.2 billion short of war levels, with fiscal restraint the recovery falls $9.2 billion short of the war level of real GNP ($22 billion short of the war level without fiscal restraint). That is, the deflationary impact of ending the war in conjunction with continued fiscal restraint exceeds the sum of the two effects taken separately. The unemployment rate follows the same pattern; the projected rate reaches 6.4 percent in 1971 and 5.6 percent in 1972.

We can also examine the impact of such a deflationary force upon the poverty population. In both simulations, the incomes of households at the bottom of the distribution would tend to decline *relative to the median* (which in turn would decline) in groups closely related to the labor force. Families with the wife in the labor force and unrelated individuals would

---

[22]The former circumstances must be suspected, since simulations with a preliminary form of the model based upon a 1969–70 end to the war indicated a 1971 boom followed by a 1972 recession under similar conditions. See Charles E. Metcalf, "The Size Distribution of Personal Income in an Econometric Model of the United States" (Ph.D. diss., Massachusetts Institute of Technology, 1968), chapter 7, pp. 341–65. Substantial revisions have been made in the model since that time.

TABLE 5.9. SELECTED SIMULATION RESULTS: WAR ENDS, 1970–71, TAX SURCHARGE AND "FISCAL RESTRAINT" CONTINUE (DIFFERENCE FROM TABLE 5.5 IN PARENTHESES)

	1970	1971	1972
Aggregate Output and Price Variables			
GNP_{58}	725.4	739.1	779.9
	(−21.2)	(−31.7)	(−9.2)
GNP	955.8	1004	1093
	(−61)	(−82)	(−52)
PGNP	1.290	1.317	1.351
	(−0.043)	(−0.064)	(−0.070)
$\Delta PGNP/PGNP_{t-1}$	0.009	0.021	0.026
	(−0.034)	(−0.015)	(−0.003)
Corporate Sector			
PROF	83.95	90.7	107.8
	(−19.65)	(−16.5)	(−0.2)
TCP	37.2	40.05	47.3
	(−8.3)	(−7.0)	(−0.1)
Employment and Income Variables			
PI	757.5	798.1	861.3
	(−32.8)	(−49.8)	(−38.8)
TFP	95.6	104.8	119.0
	(−6.2)	(−9.0)	(−6.4)
DPI	641	670.8	717.9
	(−26.7)	(−40.5)	(−32.0)
WP	399.6	414.9	449.6
	(−28.3)	(−44.2)	(−34.6)
TRAG	61.2	65.95	68.3
	(+1.9)	(+3.0)	(+1.6)
*W**	6884	7104	7404
	(−292)	(−433)	(−439)
$\Delta W^*/W^*_{t-1}$	0.016	0.032	0.042
	(−0.044)	(−0.018)	(+0.001)
U	0.049	0.064	0.056
	(+0.019)	(+0.032)	(+0.019)
Distributional Variables			
Y10	2847	3072	3316
	(−246)	(−234)	(−190)
MFAM	8992	9243	9821
	(−636)	(−947)	(−809)
Y90	18020	18330	19040
	(−500)	(−1040)	(−1040)

TABLE 5.9 (cont.)

	1970	1971	1972
HMWL	0.4581	0.4297	0.4447
	(−0.0662)	(−0.0875)	(−0.0527)
HMWN	0.3236	0.3488	0.3552
	(−0.0077)	(+0.0135)	(+0.0123)
HMOT	0.3135	0.3196	0.3329
	(−0.0215)	(−0.0149)	(+0.0008)
HFEM	0.4409	0.4270	0.4359
	(+0.0529)	(+0.0216)	(+0.0129)
HUIE	0.5308	0.4913	0.5019
	(+0.0031)	(−0.0410)	(−0.0277)
Percent Poor, by Group			
MWL	4.2	5.4	4.5
	(+2.7)	(+3.7)	(+2.2)
MWN	10.5	9.3	8.6
	(+0.9)	(0.0)	(−0.25)
MWP	8.16	7.78	6.97
	(+1.48)	(+1.29)	(+0.61)
MOT	12.4	11.75	10.4
	(+1.7)	(+1.25)	(−0.1)
FEM	36.9	36.8	36.1
	(0.0)	(+0.3)	(−0.1)
UIE	18.5	19.95	18.6
	(+0.45)	(+2.70)	(+1.60)
UIN	59.9	62.3	60.4
	(+3.0)	(+4.5)	(+0.9)

experience rather severe declines in income, whereas families with a female head or with a single earner would not be so severely affected.

Figure 5.3 indicates that the overall effect on the poverty population at the end of the war would be a differential increase of about 3,000,000 people in 1970 and 1971, most of whom would be unrelated individuals (up to 480,000 in 1971, with fiscal restraint) or in families with a male head (584,000–707,000 families). During the 1972 recovery the poverty differential is reduced to 670,000 persons in the absence of fiscal restraint and 1,330,000 persons with fiscal restraint.

In summary, an end to the war unaccompanied by a fiscal adjustment is predicted to reduce the utilization of resources substantially and to increase the incidence of poverty by three million people. This conclusion is based on the assumption that federal nondefense expenditures

FIGURE 5.3.   PROJECTED TOTAL POVERTY POPULATION
GIVEN END OF WAR IN 1970–71 WITH NO OFFSETTING
FISCAL ADJUSTMENT

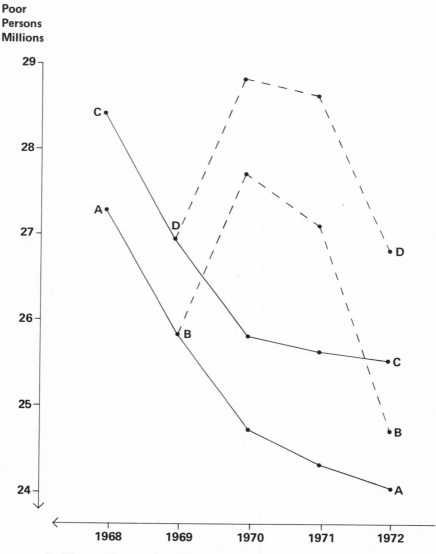

A. War continues with permanent tax surcharge (Table 5.3)
B. War ends but surcharge continues (Table 5.8)
C. War continues with surcharge and fiscal restraint (Table 5.5)
D. War ends but surcharge and restraint continue (Table 5.9)

continue to grow at the same rates as during the Kennedy-Johnson administrations. If the Nixon administration pursues a more restrictive policy, a failure to respond to the immediate deflationary effect of ending the war could mean a recession and a poverty level of more serious proportions. The decline is followed by an expansion of considerable magnitude, but there are some indications that the expansion would be of brief duration.

Compensating Fiscal Expenditures

One would expect a positive fiscal response to the end of the war. One type of response would be to absorb the decline in defense expenditures immediately into other public activities. In terms of the econometric model, this policy would reduce the influence of the end of the war to a minor impact on inventory accumulation and on civilian labor force participation. In broad terms, therefore, such an adjustment, if made quickly and smoothly, could virtually prevent the deflationary effect.

Table 5.10 compares the results of such a simulation to our original results based upon a continuation of the war. The projections are in line with what elementary production theory would have us expect: an increase of domestic labor inputs would tend to depress wage rates while increasing total output. Real output is projected to rise, while unemployment rises slightly and the rates of wage and price increase decline. There is a mild influence on the poverty population, with a differential increase of 491,000 in 1970 and 204,000 in 1971.

There are some critical omissions from the model which, if properly accounted for, would prevent us from reaching such a strong conclusion. The model does not account for sectoral or regional shifts in demand, both of which would occur in the situation described.[23] A decline in defense production would release labor which might not be readily employable in the sectors in which the compensating increase in demand occurred. This friction in transferring the labor force to peacetime activities could be due either to the nature of the skills held by the defense employees, or to their geographical location, or to both. A parallel problem of perhaps more critical nature exists with the capital equipment of defense-related industries. Similarly, the rapid expansion of demand in

[23] About 60 percent of all Department of Defense prime contracts awarded in fiscal 1968 were concentrated in ten states. About one-third of all defense contracts went to California, Texas, New York, and Connecticut. See "Where the Military Contracts Go," *Fortune* (1 August 1969), p. 75.

TABLE 5.10. SELECTED SIMULATION RESULTS: WAR ENDS, 1970–71, TAX SURCHARGE CONTINUES, CHANGE IN DEFENSE EXPENDITURES OFFSET BY EQUAL INCREASE IN NONDEFENSE GOVERNMENT PURCHASES EXPRESSED AS DIFFERENCE FROM TABLE 5.3, WAR CONTINUES

	1970	1971	1972
Aggregate Output and Price Variables			
GNP_{58}	+3.2	+8.9	+10.6
GNP	−9.0	−8.0	−4.0
$PGNP$	−0.017	−0.027	−0.026
$\Delta PGNP/PGNP_{t-1}$	−0.013	−0.007	+0.002
Corporate Sector			
$PROF$	−2.3	−0.1	+1.3
TCP	−1.0	0	+0.5
Employment and Income Variables			
PI	−5.3	−5.6	−3.4
TFP	−0.7	−0.2	+0.3
DPI	−4.7	−5.5	−3.8
WP	−4.3	−4.7	−2.8
$TRAG$	+0.3	+0.4	+0.2
W^*	−101	−163	−158
$\Delta W^*/W^*_{t-1}$	−0.015	−0.008	+0.002
U	+0.003	+0.005	+0.002
Distributional Variables			
$Y10$	−76	−67	−41
$MFAM$	−180	−260	−220
$Y90$	−150	−350	−390
$HMWL$	−0.0226	−0.0285	−0.0153
$HMWN$	−0.0039	+0.0014	+0.0036
$HMOT$	−0.0033	+0.0023	+0.0067
$HFEM$	+0.0231	+0.0187	+0.0071
$HUIE$	+0.0093	+0.0033	−0.0012
Percent Poor, by Group			
MWL	+0.46	+0.57	+0.32
MWN	+0.25	0.0	−0.10
MWP	+0.29	+0.15	+0.03
MOT	+1.0	−0.1	−0.35
FEM	−0.2	−0.2	−0.1
UIE	−0.6	−0.2	+0.05
UIN	0.0	−0.2	−0.6

the substitute activities would tend to be hindered by supply constraints not immediately alleviated by the excess capacity in defense industries.[24]

For a given level of aggregate demand, therefore, the effect of a major shift in the structure of demand would be to raise both the level of frictional unemployment and the rate of inflation. The inflationary impact could be eased by slowing down the expansion of the substitute activities at the expense of a sharper intervening deflationary impact or by diffusing the expansion across a wider cross section of the economy. One means of approaching the latter objective would be through a decrease in the personal and corporate income taxes.

Ending the Tax Surcharge (Revisited)

As an alternative means of fiscal adjustment, let us assume that the federal tax surcharge is permitted to lapse at the end of 1969, just prior to the first-year decline in defense activities; alternatively, we can assume that the surcharge is cut in half at the end of 1969 and removed at the end of 1970.[25] Otherwise, no offsetting action is presumed. Since the effects of removing the surcharge after the war are qualitatively similar to the effect discussed above of a comparable action during the war, only summary results are presented here.

Table 5.11 reports the predicted effect of terminating the tax surcharge on real GNP, the rate of inflation, the rate of wage change, the unemployment rate, and the size of the poverty population. Parts (1) and (2) repeat our earlier findings concerning the deflationary impact of the end of the war; parts (3) and (4), the effect of terminating the surcharge given a continuation of the war and fiscal restraint. Parts (5) to (8) indicate the fiscal boost provided by ending the surcharge after the war, given the alternative timing of the change and the presence or absence of fiscal restraint.

Several characteristics of the results are noteworthy. First, the tax cut has a larger impact on real output in offsetting a postwar recession than it does in a tight war economy but has *less* inflationary effect. Second, the tax cut is more expansionary in an economy without continued "fiscal restraint" than it is with the restraint package. Third, the tax cut is a more efficient instrument for restoring losses in real GNP than it is in offsetting the increase in poverty which would accompany the end of the war. For

---

[24]This statement might not be true if the substitute activities were also of a defense nature.

[25]In terms of the model, this is equivalent to removing the surcharge midway through 1970.

TABLE 5.11.   SUMMARY NET EFFECTS OF ENDING TAX SURCHARGE

A = Surcharge ends December 31, 1969
B = Surcharge cut in half, 1970; eliminated December 31, 1970

		GNP_{58}	$\dfrac{\Delta PGNP}{PGNP_{t-1}}$	$\dfrac{\Delta W^*}{W^*_{t-1}}$	U	Poor Persons (Millions)
1. (5.8) war ends,	1970	−16.5	−0.045	−0.056	+0.015	+3.03
tax continues	1971	−25.6	−0.024	−0.030	+0.028	+2.76
(compared to	1972	−3.2	−0.001	+0.003	+0.014	+0.67
war continues)						
2. (5.9) war ends,	1970	−21.2	−0.034	−0.044	+0.019	+3.05
restraint and	1971	−31.7	−0.015	−0.018	+0.032	+3.05
tax continue	1972	−9.2	−0.003	+0.001	+0.019	+1.33
(compared to war						
continues with						
restraint)						
3. (5.6) surcharge	1970	+13.2	+0.030	+0.038	−0.008	−1.45
ends (A), war	1971	+10.6	+0.002	+0.001	−0.008	−0.53
continues with	1972	+5.4	−0.001	−0.003	−0.004	−0.25
restraint (com-						
pared to sur-						
charge continues)						
4. (5.7) surcharge	1970	+6.9	+0.013	+0.017	−0.004	−0.82
ends (B), war	1971	+12.3	+0.017	+0.020	−0.008	−1.12
continues with	1972	+9.7	−0.001	−0.002	−0.007	−0.54
restraint (com-						
pared to sur-						
charge continues)						
5. Surcharge ends	1970	+15.0	+0.022	+0.029	−0.009	−2.00
(A), war ends,	1971	+14.4	−0.004	−0.006	−0.011	−0.69
no restraint	1972	+5.8	+0.006	+0.006	−0.005	−0.53
(compared to						
surcharge con-						
tinues)						
6. Surcharge ends	1970	+7.7	+0.010	+0.013	−0.005	−1.06
(B), war ends,	1971	+16.7	+0.006	+0.009	−0.011	−1.21
no restraint	1972	+9.6	+0.006	+0.006	−0.007	−0.75
(compared to						
surcharge con-						
tinues)						
7. Surcharge ends	1970	+17.2	+0.016	+0.022	−0.012	−1.74
(A), war ends,	1971	+14.9	−0.003	−0.006	−0.011	−0.76
restraint (com-	1972	+8.5	+0.006	+0.006	−0.007	−0.64
pared to sur-						
charge continues)						
8. Surcharge ends	1970	+8.7	+0.007	+0.010	−0.006	−0.76
(B), war ends,	1971	+17.8	+0.004	+0.006	−0.012	−1.16
restraint (com-	1972	+12.1	+0.005	+0.004	−0.009	−0.83
pared to sur-						
charge continues)						

instance, terminating the tax surcharge at the end of 1969 (part 5, with no "fiscal restraint") would offset 91 percent of the loss in real GNP brought about in 1970 by the end of the war and 56 percent of the loss in 1971. At the same time, only 35 and 44 percent of the increases in poverty for 1970 and 1971, respectively, are offset. A similar pattern appears in the other tax-cut simulations reported in Table 5.11.

In aggregate terms, an immediate repeal of the tax surcharge when the war ends would not prevent a decline in economic activity; it is not a powerful enough tool to cope with the hypothetical defense reduction used in the simulations. It could, however, reduce both the duration and the severity of any recession which might occur.

When evaluating the somewhat weaker effect of a tax cut on the poverty population, we must keep in mind that the first-round impact of the tax cut would be to affect the distribution of disposable personal income, given the distribution of before-tax income. Since the poor pay very little in federal income taxes, they do not share in the first-round benefits of the tax cut. Eventually they would make mild relative gains in before-tax income, as indicated in the above results.

Mixed Fiscal Action

The final alternative considered here is for the government to respond to the end of the war by both removing the tax surcharge (halfway in 1970, terminating at the end of 1970) and offsetting half the reduction in defense spending by increases in nondefense federal spending. Table 5.12 reports the net effect of pursuing this policy while simultaneously ending the war. The results are very similar to Table 5.10, where a pure expenditure policy was simulated, except that the composition of income and output is weighted more heavily toward the private sector in the current results. The mixed policy requires slightly more time to take effect as well; in the first year (1970) there is a 749,000 increase in the poverty population, compared to only 491,000 with the pure expenditure policy.

POLICY IMPLICATIONS

Are the simulations reported above reliable enough to provide meaningful predictions of the path of the economy? While many of the results appear to be reasonable, they must be viewed in light of the weaknesses of the model, particularly the absence of a financial sector and the tend-

TABLE 5.12.   SELECTED SIMULATION RESULTS: WAR ENDS 1970–71, TAX SURCHARGE CUT IN HALF IN 1970, ELIMINATED AT END OF 1970, CHANGE IN DEFENSE EXPENDITURES 50 PERCENT OFF-SET BY INCREASE IN NONDEFENSE GOVERNMENT PURCHASES, EXPRESSED AS DIFFERENCE FROM TABLE 5.3, WAR CONTINUES

	1970	1971	1972
Aggregate Output and Price Variables			
GNP_{58}	+1.0	+7.6	+12.7
GNP	−18	−13	0
$PGNP$	−0.024	−0.033	−0.026
$\Delta PGNP/PGNP_{t-1}$	−0.018	−0.005	+0.006
Corporate Sector			
$PROF$	−5.0	−0.3	+3.8
TCP	−4.2	−4.6	−3.2
Employment and Income Variables			
PI	−9.4	−8.0	−0.5
TFP	−5.4	−9.8	−9.5
DPI	−4.2	+1.3	+8.7
WP	−8.2	−8.0	−1.6
$TRAG$	+0.4	+0.5	+0.1
W^*	−145	−202	−156
$\Delta W^*/W^*_{t-1}$	−0.021	−0.007	+0.007
U	+0.004	+0.006	+0.001
Distributional Variables			
$Y10$	−117	−85	−31
$MFAM$	−277	−350	−220
$Y90$	−200	−410	−380
$HMWL$	−0.0319	−0.0342	−0.0094
$HMWN$	−0.0055	+0.0032	+0.0052
$HMOT$	−0.0062	+0.0026	+0.0096
$HFEM$	+0.0336	+0.0231	+0.0065
$HUIE$	+0.0033	+0.0039	0.0
Percent Poor, by Group			
MWL	+0.7	+0.7	+0.1
MWN	+0.35	0.0	−0.2
MWP	+0.42	+0.18	−0.10
MOT	+1.2	−0.2	−0.55
FEM	−0.2	−0.2	−0.1
UIE	−0.7	−0.3	−0.25
UIN	+0.1	−0.3	−0.9

ency to overpredict employment and price changes during periods of high demand.

Subject to the above reservations, the following general conclusions can be stated:

1. If the economy were to continue on an expansionary path, the incidence of poverty could be expected to decline steadily. The rate of decline would depend, however, on the type of fiscal action taken to restrain the war economy. For a given reduction in total output (from trend), a tax increase would cause less of a differential increase in poverty than would a reduction of government expenditures. This is primarily because the poor are spared the first-round impact of a federal tax increase. Furthermore, a reduction in federal purchases of goods and services would have a smaller impact on the poverty population than would a restriction on transfer payments. If a policy of fiscal restraint is necessary, therefore, the "mix" of the policy package is very important in terms of its impact on the poor.

2. To the extent that the federal tax surcharge has had a restraining effect on the rate of inflation, it has been at some cost to the poor, who might have benefited from even tighter labor markets. Fixed-income groups among the poor, on the other hand, were spared significant losses in real income. Although the incidence of poverty falls during a period of inflation and full employment, the composition of the poor changes substantially during such periods in the direction of more households dependent on fixed income sources and fewer households oriented toward the labor market. The converse holds during a recession.

3. Even with a tax increase and other measures of fiscal restraint present, the model did not predict a recession given a continuation of the war in Indochina at its 1968 level. In evaluating this result, two factors must be kept in mind. First, no assumptions were made concerning tight monetary policy during the period. Second, fiscal policy since 1968 has, in fact, been far tighter than what was assumed in the simulations. Compared to the trend projections used in the simulations, real government purchases of goods and services fell by $19.4 billion between 1968 and 1970. Of this total, real defense expenditures fell by $9.7 billion and real compensation of government employees fell by $7.4 billion. The 1970 level of civilian government employment was almost one million lower than the projected figure. Given such contractionary forces at work, the current recession should come as a surprise to no one.[26]

---

[26] The following table compares the projected and actual values of selected exogenous variables for 1970. Actual values are taken from the 1971 *Economic Report of the President*. Real defense expenditures are obtained by dividing cur-

When an end to the war in Indochina is simulated by the model, the reduction in defense expenditures and the decline in the armed forces is predicted to create a recession in the absence of offsetting expansionary action by the federal government. If the federal government does not take explicit expansionary steps but continues to expand nondefense expenditures and transfer payments at the rate experienced in the 1960s, the economy could be expected to pull out of the recession after the decline in total government expenditures levels off and resumes its upward path. If the government pursues more restrictive fiscal policies, the recession would be of longer duration.

4. A postwar recession would increase the numbers of the poor by a substantial amount in the short run. In differential terms, the impact on the poverty population of a given act of fiscal restraint appears to be larger during a recessionary climate than it is in a tight war economy. For the objective of reducing poverty, therefore, it is essential that any restrictive domestic policies undertaken during the war be quickly reversed at the war's end. This is particularly true in the case of restrictions on government transfers.

CONCLUDING OBSERVATIONS

The study has attempted to cover much ground, without stopping to confront a number of major problems thrown into its path. Aside from the structural weaknesses present in any econometric model, such issues as

---

rent dollar purchases of goods and services for national defense by the implicit price deflator for federal purchases of goods and services.

	Assumed in Simulation, War to Continue	1970 Actual
Armed forces (millions of persons)	3.535	3.188
Government wage and salary workers (millions of persons)	13.577	12.600
Real gross government product (billions of 1958 dollars)	68.1	60.7
Real government purchases of goods and services (billions of 1958 dollars)	161.2	141.8
Change in real defense expenditures, 1968–70 (billions of 1958 dollars)	0	−9.7

the biased nature of data relating to the income distribution, the relationship between the distribution of before-tax and after-tax income, and the theoretical implications of the rather pragmatic view taken toward describing the income distribution have all been ignored.

Yet considerable progress has been made. First, a three-parameter or "displaced" lognormal distribution, estimated by simple quantile methods, was shown to provide a convenient, flexible, and reasonably accurate description of the size distribution of personal income, either in the aggregate or for population subgroups. This claim must be qualified by acknowledging the weakness of the distributional form in describing the extreme upper tail of the distribution.

Second, the shape of the income distribution was found to respond in a significant and systematic manner to economic stimuli. Given the displaced lognormal distribution as a descriptive device, a block of equations was constructed and estimated to specify this response for each of six population groups. Special reference was made to the impact of economic changes upon the poverty population, as conventionally defined by income criteria. The heterogeneity of response of group size distributions to economic phenomena was predictable to a significant extent by differences in sources of income. It becomes clear that low income households cannot be viewed as a homogeneous group when changes in the size distribution of income are examined.

Third, the equation system describing the size distribution of income was integrated into a full scale econometric model of the United States. This involved a consideration of the impact of distributional changes upon the level and composition of consumption expenditures, upon the level of tax receipts, and upon labor force participation. While the model retains a number of weaknesses, it is a "working model" capable of simulating the path of the economy under a variety of circumstances.

Finally, a number of simulation experiments were conducted to test the usefulness of the model. In addition to revealing its limitations, the simulation experiments provided some meaningful insights into the effects of alternative fiscal policies given the present economic climate.

One could proceed in a number of directions from this point. An alternative would be to confront directly some of the issues left behind as the study proceeded. A second area of attention would concern the limitations of the econometric model as currently structured. A third direction one could take would be to adapt the model to analyze a number of policy issues relating to the distribution of income. This might include revising or refining the model to raise the level of sophistication of fiscal policies that can be examined and restructuring the distribution sector to measure the impact of economic policies on population groups other than the six chosen for treatment here.

Each of these areas reflects deficiencies in the scope and depth of the study. In order to cover the ground established at the beginning of this study, however, blinders had to be worn along much of the track. Hopefully, what has been missed along the way is not so critical as to nullify what progress has been made.

Appendix to Chapter 2

THE EMPIRICAL USAGE OF A DISPLACED LOGNORMAL DISTRIBUTION

This appendix provides a brief assessment of alternative methods of estimation to the straight quantile methods used in this study. It then presents examples of the application of the displaced lognormal distribution to postwar United States income data and compares them to alternative choices of transformations. Evidence is provided to affirm some of the empirical assertions made in chapter 2.

METHODS OF ESTIMATION: DISPLACED LOGNORMAL DISTRIBUTION

As stated in chapter 2, elegance and convenience are in conflict when methods of estimation are considered. Under "ideal" conditions, one would like to apply maximum likelihood techniques, but conditions are far from ideal in the case at hand. Aitchison and Brown say the following about applying the method of maximum likelihood estimation to the three-parameter lognormal distribution:

> The range of the variate now depends on $[c]$, one of the parameters to be estimated, so that the maximum-likelihood estimators cannot be assumed to possess the desirable properties of consistence, asymptotic normality, and minimum variance without special investigation. . . .

In our view the difficulty of computation coupled with a suspicion of the underlying theory leaves little incentive to recommend the method.[1]

The maximum likelihood equations to which they refer are quite simple in form. In the terminology of this study the equations are

$$\mu^* = (1/n) \ \Sigma \ \log(y + c^*),$$

$$(\sigma^2)^* = (1/n) \ \Sigma \ [\log(y + c^*)]^2 - (\mu^*)^2,$$

and

$$[(\sigma^2)^* - \mu^*] \cdot \Sigma \ [1/(y + c^*)] + \Sigma \ \{[\log (y + c^*)]/(y + c^*)\} = 0,$$

where starred parameters refer to estimators. A single equation containing y and c is formed by substitution, and c^* is then solved for by inverse interpolation. If an iterative procedure is used, $\log(y + c^*)$ must be recomputed for every observation each time a value of c^* is chosen.

While the above procedure is simple in form, much computation would be required, presuming the availability of individual observations. The fact that grouped observations are to be used disrupts the procedure entirely and further strengthens the incentive not to use maximum likelihood procedures.

An alternative procedure begins with the observation that if a sufficient estimator of c exists, it must be a function of the least sample value,[2] and then establishes a set of maximum likelihood equations making use of this value. Since the available grouped data have an open-ended bottom income cell, such a refinement is not available.

Once maximum-likelihood procedures are dismissed, remaining methods include graphical approximations, direct moment estimation, quantile estimation, and a wide variety of moment-quantile combinations. The graphical method[3] is a manual iteration procedure by which $(y + c)$ is plotted on logarithmic probability paper against the proportion of sample values not exceeding y, for different values of c. The objective is to find that value of c for which the graph most closely approximates a

---

[1] J. Aitchison and J. A. C. Brown, *The Lognormal Distribution* (Cambridge: At the University Press, 1957), pp. 55–56.

[2] *Ibid.*, pp. 56–57. The method referred to was suggested by A. C. Cohen in "Estimating Parameters of Logarithmic-Normal Distributions by Maximum Likelihood," *Journal of the American Statistical Association* 46 (June 1951), 206.

[3] Aitchison and Brown, *Lognormal Distribution*, p. 60.

straight line. Repeated use of this method for numerous samples does not appear to warrant serious consideration.

Direct moment estimation can be used to obtain values for α, β^2, and λ^3. The three equations involving the three known moments (on the left-hand side) can then be solved for the unknowns — μ, σ, and c. As long as $\lambda^3 > 0$, values of μ, α, and c can be obtained which are consistent with the observed moments. The difficulties involved in estimating moments from data grouped into unequal, open-ended cells have already been alluded to in chapter 2. The concern is with both bias and efficiency. Although there have been attempts to make moment corrections on the estimate of the overall mean under such circumstances,[4] to my knowledge there have not been any successful efforts to obtain unbiased estimates of higher moments with unequal, open-ended groupings.

It is also likely that moment estimation from grouped data is extremely inefficient. Even in the experiments conducted by Aitchison and Brown with individual observations, the method of moment estimation was less efficient than quantile methods.[5]

The use of moments could be retained by utilizing some mixture of moments and quantiles, since virtually any three independent pieces of data are sufficient to specify the distribution. For instance, the parameters of a displaced lognormal distribution which are consistent with observed values of the mean (α), variance (β^2), and median (d) could be found. Alternatively a second quantile measure, such as the cutoff of the bottom decile, could be utilized in place of an observed variance. Such mixed procedures vary in difficulty, but usually require an iterative solution to obtain the remaining parameters of the distribution after the three known parameters are inserted.

FAILURE OF THE DESCRIPTIVE POWER OF THE NORMAL AND LOGNORMAL DISTRIBUTIONS

It is a foregone conclusion that a normal curve does not provide an adequate description of the size distribution of income. A cursory examination of United States income data reveals that the observed distribution is positively skewed, contrary to the symmetry of a normal distribution.

---

[4] See D. J. Aigner, "A Linear Approximator for the Class Marks of a Grouped Frequency Distribution, with Especial Reference to the Unequal Interval Case," *Technometrics* 10 (November 1968), 783–809.

[5] The reader is referred to chapters 5 and 6 in Aitchison and Brown, *Lognormal Distribution*.

The following discussion utilizes the U.S. Census Current Population Survey data for 1965.[6] While these data have since been revised, the revisions or the year chosen do not affect the results of this discussion. (Specific parameter values, on the other hand, could be affected.)

Table A2.1 shows the percentage distribution of United States families by 1965 income. The sample median is $6882. With the assumption that the midpoint of each cell is the cell mean, except at the upper end where a Pareto distribution is fit to determine the mean of the open-ended cell,[7] a mean income of $7924 is observed.

For a null hypothesis of normality of the income distribution not to be rejected, one requirement is that the mean and median not be significantly different from each other. Given the sample size, the standard error of estimated percentages in the vicinity of the median is 0.4 percent of the population. In dollar terms, the standard error of the estimated median is about $40,[8] compared to the $1000 spread between the estimated mean and the sample median. Since no accounting has been made for either the standard error of the mean estimate or the covariance between the two estimates, this test is not strictly valid; the fact that over 10 percent of the cumulative distribution lies within this spread cannot be ignored, however.

Given an estimate of the variance of the distribution, moment estimation can be used to fit a normal curve to the data. One method of calculating moments for grouped data is to assume that all observations within a cell lie at the cell mean, given the assumed cell means described above. If all the cells have equal ranges, with no open-ended cells at the extremes, the estimated sample variance would be biased upward.[9] If the

---

[6] U.S. Bureau of the Census, *Current Population Reports,* Ser. P-60, No. 51, "Income in 1965 of Families and Persons in the United States" (Washington, D.C.: U.S. Government Printing Office, 1967).

[7] For a discussion of this procedure see U.S. Bureau of the Census, *Income Distribution in the United States* (1960 Census Monograph, prepared by Herman P. Miller) (Washington, D.C.: U.S. Government Printing Office, 1966), pp. 213 ff.; or U.S. Bureau of the Census, *Trends in the Income of Families and Persons in the United States 1947 to 1960* (Technical Paper No. 8, prepared by Herman P. Miller) (Washington, D.C.: U.S. Government Printing Office, 1963) (updated to 1964 and republished in 1967 as Technical Paper No. 17, prepared by Mary F. Henson).

[8] See U.S. Bureau of the Census, *Current Population Reports,* Ser. P-60, No. 51, pp. 16–17.

[9] See W. Palin Elderton, *Frequency Curves and Correlation,* 3rd ed. (Cambridge: At the University Press, 1938); also M. G. Kendall, *The Advanced Theory of Statistics,* 5th ed. (New York: Hafner, 1952), vol. 1. If in fact the true population is infinite in size and conforms to a Pareto-Lévy distribution, a finite variance does not exist.

TABLE A2.1.   FAMILIES BY TOTAL MONEY INCOME IN 1965 FOR
THE UNITED STATES, PERCENTAGE DISTRIBUTION

Total Money Income	Percent
	100.0%
Under $1,000	3.0
$ 1,000– 1,499	2.8
$ 1,500– 1,999	3.3
$ 2,000– 2,499	3.6
$ 2,500– 2,999	3.8
$ 3,000– 3,499	4.0
$ 3,500– 3,999	3.8
$ 4,000– 4,999	8.0
$ 5,000– 5,999	9.3
$ 6,000– 6,999	9.3
$ 7,000– 7,999	9.7
$ 8,000– 8,999	8.1
$ 9,000– 9,999	6.3
$10,000–11,999	9.7
$12,000–14,999	7.6
$15,000–24,999	6.1
$25,000 and over	1.5
No. (thousands)	48,297
Median income	$6,882

Source: U.S. Bureau of the Census, *Current Population Reports,* Ser. P-60, No. 51,
"Income in 1965 of Families and Persons in the United States" (Washington, D.C.: U.S.
Government Printing Office, 1967), Table 1.

distribution has high contact[10] at both ends, and if the cells are uniform
in size, Sheppard's adjustments may be applied to obtain unbiased estimates of the second and fourth moments of the distribution (the first and
third moments would already be unbiased).[11]

Sheppard's adjustments may not be used for a number of reasons:
the cells are not uniform in size, and the uppermost cell is open-ended;
the distribution may not have high contact at the lower end; and estimates for the means of the two extreme cells are not reliable. Higher
moment calculations are quite sensitive to these estimates.

Given the weakness of higher moment estimates and the removal of
conditions sufficient to determine even the direction of bias in the estimates, a simple correction procedure can guarantee no gains in reliability. In all examples where direct moment estimation is utilized, therefore, no corrections have been applied to the moment estimates.[12]

---

[10] That is, if the first derivative of the frequency distribution approaches zero
in the limit, at both ends of the curve.

[11] Elderton, *Frequency Curves and Correlation.*

[12] Ultimately, no direct moment estimation is used in this study.

The following four moments about the mean were obtained for the 1965 family income distribution, expressed in thousands of dollars:

$$\alpha = 7.924$$
$$\beta^2 = 33.876$$
$$\lambda_3 = 426.215$$
$$\lambda_4 = 41815.835$$

The coefficients of skewness and kurtosis[13] are both positive, suggesting a departure from normality:

$$\gamma_1 = \lambda_3/\beta^{2(3/2)} = 2.1617$$
$$\gamma_2 = \lambda_4/\beta^{2(2)} - 3 = 7.1068$$

In Table A2.2 a normal curve having the observed mean (7.924) and variance (33.876) is compared to the actual data. Because of the skewness of the observed data, the estimated normal distribution places too many families at incomes below $1000 and between $10,000 and $25,000. The estimated median is the sample mean with the estimated cumulative distribution lying below the observed median ($6882) being 42.8 percent. The absolute error in the estimated cumulative distribution exceeds 11 percent of the population at some points. If the true variance of the distribution were smaller than the estimated variance, the fitting of an alternative normal curve with a corrected variance would make the "fatness" of the normal curve at low incomes and at intermediate high incomes less critical, the relative absence of predicted high income families even more severe, and the already small estimate of the cumulative distribution lying below the observed median even smaller.

The following calculations are made under the assumption that the logarithm of income is $N(\mu,\sigma^2)$. With the framework of direct moment estimation, one could either estimate α and β^2 and obtain implied values of μ and σ^2, or vice versa. Similarly, while a nonzero third moment (λ_3) exists, it is strictly dependent on the values of μ and σ^2 (or α and β^2). In short, any and only two of α, β^2, λ_3, μ, and σ^2 may be estimated. If in fact the lognormal distribution describes the empirical data poorly, this will be reflected in a significant inconsistency of unrestricted estimates of the five parameters with their theoretical relationships.

Again using the direct estimates $\alpha = 7.924$ and $\beta^2 = 33.876$, the following implied values for μ and σ^2 are derived:

$$\alpha = 7.92446 = e^{\mu+.5\sigma^2}$$
$$\beta^2 = 33.87602 = e^{2\mu+\sigma^2}(e^{\sigma^2} - 1)$$

---

[13] Aitchison and Brown, *Lognormal Distribution*, p. 8.

TABLE A2.2. ESTIMATED AND ACTUAL FAMILY INCOME, 1965 UNDER ASSUMPTION
OF NORMALITY, PERCENTAGE DISTRIBUTIONS

Assumption: Moment method; $\alpha = 7.924$, $\beta^2 = 33.876$ estimated directly from data. (See text.)

Income (thousands of dollars)	Actual Distribution	Cumulative Distribution	Estimated Distribution	Cumulative Estimate	Error	Cumulative Error
0– 1.0	3.0	3.0	11.7	11.7	+8.7	+8.7
1.0– 1.5	2.8	5.8	1.9	13.6	−0.9	+7.8
1.5– 2.0	3.3	9.1	1.8	15.4	−1.5	+6.3
2.0– 2.5	3.6	12.7	2.2	17.6	−1.4	+4.9
2.5– 3.0	3.8	16.5	2.2	19.8	−1.6	+3.3
3.0– 3.5	4.0	20.5	2.6	22.4	−1.4	+1.9
3.5– 4.0	3.8	24.3	2.6	25.0	−1.2	+0.7
4.0– 5.0	8.0	32.3	5.8	30.8	−2.2	−1.5
5.0– 6.0	9.3	41.6	6.3	37.1	−3.0	−4.3
6.0– 7.0	9.3	50.9	6.5	43.6	−2.8	−7.3
7.0– 8.0	9.7	60.6	6.9	50.5	−2.8	−10.1
8.0– 9.0	8.1	68.7	6.8	57.3	−1.3	−11.4
9.0–10.0	6.3	75.0	6.4	63.7	+0.1	−11.3
10.0–12.0	9.7	84.7	12.1	75.8	+2.4	−8.9
12.0–15.0	7.6	92.3	13.1	88.9	+5.5	−3.4
15.0–25.0	6.1	98.4	10.9	99.8	+4.8	+1.4
25.0+	1.5	99.9	0.2	100.0	−1.3	–

$$\beta^2/\alpha^2 = 0.53945 = e^{\sigma^2} - 1$$
$$\sigma^2 = 0.43144$$
$$e^{\mu + .21572} = 7.92446$$
$$\mu = 1.85428$$
$$\text{median } (e^\mu) = 6.387$$

In the above calculation, the observed median is underestimated by about $500. Part of this underestimation would come from an upward bias in the variance measure, if such a bias is present. In Table A2.3, Assumption A, a lognormal distribution is fitted to the 1965 data according to the above procedure. Any improvement in the estimate of the median coming from a lower variance measure would be accompanied by a worsening of the fit on the lower tail of the data.

As an alternative, μ and σ^2 could be estimated directly from the logarithmic data. Since the bottom cell of the grouped data has a logarithmic range of log($1000) to minus infinity (ruling out negative incomes), the estimates are quite sensitive to the form of the estimation procedure. The results of two such estimation procedures are given in Table A2.3 under Assumptions B and C. Under Assumption B, all persons are assumed to lie at the logarithmic midpoint of their respective cells, such as the point [log($1000) + log($1500)]/2 for the $1000–$1500 cell. The cell for incomes under $1000 is assumed to have a lower bound of $1. Therefore all persons in that cell are assigned the value [log($1000)]/2. At the upper end of the distribution the assumed logarithmic mean is found by fitting a Pareto curve to the logarithmic data.

When Assumption B is followed, the directly estimated logarithmic mean has an antilogarithm (median income) of $5545, far below the observed value of $6882. Too many families are assigned to the lower income brackets, and also to incomes in excess of $15,000. The observed coefficient of skewness in the logarithmic data is −2.699, compared to a positive coefficient of 2.162 in the nontransformed data. To a large extent, these results are a consequence of the assumptions made concerning the distribution of families having less than $1000 income.

Under Assumption C, all families are assumed to lie at the arithmetic midpoint of their respective cells, except as described previously for the upper income tail. For instance, the value log($1250) is assigned to the $1000–$1500 class, and log($500) is assigned to the under-$1000 class. This change in assumption lowers the variance estimate and increases the median estimate. Estimated median income is now $6058, above the $5545 value obtained from Assumption B, but well below the sample median of $6882. As Table A2.3 indicates, too few families are now assigned to incomes below $1000 and between $5000 and $15,000, while too many families are assigned to incomes between $1000 and $5000. While the curve fitted under Assumption C describes the data far better than the curve fitted under Assumption B, the error in the estimated cumulative distribution exceeds 8 percent of the population in the vicinity of the median. While the assumption of lognormality presumes the presence of positive skewness in the absolute data, the transformation into logarithmic form is supposed to negate that skewness. Under Assumption C the coefficient of skewness is -0.8672, negative but smaller than under Assumption B. Under the assumption of normality the estimate of the coefficient of skewness has a known variance, based on the number of observations.[14] The variance measure could be used to provide an approximate test of the departure from normality (or in this case departure from lognormality); here the test is obscured by the complications imposed by the grouped data, particularly in the logarithmic form.

All the above moment estimation procedures yield a median estimate which is considerably smaller than the observed sample median. Quantile methods could be utilized to circumvent the instability of these procedures. One alternative would be to accept the antilogarithm of the sample median as the mean of the logarithmic distribution, and then to use one additional quantile to derive a variance estimate. As a result, values of μ and σ^2 for a lognormal distribution which are consistent with a zero cumulative error at the median and at the other specified quantile could be obtained. In specifying quantiles one may either name a quantile and observe what dollar level (or fraction of the median) it represents, or name a predetermined income fraction of the median and observe what quantile it represents.

By interpolation of 1965 family income data, it is observed that 20 percent of all families received less than $3441, or half the observed median. Using this information and the observed median, an implied logarithmic standard error (σ) of 0.8232 is obtained. The estimated income distribution is shown under Assumption D of Table A2.4.

The estimated distribution derived in this manner provides a closer fit to the actual data on the lower half of the distribution than any of the previously used procedures, but above the median the predicted distribution fares quite poorly. In particular, 17.2 percent of all families are predicted to have incomes in excess of $15,000, compared to an observed percentage of only 7.6 percent.

Alternatively, for Assumption E, 23.3 percent of all families reported incomes greater than 1.5 times the observed median. The estimate $\sigma =$

---

[14] Kendall, *Advanced Theory,* 3rd ed., 2:105.

TABLE A2.3. ESTIMATED FAMILY INCOME, 1965, UNDER ASSUMPTION OF LOGNORMALITY, MOMENT METHODS, PERCENTAGE DISTRIBUTIONS

Assumption A: $\alpha = 7.924$, $\beta^2 = 33.876$ estimated directly from data, and implied logarithmic moments solved for. (See text.)

Assumption B: μ, σ^2 estimated directly from logged data. Cell midpoints assumed to be midpoint of logarithmic range, i.e., midpoint of $1000–$1500 cell assumed to be [log($1000) + log($1500)]/2. The y < $1000 group is assigned a range of $1–$1000.

Income (thousands of dollars)	Estimated Distribution (Assumption A)	Error	Cumulative Estimate	Error	Estimated Distribution (Assumption B)	Error	Cumulative Estimate	Error
0– 1.0	0.2	−2.8	0.2	−2.8	5.9	+2.9	5.9	+2.9
1.0– 1.5	1.1	−1.7	1.4	−4.4	5.8	+3.0	11.7	+5.9
1.5– 2.0	2.5	−0.8	3.8	−5.3	5.9	+2.6	17.6	+8.5
2.0– 2.5	3.8	+0.2	7.6	−5.1	5.6	+2.1	23.3	+10.6
2.5– 3.0	4.9	+1.1	12.5	−4.0	5.5	+1.7	28.8	+12.3
3.0– 3.5	5.4	+1.4	17.9	−2.6	5.0	+0.9	33.7	+13.2
3.5– 4.0	6.0	+2.2	23.9	−0.4	4.5	+0.7	38.2	+13.9
4.0– 5.0	11.7	+3.7	35.6	+3.3	8.4	+0.4	46.0	+14.3
5.0– 6.0	10.4	+1.1	46.6	+4.4	6.2	−3.0	52.9	+11.3
6.0– 7.0	9.6	+0.3	55.6	+4.7	5.6	−3.8	58.4	+7.5
7.0– 8.0	7.7	−2.0	63.3	+2.7	5.0	−3.6	63.5	+2.9
8.0– 9.0	6.5	−1.6	69.8	+1.1	3.6	−4.5	67.1	−1.6
9.0–10.0	5.3	−1.0	75.2	+0.2	3.4	−2.9	70.5	−4.5
10.0–12.0	8.0	−1.7	83.2	−1.5	5.4	−4.3	75.9	−8.8
12.0–15.0	7.2	−0.4	90.3	−2.0	5.9	−1.7	81.8	−10.5
15.0–25.0	7.8	+1.7	98.1	−0.3	9.7	+3.6	91.5	−6.9
25.0+	1.9	+0.4	100.0	–	8.5	+6.9	100.0	–

Assumption C: μ, σ^2 estimated directly from logged data. Group cells assumed to be rectangular prior to taking of logarithms, e.g., midpoint of $0–$1000 cell assumed to be log($500).

Income (thousands of dollars)	Estimated Distribution (Assumption C)	Error	Cumulative Estimate	Cumulative Error
0– 1.0	1.2	−1.8	1.2	−1.8
1.0– 1.5	2.9	+0.1	4.1	−1.7
1.5– 2.0	4.3	+1.0	8.4	−0.7
2.0– 2.5	5.2	+1.6	13.6	+0.9
2.5– 3.0	5.5	+1.7	19.1	+2.6
3.0– 3.5	5.6	+1.6	24.7	+4.2
3.5– 4.0	5.5	+1.7	30.2	+5.9
4.0– 5.0	10.3	+2.4	40.6	+8.3
5.0– 6.0	9.0	−0.4	49.5	+7.9
6.0– 7.0	7.6	−1.7	57.1	+6.2
7.0– 8.0	6.4	−3.2	63.6	+3.0
8.0– 9.0	5.4	−2.8	68.9	+0.2
9.0–10.0	4.5	−1.8	73.4	−1.6
10.0–12.0	6.9	−2.8	80.3	−4.4
12.0–15.0	6.8	−0.8	87.1	−5.2
15.0–25.0	9.1	+2.9	96.1	−2.3
25.0+	3.9	+2.3	100.0	–

TABLE A2.4. ESTIMATED FAMILY INCOME, 1965, UNDER ASSUMPTION OF LOGNORMALITY, QUANTILE METHODS, PERCENTAGE DISTRIBUTIONS

Assumption D: $\mu = \log_e 6.882 = 1.92891$ where \$6882 is empirically observed median.
$\sigma = 0.8232$ based on 20 percent of population lying below 0.5μ, $e^{.5\mu} = 3.441$.

Assumption E: $\mu = \log_e 6.882 = 1.92891$, $\sigma = 0.556$ based on 23.3 percent of population lying above 1.5μ, $e^{1.5\mu} = 10.323$.
Also consistent with 10.7 percent of population lying above 2μ, $e^{2\mu} = 13.764$.

Income (thousands of dollars)	Estimated Distribution (Assumption D)	Error	Cumulative Estimate	Error	Estimated Distribution (Assumption E)	Error	Cumulative Estimate	Error
0- 1.0	1.0	−2.0	1.0	−2.0	0.0	−3.0	0.0	−3.0
1.0- 1.5	2.2	−0.6	3.2	−2.6	0.3	−2.5	0.3	−5.5
1.5- 2.0	3.5	+0.2	6.7	−2.4	1.1	−2.2	1.4	−7.7
2.0- 2.5	4.2	+0.6	10.9	−1.8	2.2	−1.4	3.6	−9.1
2.5- 3.0	4.7	+0.9	15.6	−0.9	3.6	−0.2	7.2	−9.3
3.0- 3.5	5.0	+1.0	20.6	+0.1	4.5	+0.5	11.6	−8.9
3.5- 4.0	4.9	+1.1	25.5	+1.2	5.3	+1.5	16.9	−7.4
4.0- 5.0	9.4	+1.4	34.8	+2.5	12.0	+4.0	28.9	−3.4
5.0- 6.0	8.5	−0.8	43.4	+1.8	12.0	+2.7	40.9	−0.7
6.0- 7.0	7.4	−1.9	50.8	−0.1	11.0	+1.7	51.9	+1.0
7.0- 8.0	6.5	−3.2	57.3	−3.3	9.5	−0.2	61.3	+0.7
8.0- 9.0	5.5	−2.6	62.8	−5.9	7.8	−0.3	69.1	+0.4
9.0-10.0	4.7	−1.6	67.5	−7.5	6.3	0	75.4	+0.4
10.0-12.0	7.5	−2.2	75.0	−9.7	9.1	−0.6	84.5	−0.2
12.0-15.0	7.8	+0.2	82.8	−9.5	7.6	0	92.1	−0.2
15.0-25.0	11.4	+5.3	94.2	−4.2	6.9	+0.8	99.0	+0.6
25.0+	5.8	+4.3	100.0	—	1.0	−0.5	100.0	—

If we use the 20 percent and 76.7 (100−23.3) percent quantiles and *not* the median we have $\sigma = 0.6993$, $e^{\mu} = 6.200$, i.e., the median is underestimated by \$682.

0.556, a value considerably smaller than the standard error predicted from the lower tail of the distribution, is derived from this information. When the value $\sigma = 0.556$ is used to plot an estimated distribution (Table A2.4, Assumption E), the upper tail of the observed distribution is plotted quite closely, while the estimated lower tail is concentrated much closer to the median than is actually the case.

The fact that a variance measure based upon the upper tail of the distribution is considerably smaller than one based on the lower tail is merely another form of the evidence that in logarithmic form United States income data is negatively skewed.

Furthermore, the null hypothesis of lognormality implies that the cumulative distribution lying below 0.5μ is not significantly different from the cumulative distribution lying above 2.0μ. The observed percentages, however, are 20.0 and 10.7 respectively. According to sampling error tables published by the Census Bureau,[15] the standard errors of estimate on the observed percentages are about 0.5 and 0.3 percentage points, respectively. Assuming zero covariance in the two sampling errors, the standard error of the difference of the two percentages is about 0.6 percent. The hypothesis of equal density in the two tails can therefore be rejected.

ESTIMATION OF DISPLACED LOGNORMAL DISTRIBUTION

Total Families

The displaced lognormal distribution fits the observed data much closer than either the normal or the lognormal distributions, regardless of the method of estimation. Quantile methods provided better results than methods based on moments.

Table A2.5 presents estimated family income for 1965, based on a displaced lognormal distribution calculated by direct moment estimation. The results are directly comparable to Tables A2.2 (normal distribution) and A2.3 (lognormal distribution, Assumption A), except that in addition to the mean and variance the third moment about the mean is utilized. As before, no corrections are applied to the moment estimates.

---

[15] See, for instance, U.S. Bureau of the Census, *Current Population Reports,* Ser. P-60, No. 51, p. 17.

TABLE A2.5. ESTIMATED FAMILY INCOME, 1965, UNDER AS-
SUMPTION OF DISPLACED LOGNORMALITY, MOMENT METHOD,
PERCENTAGE DISTRIBUTIONS

Assumption A: Direct (uncorrected) moment estimation, using $\alpha = 7.924$,
$\beta^2 = 33.876$, $\lambda^3 = 426.215$.

Calculate $\gamma^3 = \lambda^3/\beta^3 = 2.1617$, then $e^{\sigma^2} = (A + B)^2 + 1$ where

$$A,B = \sqrt[3]{\gamma^3/2 \pm \sqrt{\gamma^6/4 + 1}}$$

and $c = [\beta/(A + B)] - \alpha$; then $c = 1.240$, $\sigma^2 = 0.33886$, and $d = 6.496$.

Income (thousands of dollars)	Estimated Distribution (Assumption A)	Error	Cumulative Estimate	Cumulative Error
0– 1.0	1.66	−1.34	1.66	−1.34
1.0– 1.5	2.09	−0.71	3.75	−2.05
1.5– 2.0	2.99	−0.31	6.74	−2.36
2.0– 2.5	3.86	+0.26	10.60	−2.10
2.5– 3.0	4.50	+0.70	15.10	−1.40
3.0– 3.5	4.89	+0.89	19.99	−0.51
3.5– 4.0	5.15	+1.35	25.14	+0.84
4.0– 5.0	10.43	+2.43	35.57	+3.27
5.0– 6.0	9.89	+0.59	45.46	+3.86
6.0– 7.0	9.84	+0.54	54.30	+3.40
7.0– 8.0	7.68	−2.02	61.98	+1.38
8.0– 9.0	6.50	−1.60	68.48	+0.78
9.0–10.0	5.48	−0.82	73.96	−1.04
10.0–12.0	8.24	−1.46	82.20	−2.50
12.0–15.0	7.63	+0.03	89.83	−2.47
15.0–25.0	8.38	+2.28	98.21	−0.19
25.0+	1.79	+0.29	100.00	−

Compared to the observed median of $6882, the median estimated
with a displaced lognormal distribution is $6496, about $100 higher than
that obtained from the lognormal distribution. While the lognormal distribution has cumulative descriptive errors in excess of (−)5 percent in
the vicinity of $2000 and (+)4.5 percent in the vicinity of the median, the
displaced lognormal distribution has errors of less than (−)2.4 percent in
the lower tail and (+)3.9 percent near the median.

Table A2.6 presents a mixed estimate utilizing the mean ($7924) in
addition to the median ($6882) and the 20 percent quantile. Given the
constrained zero cumulative error at both the median and the 20 percent
quantile, this procedure is far more accurate for incomes in the $1000–
$7000 range than for any of the previous procedures. Where the pro-
cedure fails is for incomes above $7000, with the cumulative error ex-
ceeding (−)4 percent in the vicinity of $12,000.

TABLE A2.6. ESTIMATED FAMILY INCOME, 1965, UNDER
ASSUMPTION OF DISPLACED LOGNORMALITY, MIXED
METHOD, PERCENTAGE DISTRIBUTIONS

Assumption B: (1) α = mean = 7.924
(2) d = median = 6.882; $0.5d$ = 3.441
(3) 20 percent families < $0.5d$, g = 0.8418

By iteration we solve for value of c, for which the following two
relations are true:

(a) $e^{g\sigma} = (d + c)/(0.5d + c)$
(b) $e^{.5\sigma^2} = (\alpha + c)/(d + c)$

The iterated solution for c = 4.847; then σ = 0.4211,
e^{μ} = 11.729.

Income (thousands of dollars)	Estimated Distribution (Assumption B)	Error	Cumulative Estimate	Cumulative Error
0– 1.0	4.85	+1.85	4.85	+1.85
1.0– 1.5	2.36	−0.44	7.21	+1.41
1.5– 2.0	2.82	−0.48	10.03	+0.93
2.0– 2.5	3.32	−0.28	13.35	+0.65
2.5– 3.0	3.63	−0.17	16.98	+0.48
3.0– 3.5	3.92	−0.08	20.90	+0.40
3.5– 4.0	4.24	+0.44	25.14	+0.84
4.0– 5.0	8.76	+0.76	33.90	+1.60
5.0– 6.0	8.73	−0.57	42.63	+1.03
6.0– 7.0	8.33	−0.97	50.96	+0.06
7.0– 8.0	7.59	−2.11	58.55	−2.05
8.0– 9.0	6.80	−1.30	65.35	−3.35
9.0–10.0	5.88	−0.42	71.23	−3.87
10.0–12.0	9.28	−0.42	80.51	−4.19
12.0–15.0	8.93	+1.33	89.44	−2.86
15.0–25.0	9.25	+3.15	98.68	+0.28
25.0+	1.32	−0.18	100.00	−

Similar results were obtained for 1960 total families, and in varying degrees of accuracy for several disaggregated family groups.

In Table A2.7, a symmetric quantile method is used to apply the displaced lognormal distribution to the data, first with the median and the 20 percent quantiles (Assumption C), then with the median and the 10 percent quantiles (Assumption D). Under Assumption C, the proportion of families with incomes under $1000 is overestimated, with the negative income tail stretching down to −$13,923, the value of −$c$. This over-estimate is offset by an underestimate of the cumulative distribution lying between $1000 and $3500. Slightly too few families are placed

TABLE A2.7. ESTIMATED FAMILY INCOME, 1965, UNDER ASSUMPTION OF DISPLACED LOGNORMALITY, QUANTILE METHODS, PERCENTAGE DISTRIBUTIONS

Assumption C: Median, lower and upper quintiles: $g = 0.8418$, $h = 3.4375/6.882 = 0.4995$, $j = 11.010/6.882 = 1.5998$, $c = 13,923$, $\sigma = 0.215$.

Assumption D: Median, lower and upper deciles: $g = 1.2817$, $h = 2.125/6.882 = 0.309$, $j = 14.053/6.882 = 2.042$, $c = 7.235$, $\sigma = 0.3206$.

Income (thousands of dollars)	Estimated Distribution (Assumption C)	Error	Cumulative Estimate	Error	Estimated Distribution (Assumption D)	Error	Cumulative Estimate	Error
0– 1.0	6.09	+3.09	6.09	+3.09	4.65	+1.65	4.65	+1.65
1.0– 1.5	2.11	−0.69	8.20	+2.40	2.03	−0.77	6.68	+0.88
1.5– 2.0	2.47	−0.83	10.67	+1.57	2.60	−0.70	9.28	+0.18
2.0– 2.5	2.90	−0.70	13.57	+0.87	3.02	−0.58	12.30	−0.40
2.5– 3.0	3.28	−0.52	16.85	+0.35	3.50	−0.30	15.80	−0.70
3.0– 3.5	3.62	−0.38	20.47	−0.03	3.86	−0.14	19.66	−0.84
3.5– 4.0	3.91	+0.11	24.38	+0.08	4.17	+0.37	23.83	−0.47
4.0– 5.0	8.58	+0.58	32.96	+0.66	8.95	+0.95	32.78	+0.48
5.0– 6.0	9.07	−0.23	42.03	+0.43	9.25	−0.05	42.03	+0.43
6.0– 7.0	9.01	−0.29	51.04	+0.14	9.01	−0.29	51.04	+0.14
7.0– 8.0	8.56	−1.14	59.60	−1.00	8.36	−1.34	59.40	−1.20
8.0– 9.0	7.80	−0.30	67.40	−1.30	7.46	−0.64	66.86	−1.84
9.0–10.0	6.82	+0.52	74.22	−0.78	6.55	+0.25	73.31	−1.69
10.0–12.0	10.46	+0.76	84.68	−0.02	9.96	+0.26	83.27	−1.43
12.0–15.0	9.04	+1.44	93.72	+1.42	8.91	+1.31	92.18	−0.12
15.0–25.0	6.10	0	99.82	+1.42	7.32	+1.22	99.50	+1.10
25.0+	0.18	−1.32	100.00	—	0.50	−1.00	100.00	—

between $5000 and $9000, too many between $9000 and $15,000, and too few over $25,000.

When the quantiles are moved out to the 10 percent points (Assumption D), considerably higher accuracy is obtained in the tails at the expense of larger errors at intermediate upper income levels, although the general error pattern is similar. Specifically, the overestimate of density below $1000 is considerably reduced, and in no case does either the cumulative error or the error for any income cell between $1000 and $7000 reach 1 percent of the total distribution. The largest error in the estimated cumulative distribution is (−)1.84 percent at the $9000 level. This level of accuracy dominates that achieved by other estimation methods and by normal and lognormal distributions. A slightly lower error level can be achieved by disaggregating the family estimates.

Some general observations can be made about the empirical properties of displaced lognormal distributions when applied to United States income data. While reference is made here explicitly to aggregate family data for 1965, the same properties tend to reappear for other years and for disaggregated groups.

1. Because the frequency distribution extends to $-c$ as the lower income bound, the displaced lognormal distribution tends to place too many units at incomes under $1000, offset by an underestimate of the density of other cells in the poverty region. The offsetting effect is necessarily present due to the constrained zero error at the decile cutoff. If the bottom two cells are combined when the distribution is applied to data, however, the practical significance of this distortion is quite limited.

2. At the upper extreme, the displaced lognormal distribution "tails off" too quickly to describe the allocation of families to high income cells. This observation corresponds to the common assertion that a Pareto-Lévy distribution, with its infinite variance, approximates the upper end of the income distribution quite closely. This rapid "tailing off," combined with the zero-cumulative-error constraint at the upper decile cutoff, produces a counteracting concentration of density in the $10,000–$25,000 (or some other comparable) range. Further evidence of this slight distortion of shape along the upper tail is provided by the general presence of an underestimate of density immediately above the median.

3. The tendencies to place too many units at negative incomes and too few at extremely high incomes combine to produce a *mean* estimate (derived from the symmetric quantile method) which is biased downward. The mean implied by Assumption D is $7626, compared to the directly observed mean of $7924.

The above distortions reappear sufficiently often to suggest that a nonrandom pattern exists in the error structure. Compared to the errors created by crude moment estimation or by the application of conventional normal or lognormal distributions, however, the problems created by these distortions are small in magnitude.

Disaggregated Family Groups

In the previous section, the displaced lognormal distribution is used to approximate the size distribution of income for total families in the aggregate. In this section, the same procedure is applied to four exhaustive subgroups of families and to two groups of unrelated individuals.

At least two possibilities justify a disaggregation procedure. First, by disaggregation of families into relatively homogeneous groups, the descriptive power of simple functional forms may be improved. Second, a more detailed picture of distributional shifts should be obtained by observing changes in the structure of disaggregated income groups than by observing only the aggregate.

Both possibilities bear fruit. The subgroups are described quite well by displaced lognormal distributions; when disaggregated estimates are recombined to provide a global estimate, global accuracy is improved. These observations are even more appropriate in the case of unrelated individuals; if taken as a group, the distribution takes on a bimodal appearance unconducive to simple curve fitting. In retrospect, if total families plus unrelated individuals had been considered earlier rather than just total families, the initial global approximations would have been considerably less accurate.

The availability of disaggregated data makes it possible to estimate a disaggregated model of the income distribution in this study. It is generally possible to find meaningful empirical relationships governing each of the six groups, thus allowing the study of differential impacts of economic forces on various types of living units.

Disaggregation has its price, however. First, because the lognormal family of distributions does not possess convenient additivity properties, the hypothesis of displaced lognormality can be stated at only one level of aggregation. If, therefore, each of four subgroups of families is assumed to obey a displaced lognormal distribution, the same claim cannot be made (in a strict sense) about total families. Since the distribution is applied pragmatically and not out of belief in an underlying generation process, the observation that the sum of disaggregated distributions given below is similar to the aggregate distribution generated in the previous section, is utilized in constructing the model.

Second, since the *Current Population Reports* is based upon sample data, disaggregation increases the presence of sampling error in the cell estimates; this translates into a larger variance in the estimates of the distribution parameters. The larger the sampling variance compared to the variance related to economic phenomena, the more difficult it is to discern significant economic impacts on the group distributions.

Tables A2.8–A2.11 present the estimated distribution of 1965 income for each of four family groups: families (1) with a male head, wife in paid labor force; (2) with a male head, wife not in paid labor force; (3) with a male head, other marital status; and (4) with a female head. This breakdown is governed by two heterogeneous features of family composition relating to the economic structure. First, families with wives in the labor force are quite distinct from those with wives not in the labor force in terms of income sources, the shape of the size distribution, and reactions to economic phenomena. Furthermore, the breakdown of families into these two groups can be linked fairly easily to the labor force sector of an econometric model. Second, families with a female head have a decidedly different relation to the economy than do families with a male head. Families with a male head but no wife present are a residual group constituting less than 2.5 percent of all families.

Most families (57.8 percent) fall into the second group, those with the wife not in the labor force, although the proportion of families in the wife-in-labor-force group has been increasing (29.4 percent of total in 1965). Group two, as the largest group, is perhaps the most heterogeneous and deviates more seriously from functional estimates of the distribution than do the other groups.

Disaggregation of families into more homogeneous groupings on other grounds (such as age, race, or education) is recommended for future research both to test the applicability of the displaced lognormal distribution to other breakdowns and to determine the differential distributional changes which may occur according to these breakdowns with a given impact of economic events.

In Table A2.8 the displaced lognormal distribution is applied to families with the wife in the paid labor force. As a group, these families have a higher mean than families with wives not in the labor force, and a considerably smaller proportion of families at very low incomes. The lower decile cutoff is 44 percent of the median, compared to 32 percent for families with wives not in the labor force.

The latter group, presented in Table A2.9, has relatively more families at extremely high income levels, with the upper decile cutoff being 2.04 compared to 1.74 for the first group.

The errors of estimate for the wife-in-labor-force group (Table A2.8) are quite small, especially under Assumption B. Except for a brief range

TABLE A2.8. ESTIMATED INCOME, FAMILIES, MALE HEAD WITH WIFE IN PAID LABOR FORCE, 1965, QUANTILE METHODS, PERCENTAGE DISTRIBUTIONS

Assumption A: Median, 15.87 percent, 84.13 percent quantiles (corresponding to one standard deviation), $d = 8.597$, $h = 0.5633$, $j = 1.5769$, $c = 6.846$, $\sigma = 0.2785$.

Assumption B: Median, lower and upper deciles, $d = 8.597$, $h = 0.4443$, $j = 1.7448$, $c = 10.217$, $\sigma = 0.2285$.

Income (thousands of dollars)	Estimated Distribution (Assumption A)	Error	Cumulative Estimate	Error	Estimated Distribution (Assumption B)	Error	Cumulative Estimate	Error
0– 1.0	0.75	−0.35	0.75	−0.35	1.19	+0.09	1.19	+0.09
1.0– 1.5	0.61	−0.09	1.36	−0.44	0.73	+0.03	1.92	+0.12
1.5– 2.0	0.91	+0.01	2.27	−0.43	1.02	+0.12	2.94	+0.24
2.0– 2.5	1.32	−0.08	3.59	−0.51	1.39	−0.01	4.33	+0.23
2.5– 3.0	1.73	−0.27	5.32	−0.78	1.79	−0.21	6.12	+0.02
3.0– 3.5	2.17	−0.13	7.49	−0.91	2.23	−0.07	8.35	−0.05
3.5– 4.0	2.71	+0.21	10.20	−0.70	2.68	+0.18	11.03	+0.13
4.0– 5.0	6.91	+1.01	17.11	+0.31	6.59	+0.69	17.62	+0.82
5.0– 6.0	8.35	−0.05	25.46	+0.26	8.16	−0.24	25.78	+0.58
6.0– 7.0	9.37	+0.47	34.83	+0.73	9.12	+0.22	34.90	+0.80
7.0– 8.0	9.60	−0.20	44.43	+0.53	9.49	−0.31	44.39	+0.49
8.0– 9.0	9.26	−0.94	53.69	−0.41	9.32	−0.98	53.71	−0.49
9.0–10.0	8.48	−0.92	62.17	−1.33	8.65	−0.75	62.36	−1.24
10.0–12.0	14.09	−0.11	76.26	−1.44	14.37	+0.17	76.73	−1.07
12.0–15.0	13.09	+0.89	89.35	−0.55	13.27	+1.07	90.00	0
15.0–25.0	10.18	+1.48	99.53	+0.93	9.69	+0.99	99.69	+0.99
25.0+	0.47	−0.93	100.00	—	0.31	−0.99	100.00	—

TABLE A2.9. ESTIMATED INCOME, FAMILIES, MALE HEAD WITH WIFE NOT IN PAID LABOR FORCE, 1965, QUANTILE METHODS, PERCENTAGE DISTRIBUTIONS

Assumption A: Median, 15.87 percent, 84.13 percent quantiles, $d = 6.592$, $h = 0.4337$, $j = 1.7403$, $c = 9.289$, $\sigma = 0.268$.

Assumption B: Median, lower and upper deciles, $d = 6.592$, $g = 1.2817$, $h = 0.3224$, $j = 2.0391$, $c = 6.247$, $\sigma = 0.33358$.

Income (thousands of dollars)	Estimated Distribution (Assumption A)	Error	Cumulative Estimate	Error	Estimated Distribution (Assumption B)	Error	Cumulative Estimate	Error
0– 1.0	5.26	+2.66	5.26	+2.66	4.27	+1.67	4.27	+1.67
1.0– 1.5	2.23	−0.57	7.49	+2.09	2.28	−0.52	6.55	+1.15
1.5– 2.0	2.71	−0.89	10.20	+1.20	2.63	−0.97	9.18	+0.18
2.0– 2.5	3.15	−0.85	13.35	+0.35	3.33	−0.67	12.51	−0.49
2.5– 3.0	3.58	−0.42	16.93	−0.07	3.72	−0.28	16.23	−0.77
3.0– 3.5	3.97	−0.33	20.90	−0.40	4.21	−0.09	20.44	−0.86
3.5– 4.0	4.40	+0.40	25.30	−0.00	4.47	+0.47	24.91	−0.39
4.0– 5.0	9.38	+0.68	34.68	+0.68	9.62	+0.92	34.53	+0.53
5.0– 6.0	9.67	−0.33	44.35	+0.35	9.83	−0.17	44.36	+0.36
6.0– 7.0	9.44	−0.56	53.79	−0.21	9.39	−0.61	53.75	−0.25
7.0– 8.0	8.65	−1.75	62.44	−1.96	8.50	−1.90	62.25	−2.15
8.0– 9.0	7.61	−0.29	70.05	−2.25	7.46	−0.44	69.71	−2.59
9.0–10.0	6.49	+0.99	76.54	−1.26	6.28	+0.78	75.99	−1.81
10.0–12.0	9.76	+1.16	86.30	−0.10	9.41	+0.81	85.40	−1.00
12.0–15.0	8.06	+1.56	94.36	+1.66	8.05	+1.75	93.45	−0.75
15.0–25.0	4.53	−0.07	99.79	+1.59	6.17	+0.67	99.62	+1.42
25.0+	0.21	−1.59	100.00	–	0.38	−1.42	100.00	–

Assumption C, using 8 percent tails, has cumulative errors of +1.28 at $1.0, −0.97 at $3.5, −3.04 at $9.0, +1.21 at $25.0.
Assumption D, using 25 percent tails, has cumulative errors of +3.75 at $1.0, +1.97 at $2.0, −1.28 at $8.0, +3.67 at $15.0, +1.77 at $25.0.
Assumption E, using 8 percent, 35.74 percent, and 75 percent quantiles, has cumulative errors of +1.49 at $1.0, −1.95 at $3.5, 0 at $6.0, −1.17 at $8.0, +2.72 at $15.0, +1.69 at $25.0.

TABLE A2.10. ESTIMATED INCOME, FAMILIES, MALE HEAD OTHER MARITAL STATUS, 1965, QUANTILE METHODS, PERCENTAGE DISTRIBUTIONS

Assumption A: Median, 15.87 percent, 84.13 percent quantiles, $d = 6.148$, $h = 0.3925$, $j = 1.8076$, $c = 8.9255$, $\sigma = 0.2847$.

Assumption B: Median, lower and upper deciles, $d = 6.148$, $h = 0.2967$, $j = 2.1091$, $c = 5.669$, $\sigma = 0.3554$.

Income (thousands of dollars)	Estimated Distribution (Assumption A)	Error	Cumulative Estimate	Error	Estimated Distribution (Assumption B)	Error	Cumulative Estimate	Error
0– 1.0	7.14	+3.44	7.14	+3.44	5.37	+1.67	5.37	+1.67
1.0– 1.5	2.62	−1.48	9.76	+1.96	2.61	−1.49	7.98	+0.18
1.5– 2.0	3.16	−0.24	12.92	+1.72	3.22	−0.18	11.20	0
2.0– 2.5	3.53	−2.37	16.45	−0.65	3.72	−2.18	14.92	−2.18
2.5– 3.0	4.08	+0.48	20.53	−0.17	4.24	+0.64	19.16	−1.54
3.0– 3.5	3.23	−1.67	23.76	−1.84	4.61	−0.29	23.77	−1.83
3.5– 4.0	5.70	+0.80	29.46	−1.04	4.83	−0.07	28.60	−1.90
4.0– 5.0	9.59	+0.49	39.05	−0.55	10.07	+0.97	38.67	−0.93
5.0– 6.0	9.55	+0.35	48.60	−0.20	9.91	+0.71	48.58	−0.22
6.0– 7.0	9.05	+0.75	57.65	+0.55	9.19	+0.89	57.77	+0.67
7.0– 8.0	8.15	−1.55	65.80	−1.00	8.14	−1.56	65.91	−0.89
8.0– 9.0	7.11	+0.21	72.91	−0.79	6.93	+0.03	72.84	−0.86
9.0–10.0	5.91	−0.30	78.81	−1.09	5.80	−0.40	78.64	−1.26
10.0–12.0	8.68	+1.08	87.49	−0.01	8.50	+0.90	87.14	−0.36
12.0–15.0	7.29	+1.29	94.78	+1.28	7.07	+1.07	94.21	+0.71
15.0–25.0	5.00	−0.60	99.78	+0.68	5.42	−0.18	99.63	+0.53
25.0+	0.22	−0.68	100.00	—	0.37	−0.53	100.00	—

TABLE A2.11. ESTIMATED INCOME, FAMILIES WITH
FEMALE HEAD, 1965, QUANTILE METHOD,
PERCENTAGE DISTRIBUTION

Assumption A: Median, 15.87 percent, 84.13 percent quantiles, $d = 3.532$, $h = 0.3746$, $j = 2.1492$, $c = 1.315$, $\sigma = 0.608$.

Income (thousands of dollars)	Estimated Distribution (Assumption A)	Error	Cumulative Estimate	Cumulative Error
0– 1.0	11.22	+0.52	11.22	+0.52
1.0– 1.5	7.37	−0.63	18.59	−0.11
1.5– 2.0	8.00	−0.60	26.59	−0.71
2.0– 2.5	8.09	+0.79	34.68	+0.08
2.5– 3.0	7.79	−0.01	42.47	+0.07
3.0– 3.5	7.13	−0.07	49.60	0
3.5– 4.0	6.36	+0.06	55.96	+0.06
4.0– 5.0	10.86	+0.26	66.82	+0.32
5.0– 6.0	8.22	−0.08	75.04	+0.24
6.0– 7.0	6.29	−0.01	81.33	+0.23
7.0– 8.0	4.51	−0.79	85.84	−0.56
8.0– 9.0	3.41	−0.29	89.25	−0.85
9.0–10.0	2.57	+0.27	91.82	−0.58
10.0–12.0	3.33	+0.03	95.15	−0.55
12.0–15.0	2.58	+0.38	97.73	−0.17
15.0–25.0	2.00	+0.17	99.73	≅0
25.0+	0.27	≅0	100.00	0

of incomes above $10,000, the cumulative error remains well under 1 percent of the total density of the distribution.

The errors of estimate for the second group, as the dominant family group, follow essentially the same pattern of errors as the total family estimates. There is a positive distortion at incomes below $1500 and a substantial underestimate of density immediately above the median. The tendency to underestimate incomes at the upper end is quite severe. In general, any distortion in the estimated distribution for total families is magnified slightly in the group with wives not in the labor force. This is to be expected, because (1) the estimation weaknesses in this group can be expected to dominate the aggregate picture, (2) the group is more heterogeneous than the others, and (3) the pattern of incomes at the upper end of this group is more likely to obey Pareto's law than the pattern for other groups, which do not have the same frequency of high-salaried heads of households.

Table A2.10 presents the estimated distributions for families with

TABLE A2.12. ESTIMATED INCOME, TOTAL FAMILIES, 1965, SUM OF QUANTILE METHODS APPLIED TO FOUR DISAGGREGATED GROUPS,* PERCENTAGE DISTRIBUTIONS

Income (thousands of dollars)	Disaggregated Cumulative Estimates				Total Families, Estimated Distribution	Error	Cumulative Estimate	Cumulative Error
	Male Head, Wife in Labor Force	Male Head, Wife Not in Labor Force	Male Head, Other Marital Status	Female Head				
0– 1.0	1.19	4.27	5.37	11.22	4.12	+1.12	4.12	+1.12
1.0– 1.5	1.92	6.55	7.98	18.59	2.35	−0.45	6.47	+0.67
1.5– 2.0	2.94	9.18	11.20	26.59	2.73	−0.57	9.20	+0.10
2.0– 2.5	4.33	12.51	14.92	34.68	3.27	−0.33	12.47	−0.23
2.5– 3.0	6.12	16.21	19.16	42.47	3.58	−0.22	16.05	−0.45
3.0– 3.5	8.35	20.44	23.77	49.60	3.95	−0.05	20.00	−0.50
3.5– 4.0	11.03	24.91	28.60	55.96	4.15	+0.35	24.15	−0.15
4.0– 5.0	17.62	34.53	38.67	66.82	8.87	+0.87	33.02	+0.72
5.0– 6.0	25.78	44.36	48.58	75.04	9.17	−0.13	42.19	+0.59
6.0– 7.0	34.90	53.75	57.77	81.33	8.99	−0.31	51.18	+0.28
7.0– 8.0	44.39	62.25	65.91	85.84	8.37	−1.33	59.55	−1.05
8.0– 9.0	53.71	69.71	72.84	89.25	7.56	−0.54	67.11	−1.59
9.0–10.0	62.36	75.99	78.64	91.82	6.57	+0.27	73.68	−1.32
10.0–12.0	76.73	85.40	87.14	95.15	10.25	+0.55	83.93	−0.77
12.0–15.0	90.00	93.45	94.21	97.73	8.97	+1.37	92.90	+0.60
15.0–25.0	99.69	99.62	99.63	99.73	6.75	+0.65	99.65	+1.25
25.0+	100.00	100.00	100.00	100.00	0.35	−1.25	100.00	—
Number of families (millions)	14.183	27.925	1.179	4.992	48.279			
Proportion of families	0.294	0.578	0.024	0.104				

*Assumption B in Table A2.8, Assumption B in Table A2.9, Assumption B in Table A2.10, Assumption A in Table A2.11

male head, other marital status. While some of the errors of estimate are large, there is a substantial component of random sampling error built into the observed values.

Table A2.11 presents the estimated distribution for families with female heads. In this case the displaced lognormal distribution fits extremely well, with no individual or cumulative error term exceeding 0.85 percent of the population.

In Table A2.12 the aggregate family income distribution produced by summing the four components is constructed. While the "best" aggregate estimate (Table A2.7, Assumption D) produces a 1.65 percentage point overestimate of density in the bottom cell and a peak cumulative error of (−)1.84 percent at $9000, the estimate in Table A2.12 produces comparable errors of only (+)1.12 percent and (−)1.59 percent respectively. The "tailing-off" problem at the upper end is slightly more severe, however.

Unrelated Individuals

Tables A2.13 and A2.14 present distribution estimates for unrelated individuals divided into two groups, earners and nonearners. An alternative to the above breakdown is a division by sex, but the bimodal appearance of the unrelated individual distribution is best combated by utilizing a labor market division.

In Table A2.13 the earner group is estimated by a quantile method. Again, the density of the bottom cell is overestimated due to a substantial presence of estimated negative income units. Otherwise, the size of the error of estimate is quite respectable.

For nonearners, the median is so close to the bottom cell that it is not feasible to calibrate a quantile below the median. Consequently, Assumption A utilizes the median, the 79.4 percent, and the 95 percent quantiles; these are equidistant in normal standard deviate terms. Because the negative value of c implies that all incomes exceed $758, the estimates below the median are not to be taken seriously. Given the data groupings, the median itself is sufficiently low ($1155 in 1965) to provide as much information as is available for the bottom of the distribution. The function works quite well for the distribution above the median. For comparison, a two-parameter lognormal distribution is fitted to the median and the 95 percent quantile under Assumption B.

TABLE A2.13.　ESTIMATED INCOME, UNRELATED
INDIVIDUALS WHO WERE EARNERS, 1965,
QUANTILE METHOD, PERCENTAGE
DISTRIBUTION

Assumption A:　Median $= 3.657$; lower and upper quartiles: $h = 0.5108$, $j = 1.5892$; $c = 6.886$, $\sigma = 0.2757$.

Income (thousands of dollars)	Estimated Distribution (Assumption A)	Error	Cumulative Estimate	Cumulative Error
0– 1.0	14.69	+2.99	14.69	+2.99
1.0– 1.5	5.64	−2.06	20.33	+0.93
1.5– 2.0	6.43	−1.17	26.76	−0.24
2.0– 2.5	6.89	−1.51	33.65	−1.75
2.5– 3.0	7.04	+1.04	40.79	−0.71
3.0– 3.5	7.16	+0.46	47.85	−0.25
3.5– 4.0	6.77	+0.87	54.62	+0.62
4.0– 5.0	12.20	+0.40	66.82	+1.02
5.0– 6.0	10.05	−0.95	76.67	+0.07
6.0– 7.0	7.26	−0.14	84.13	−0.97
7.0– 8.0	5.31	+0.11	89.44	+0.04
8.0– 9.0	3.88	+0.48	93.32	+0.52
9.0–10.0	2.32	+0.32	95.64	+0.84
10.0–15.0	3.96	+0.26	99.60	+1.10
15.0–25.0	0.40	−0.80	100.00	+0.30
25.0+	−	−0.30	100.00	−

DISPLACED LOGNORMAL DISTRIBUTION: EARLIER YEARS

Some calculations are presented for 1958 and 1953 to verify the overall pattern of results that are derived from the 1965 data. Some results are presented in Tables A2.15 and A2.16 for families with wife in the labor force, and with wife not in the labor force. In both cases the qualitative structure of the errors of estimate remains the same.

Since each estimated distribution requires only the values of three specified quantiles in order to be determined, it is not necessary to record detailed estimates of the distribution of income for each year before proceeding with the econometric model building. The distribution sector requires three endogenous variables for each group distribution to be included in the model. Since these endogenous variables are derivable from the quantiles, it is necessary to have time series data for each set of

TABLE A2.14. ESTIMATED INCOME, UNRELATED INDIVIDUALS WHO WERE NOT EARNERS, 1965, QUANTILE METHODS, PERCENTAGE DISTRIBUTIONS

Assumption A: Median (1.555), 79.46 percent quantile ($k = 1.6710$), 95 percent quantile ($j = 3.6528$), $c = -0.758$, $\sigma = 1.316$.

Assumption B: Lognormal distribution using median and 95 percent quantile, $c = 0$, $\sigma = 0.7875$.

Income (thousands of dollars)	Estimated Distribution (Assumption A)	Error	Cumulative Estimate	Cumulative Error	Estimated Distribution (Assumption B)	Error	Cumulative Estimate	Cumulative Error
0– 1.0	35.35	−6.35	35.35	−6.35	42.74	+1.04	42.74	+1.04
1.0– 1.5	32.91	+6.31	68.26	−0.04	20.32	−6.28	63.06	−5.24
1.5– 2.0	12.39	−0.11	80.65	−0.15	12.62	+0.12	75.68	−5.12
2.0– 2.5	6.32	−0.78	86.97	−0.93	7.92	+0.82	83.60	−4.30
2.5– 3.0	3.60	+1.10	90.57	+0.17				
3.0– 3.5	2.32	−0.18	92.89	−0.01	13.26	+4.66		
3.5– 4.0	1.57	−0.03	94.46	−0.04				
4.0– 5.0	1.95	−0.05	96.41	−0.09			96.86	+0.36
5.0– 6.0	1.09	−0.01	97.50	−0.10				
6.0– 7.0	0.69	−0.11	98.19	−0.21				
7.0– 8.0	0.43	−0.27	98.62	−0.48	3.14	−0.36		
8.0– 9.0	0.31	+0.01	98.93	−0.47				
9.0–10.0	0.23	+0.03	99.16	−0.44				
10.0–15.0	0.51	+0.21	99.67	−0.23				
15.0–25.0	0.24	+0.14	99.91	−0.09				
25.0+	0.09	+0.09	100.00	0	100.00		100.00	0

TABLE A2.15.   ESTIMATED INCOME; FAMILIES; MALE HEAD
WITH WIFE IN PAID LABOR FORCE; 1965, 1958, 1953;*
PERCENTAGE DISTRIBUTIONS

Assumption: Median, lower and upper deciles

Income*	1965 Estimated Distribution	1965 Error	1958 Estimated Distribution	1958 Error	1953 Estimated Distribution	1953 Error
0– 2.0	2.95	+0.25	6.60	+0.20	7.39	+0.39
2.0– 4.0	8.06	−0.14	16.39	+0.69	17.81	+0.51
4.0– 6.0	14.77	+0.47	24.34	−0.76	26.39	−1.01
6.0– 8.0	18.61	+0.11	22.83	−0.56	23.87	+1.01
8.0–10.0	17.97	−1.63	15.51	−0.56	14.64	+1.01
10.0+	37.64	+1.14	14.33	+0.43	9.90	0

Income*	1965 Cumulative Estimate	Error	1958 Cumulative Estimate	Error	1953 Cumulative Estimate	Error
0– 2.0	2.95	+0.25	6.60	+0.20	7.39	+0.39
2.0– 4.0	11.01	+0.11	22.99	+0.89	25.20	+0.90
3.0– 6.0	25.78	+0.58	47.33	+0.13	51.59	+0.11
6.0– 8.0	44.39	+0.49	70.16	0	75.46	0
8.0–10.0	62.36	−1.14	85.67	−0.43	90.10	0
10.0+	100.00	0	100.00	0	100.00	0

* 1958 and 1965 in current dollars, 1953 in 1959 dollars.

quantiles used, but nothing more. It has been the objective of chapter 2 to argue that a meaningful description of a group distribution can be reduced into three pieces of information which can be treated as endogenous variables in an econometric model.

PEARSON CURVES AND BOX-COX TRANSFORMATIONS

Tables A2.17–A2.19 present sample computations for 1965 family income estimates by the fitting of a Pearson curve and by the fitting of a simple Box-Cox transformation, i.e., $y^\lambda = N(\mu, \sigma^2)$.

The Pearson curve procedure shown in Table A2.17 begins with uncorrected direct estimates of the first four moments of the income distribution as described earlier in this appendix. The distribution is then classified and specified; the results underscore the instability of Pearson curve estimates in the absence of good moment estimates. While the

TABLE A2.16. ESTIMATED INCOME; FAMILIES; MALE HEAD
WITH WIFE NOT IN PAID LABOR FORCE; 1965, 1958;
PERCENTAGE DISTRIBUTIONS

Assumption: Median, lower and upper deciles

Income (thousands of dollars)	1965 Estimated Distribution	Error	1958 Estimated Distribution	Error
0- 1	4.32	+1.72	5.63	+0.73
1- 2	4.90	−1.50	7.53	−1.17
2- 3	7.03	−0.97	10.98	+1.18
3- 4	8.70	+0.30	12.93	+1.23
4- 5	9.62	+1.02	13.13	−1.87
5- 6	9.82	−0.18	12.05	−2.75
6- 7	9.36	−0.64	10.12	−0.68
7-10	22.24	−1.56	18.39	+3.49
10-15	17.46	+3.56	8.12	+1.52
15-25	6.17	−0.33	1.107	−0.993
25+	0.38	−1.42	0.013	−0.687

Income (thousands of dollars)	1965 Cumulative Distribution	Error	1958 Cumulative Distribution	Error
0- 1	4.32	+1.72	5.63	+0.73
1- 2	9.22	+0.22	13.16	−0.44
2- 3	16.25	−0.75	24.14	+0.74
3- 4	24.95	+0.45	37.07	+1.97
4- 5	34.57	+0.57	50.20	+0.10
5- 6	44.39	+0.39	62.25	−2.65
6- 7	53.75	−0.25	72.37	−3.33
7-10	75.99	−1.81	90.76	+0.16
10-15	93.45	+1.75	98.88	+1.68
15-25	99.62	+1.42	99.987	+0.687
25+	100.00	0	100.00	0

distribution is not actually calibrated, the given calculations are sufficient to establish that all families are predicted to have incomes in excess of $2321, and that the distribution is *J*-shaped, with the "mode" *below* $2321.

The estimated distribution in Table A2.18, based on the assumption that y^λ is normally distributed, is comparable in accuracy to estimates based on the displaced lognormal distribution. Although negative incomes are not defined, there is still a slight tendency to overestimate the density below $1000 and to underestimate the density immediately above

TABLE A2.17.   ESTIMATED FAMILY INCOME, 1965, UNDER
ASSUMPTION OF PEARSON CURVE SYSTEM, BASED ON
UNCORRECTED ESTIMATION OF FIRST FOUR
MOMENTS (HIGHER MOMENTS ARE ABOUT
MEAN)

$$\mu_1 = 7.924$$
$$\mu_2 = 33.876$$
$$\mu_3 = 426.215$$
$$\mu_4 = 11598.358$$

To classify in Pearson system:

$$\beta_1 = \frac{\mu_3^2}{\mu_2^3} = 4.67283$$

$$\beta_2 = \frac{\mu_4}{\mu_2^2} = 10.10675$$

$$K = \frac{\beta_1(\beta_2 + 3)^2}{4(2\beta_2 - 3\beta_1 - 6) \cdot (4\beta_2 - 3\beta_1)} = 38.96811$$

With $K > 1$, we have basic Type VI, $y = y_0 (x - a)^{q_2} x^{-q_1}, x > a$.

Calculate

$$r = \frac{6(\beta_2 - \beta_1 - 1)}{6 + 3\beta_1 - 2\beta_2} = -136.421$$

$$a = \tfrac{1}{2} \sqrt{\mu_2} \cdot \sqrt{\beta_1(r + 2)^2 + 16(r + 1)} = 856.407$$

$$q_2, -q_1 = \frac{r - 2}{2} \pm \frac{r(r + 2)}{2} \sqrt{\beta_1/[\beta_1(r + 2)^2 + 16(r + 1)]} = -69.2105 \pm 69.1032$$

$$q_2 = -0.1073$$
$$-q_1 = -138.3137$$
$$y = y_0 \cdot (x - 856.407)^{-.1073} x^{-138.3137},$$

where

$$y_0 = \frac{Na^{q_1-q_2-1} \cdot \Gamma(q_1)}{\Gamma(q_1-q_2-1) \cdot \Gamma(q_2 + 1)}, \quad N = 0.999;$$

$$y_0 = \frac{0.999(856.407)^{137.421} \cdot \Gamma(138.3137)}{\Gamma(137.421) \cdot \Gamma(0.8927)} \quad \text{[where } \Gamma(x + 1) \cong (2\pi x) x^x e^{-x} e^{-1/12x}].$$

$$\text{Origin} = \text{mean} - \frac{a(q_1 - 1)}{q_1 - q_2 - 2} = 7.924 - \frac{856.407(137.314)}{(136.421)} = -854.086.$$

Given origin and $a = 856.407$, all families are predicted to have incomes greater than 2.321, i.e., $2321.

$$\text{Mode} = \text{mean} - \tfrac{1}{2}\frac{\mu_3}{\mu_2} \cdot \left(\frac{r + 2}{r - 1}\right) = 1.8155, \text{ to the left of beginning of defined}$$
distribution, indicating a predicted J-shaped distribution.

Estimation procedures discussed in W. Palin Elderton, *Frequency Curves and Correlations,* 3rd ed. (Cambridge: At the University Press, 1938), chapter 5.

the median. The aggregate estimate in Table A2.18 is relatively better than the two group estimates in Table A2.19.

The displaced lognormal distribution is preferred to an exponential distribution because of the convenience of its functional form. Since the model estimation will not be bound to the assumption of displaced lognormality it will be possible, for one so inclined, to work back from the model to a three-parameter Box-Cox transformation rather than to a displaced lognormal distribution, through iterative procedures.

TABLE A2.18.   ESTIMATED INCOME, TOTAL FAMILIES, 1965, UNDER ASSUMPTION OF EXPONENTIAL BOX-COX TRANSFORMATION, PERCENTAGE DISTRIBUTION

y^λ assumed normally distributed, λ iterated from median, lower and upper deciles; $\lambda \cong 0.58$, $\sigma = 1.1805$.

Income (thousands of dollars)	Estimated Distribution	Error	Cumulative Estimate	Cumulative Error
0– 1.0	4.05	+1.05	4.05	+1.05
1.0– 1.5	2.38	−0.42	6.43	+0.63
1.5– 2.0	2.81	−0.49	9.24	+0.14
2.0– 2.5	3.23	−0.37	12.47	−0.23
2.5– 3.0	3.64	−0.16	16.11	−0.39
3.0– 3.5	3.91	−0.09	20.02	−0.48
3.5– 4.0	4.18	+0.38	24.20	−0.10
4.0– 5.0	8.84	+0.84	33.04	+0.74
5.0– 6.0	9.11	−0.19	42.15	+0.55
6.0– 7.0	8.85	−0.45	51.00	+0.10
7.0– 8.0	8.33	−1.47	59.33	−1.37
8.0– 9.0	7.56	−0.44	66.89	−1.81
9.0–10.0	6.58	+0.28	73.47	−1.53
10.0–12.0	10.35	+0.65	83.82	−0.88
12.0–15.0	9.24	+1.64	93.06	+0.76
15.0–25.0	4.87	−1.23	97.93	−0.47
25.0+	2.07	+0.47	100.00	0

TABLE A2.19. ESTIMATED INCOME, FAMILIES, MALE HEAD WITH WIFE PRESENT, 1965, UNDER ASSUMPTION OF EXPONENTIAL BOX-COX TRANSFORMATION, PERCENTAGE DISTRIBUTIONS

y^A assumed normally distributed, λ iterated from median, lower and upper deciles.
Group A: Wife in paid labor force, λ = 0.56, σ = 0.9503.
Group B: Wife not in paid labor force, λ = 0.51, σ = 0.8949.

Income (thousands of dollars)	Estimated Distribution (Group A)	Error	Cumulative Distribution (Group A)	Error	Estimated Distribution (Group B)	Error	Cumulative Distribution (Group B)	Error
0– 1.0	0.69	−0.41	0.69	−0.41	3.55	+0.95	3.55	+0.95
1.0– 1.5	0.74	+0.04	1.43	−0.37	2.53	−0.27	6.08	+0.68
1.5– 2.0	1.07	+0.17	2.50	−0.20	3.07	−0.53	9.15	+0.15
2.0– 2.5	1.45	+0.05	3.95	−0.15	3.56	−0.44	12.71	−0.29
2.5– 3.0	1.94	−0.06	5.89	−0.21	3.99	−0.01	16.70	−0.30
3.0– 3.5	2.34	+0.04	8.23	−0.17	4.29	−0.01	20.99	−0.31
3.5– 4.0	2.78	+0.28	11.01	+0.11	4.57	+0.57	25.56	+0.26
4.0– 5.0	6.87	+0.97	17.88	+1.08	9.45	+0.75	35.01	+1.01
5.0– 6.0	8.23	−0.17	26.11	+0.91	9.58	−0.42	44.59	+0.59
6.0– 7.0	9.02	+0.12	35.13	+1.03	9.08	−0.92	53.67	−0.33
7.0– 8.0	9.34	−0.46	44.47	+0.57	8.27	−2.13	61.94	−2.46
8.0– 9.0	9.20	−1.10	53.67	−0.53	7.32	−0.58	69.26	−3.04
9.0–10.0	8.50	−0.90	62.17	−1.43	6.32	+0.82	75.58	−2.22
10.0–12.0	14.25	+0.05	76.42	−1.38	9.64	+1.04	85.22	−1.18
12.0–15.0	13.60	+1.40	90.02	+0.92	8.44	+2.14	93.66	+0.96
15.0–25.0	9.77	+1.07	99.79	+1.09	6.12	+0.62	99.78	+1.58
25.0+	0.21	−1.09	100.00	0.00	0.22	−1.58	100.00	0.00

Appendix to Chapter 4

NOTES ON ESTIMATION

The regressions reported in chapter 4, as well as the regressions for the full model reported in the appendix to chapter 5, were estimated by two-stage least squares. Because the number of exogenous variables in the system far exceeded the available nineteen observations, the number of predetermined variables appearing in the first stage of estimation had to be reduced to a manageable level. This reduction was achieved by the use of principle components.[1]

Because all right-hand variables in the distribution sector appear endogenously elsewhere in the model, all exogenous variables appear somewhere within the remaining blocks of the model. The initial form of the model[2] consisted of three blocks determining income, expenditures, and labor force and employment levels. The model presented here includes a fourth block to determine price levels endogenously.

With only nineteen observations and approximately fifty exogenous variables, principle components were drawn separately from subsets of exogenous variables corresponding to the three blocks of the initial model. This procedure left fewer than nineteen exogenous variables in

---

[1] See T. Kloeck and L. B. M. Mennes, "Simultaneous Equations Estimation Based on Principle Components of Predetermined Variables," *Econometrica* 28 (January 1960), 45–61.
[2] See Charles E. Metcalf, "The Size Distribution of Personal Income in an Econometric Model of the United States" (Ph.D. diss., Massachusetts Institute of Technology, 1968).

Econometric Model of the Income Distribution

each set. For this purpose, lagged endogenous variables were excluded from the list of predetermined variables.

The above procedure provided three sets of principle components, orthogonal within but not across sets. The distribution sector contains right-hand endogenous variables determined within the income and labor force-employment blocks, but not in the expenditure block. By causal-ordering criteria,[3] the former two blocks are more closely linked to the distribution sector than is the expenditure block. Accordingly, for the distribution sector, the first stage was estimated with the first four (or five, depending on the number of right-hand variables in the structural equation) components each from the income and labor force sectors.

Outside the distribution sector, all three sets of principle components were used with one modification. Since the first component of each set was essentially a time trend, the inclusion of all three first components in the first stage of estimation would create a near-singular $(X'X)$ matrix of exogenous variables. To avoid this problem, the first two principle components were drawn in turn from the three "first components." These two components were then used in conjunction with the second and third principle components drawn from each of the three sectors. In equations containing several *included* predetermined variables, the number of principle components used in the first stage was reduced. While not included in the principle component set, lagged endogenous variables were treated as predetermined variables in their respective equations.

Although many of the equations in the following chapters are non-linear, all stochastic equations are linear in the coefficients. Each cluster of variables corresponding to a given coefficient was treated like a single right-hand endogenous variable, unless every element of the cluster was predetermined. Equivalently, each right-hand term was defined as a single variable by a nonlinear identity and then regressed linearly against the model instruments in the first stage of estimation.

The legitimacy of using two-stage least squares in the above manner is open to question. While the first stage of estimation assumes the existence of a linear reduced form, the actual reduced form corresponding to the structural model is nonlinear in the structural disturbances.

The methodological issues raised by the procedure are beyond the scope of this study;[4] while the simultaneity of the model calls for something other than ordinary least squares, conventional two-stage least

[3] See Franklin M. Fisher, in J. S. Duesenberry et al., *The Brookings Quarterly Econometric Model of the United States* (Chicago: Rand McNally, 1965), pp. 621–33.

[4] See H. Eisenpress and J. Greenstadt, "The Estimation of Nonlinear Econometric Systems," *Econometrica* 34 (October 1966), 851–61; also Harry Kelejian,

squares was chosen for its simplicity despite possible problems with reduced form disturbances.[5]

Since the specifications in chapter 4 are patterned after identities stating sums of income components, there is no reason to expect a non-zero intercept term unless it is implied by one of the component elements of the specification. In practice, all regressions were estimated both with a free and with a zero intercept. Generally, a free intercept was retained only if it reduced the standard error of estimate.

In cases where the intercept has been restricted to zero, caution must be exercised in interpreting the test statistics of the regression. The values of R^2, F, and the standard error of estimate are all constructed from the sum of the squared error terms, with degree of freedom corrections. With a free intercept, a least squares regression produces a zero mean error. Summing the squares of the error terms is equivalent to summing the squares of deviations from the mean error. In a regression constrained to have a zero intercept, however, the mean error no longer has to equal precisely zero. All test statistics in the constrained regressions estimated in this study are based upon deviations from a zero error, not from the mean error.

If we interpret the correct standard error to be based upon deviations from a zero error, then all test statistics are in order. If we believe the standard of comparison should be the mean error, our estimate of the

standard error is biased upward, since $\dfrac{\sqrt{\sum(e_i)^2}}{n-k} > \dfrac{\sqrt{\sum(e_i - \bar{e})^2}}{n-k}$ for $\bar{e}$ not

equal to zero. The values of R^2, F, and all t-statistics are correspondingly too small. If the *expected* value of the error term is zero, despite the possibility of a nonzero mean sample error, we could argue that the goodness of fit is slightly better than the reported test statistics would indicate.

"Two Stage Least Squares and Nonlinear Systems" (mimeo.). Kelejian argues that nonlinear structural systems which are linear in the coefficients can in some cases be consistently estimated by two-stage least squares.

[5] All equations in chapter 4 were estimated on an IBM 1620-II computer using the Time Series Processor written by R. E. Hall and others. The principle component procedure involves the normalization of all exogenous variables to zero mean, unit standard deviation before components are taken. The procedure is described in H. H. Harman, *Modern Factor Analysis* (Chicago: University of Chicago Press, 1963), and was adapted to the TSP estimation package by J. Phillip Cooper. Equations appearing in the appendix to chapter 5 which correspond to the initial model were also estimated on the 1620–II. Revised versions of specifications appearing in the wage, price, and consumption sectors of the model were estimated on a Univac 1108 computer, also with the Time Series Processor estimation package.

As a practical issue, we may set aside the test statistic question. If the intercept term has a statistically insignificant value before being constrained to zero, the mean error should assume a value correspondingly close to zero. The "correct" statistics, by the latter interpretation, should not be substantively different from the reported statistics. In cases where a free intercept did assume a significant value, it was retained in the regression.

Appendix to Chapter 5

EQUATION ESTIMATES: AN ECONOMETRIC MODEL OF THE UNITED STATES

This appendix reports the estimated equations of the full econometric model summarized at the beginning of chapter 5. A detailed listing of the exogenous variable specifications used in the policy simulations appears at the end of the appendix.

ALLOCATION AND AGGREGATION EQUATIONS

In addition to the equations reported in chapter 4, the distribution model includes two allocation functions to determine the proportion of wives who are in the labor force and the proportion of unrelated individuals who are earners. In addition, estimates of five aggregate distribution variables are constructed for use in the remainder of the econometric model. These allocation and aggregation equations are reported in equations (A5.1)–(A5.7).

EQUATIONS (A5.1)–(A5.7). ALLOCATION AND AGGREGATION EQUATIONS

$PAR1 = 0.215 + 0.199 HMWN - 0.209 HMWL + 0.00786T$
$\qquad (0.036)\ \ (0.086) \qquad\quad (0.075) \qquad\qquad (0.00037)$

$\qquad\qquad\quad R^2 = .991 \qquad F(3,\ 13) = 493$
$\qquad\qquad\quad D\text{-}W = 2.04 \qquad \text{s.e.} = 0.0040$
$\qquad\qquad\quad 1949\text{–}65$

$\qquad\qquad\qquad\qquad\qquad\qquad\qquad\qquad\qquad\qquad$ (A5.1)

$PAR3 = 0.899 - 2.142(PP65/PP14) - 2.593(U26/PP14)$
      (0.044) (0.408)   (2.401)

$$R^2 = .785 \qquad F(2,\ 14) = 25.6$$
$$D\text{-}W = 2.30 \qquad \text{s.e.} = 0.0123$$
$$1949\text{--}65$$

(A5.2)

$MFAM = -42.18 + 0.856(NMWL \cdot PGNP) \cdot PAR1$
        (117.96) (0.061)

$+ 0.935(NMWN \cdot PGNP) \cdot (1 - PAR1)$
  (0.044)

$+ 0.098(NFEM \cdot PGNP)$
  (0.068)

(A5.3)

$$R^2 = .9998 \qquad F(3,\ 13) = 30{,}435$$
$$D\text{-}W = 1.58 \qquad \text{s.e.} = 15.0$$
$$1949\text{--}65$$

$(Y10/MFAM) = HFAM = 0.0128 + 0.616HMWN + 0.038HFEM$
                     (0.0154) (0.059)   (0.038)

$+ 0.027(NFEM/1000)$
  (0.008)

(A5.4)

$$R^2 = .968 \qquad F(3,\ 13) = 130$$
$$D\text{-}W = 1.60 \qquad \text{s.e.} = 0.0033$$
$$1949\text{--}65$$

$(Y90/MFAM) = JFAM = 0.1720 + 0.890JMWL \cdot PAR1$
                     (0.1314) (0.062)

$+ 0.883JMWN \cdot (1 - PAR1)$
  (0.049)

$+ 0.053JFEM$
  (0.045)

(A5.5)

$$R^2 = .968 \qquad F(3,\ 13) = 130$$
$$D\text{-}W = 1.49 \qquad \text{s.e.} = 0.0089$$
$$1949\text{--}65$$

$MMWP = 158.7 + 1.112(NMWL \cdot PGNP) \cdot PAR1$
        (94.3) (0.048)

$+ 0.887(NMWN \cdot PGNP) \cdot (1 - PAR1)$
  (0.052)

(A5.6)

$$R^2 = .9998 \qquad F(2,\ 14) = 3742$$
$$D\text{-}W = 2.09 \qquad \text{s.e.} = 17.8$$
$$1949\text{--}65$$

$(Y10P/MMWP) = HMWP = 0.0047 + 1.057HMWN \cdot (1 - PAR1)$
                     (0.0247) (0.100)

$$+ 0.765 HMWL \cdot PAR1$$
$$(0.044) \qquad\qquad (A5.7)$$

$$R^2 = .964 \qquad F(2, 14) = 186$$
$$D\text{-}W = 1.40 \qquad \text{s.e.} = 0.0034$$

Included variables not reported in Table 4.1:

HFAM	Y10/MFAM
HMWP	Y10/MMWP
JFAM	Y90/MFAM
MFAM	Median income, all families (current dollars)
MMWP	Median income, families with male head, wife present (current dollars) (MWL + MWN groups)
PP14	Noninstitutional civilian population aged 14+ (millions of persons)
PP65	Noninstitutional civilian population aged 65+ (millions of persons)
U26	Civilian unemployment, 26 or more weeks (millions of persons)
Y10	Income below which 10 percent of all families lie (current dollars)
Y10P	Income below which 10 percent of families in MWP (MWL + MWN) group lie (current dollars)
Y90	Income above which 10 percent of all families lie (current dollars)

Two-stage least squares; coefficient standard errors in parentheses.

Equation (A5.1) determines the proportion of wives who are in the labor force. Specifying the function as a standard labor force participation function was difficult, since the participation data[1] refer to the March interviewing period following the year for which income data are pertinent. Attempts to relate the March data to annual data used elsewhere in the model were relatively unsuccessful. Equation (A5.1) should not be interpreted as a structural or causal relationship. The participation function is dominated by a positive time trend; exclusive of the trend, higher participation rates are associated with higher levels of HMWN and lower levels of HMWL. The direction of causality is probably from left to right: as families shift from the MWN to the MWL group, the value of HMWN rises and HMWL falls.

Equation (A5.2) determines the proportion of unrelated individuals who are earners. It differs from a labor force participation function, since the proportion of individuals who earn income during the year is greater than the proportion who are in the labor force at a given point in time. Once again, the chosen specification leaves much to be desired. The proportion of unrelated individuals who are earners declines as the pro-

---

[1] The data referred to are the CPS classifications of households into the wife-in-labor-force and wife-not-in-labor-force groups.

portion of the population over age 65 increases and when the long-term unemployment rate rises. This latter tendency is not statistically significant when the equation is estimated by two-stage least squares, however.

Despite the warning from chapter 2 that the aggregate size distribution of income would not adhere to the same functional form as the group distributions, no difficulty was encountered in approximating aggregate quantiles from corresponding group statistics.

Median income for total families (A5.3) is a linear function of median incomes for the three largest family groups, with the MWL and MWN medians weighted by the participation rate of wives to account for the changing proportions of these two groups over time.[2] The lower tail variable for total families (A5.4) is a function of lower tail variables of the MWN and FEM groups and of the median of the female head group. The decile variable for the MWL group was not significant in the equation, presumably due to the relative affluence of that group. Since the female head group has relatively low incomes as a whole, on the other hand, the FEM median had a significant impact on the equation.

The upper tail variable for total families (A5.5) is a function of the upper tail variables of the three groups; again, the first two groups are weighted by the participation rate of wives.

Similar approximations were required for all families with a male head, wife present. Since this category is the sum of the MWL and MWN groups, the median can be approximated as a weighted sum of the two medians. Similarly, the lower decile variable is a weighted function of HMWL and HMWN. An upper decile variable was not required for the male head, wife present group.

THE EXPENDITURE SECTOR

This section reports estimates of equations predicting real annual levels of consumption and investment expenditures.

Private Consumption Expenditures

An attempt was made to examine the impact of changes in the distribution of income upon aggregate consumption expenditures. While a

---

[2]The MOT median was omitted because the group was too small a share of total families to be a statistically significant factor.

number of significant relationships were uncovered, it is not yet clear how
the results should be interpreted. The questions raised in this section will
be more thoroughly pursued, beyond the limitations of this study.

Equations (A5.8)–(A5.12) report some preliminary estimates of
aggregate consumption expenditures for the years 1947 through 1965.
Equation (A5.8) specifies total real consumption as a function of real
disposable personal income and lagged consumption.[3] Equation (A5.9)
permits the relative position of the tails of the United States family income distribution to influence the marginal propensity to consume out of
disposable personal income.

EQUATIONS (A5.8)–(A5.12). ESTIMATES OF AGGREGATE
CONSUMPTION EXPENDITURES, 1947–65

$$C_{58} = -0.660 + 0.801 DPI_{58} + 0.136 C_{58_{t-1}}$$
$$(3.558) \quad (0.110) \qquad\quad (0.130)$$
$$R^2 = .998$$
$$D\text{-}W = 1.48 \qquad \text{s.e.} = 2.59$$
(A5.8)

$$C_{58} = -2.053 + 0.635 DPI_{58} + 0.023 HFAM \cdot DPI_{58}$$
$$(3.858) \quad (0.102) \qquad\quad (0.137)$$
$$+ 0.127 JFAM \cdot DPI_{58} + 0.036 C_{58_{t-1}}$$
$$(0.038) \qquad\qquad\qquad (0.114)$$
$$R^2 = .999$$
$$D\text{-}W = 2.52 \qquad \text{s.e.} = 2.07$$
(A5.9)

$$\bar{C}_{58}/\overline{DPI}_{58} = -9.573/\overline{DPI}_{58} + 0.932 \overline{PERM}_{58}/\overline{DPI}_{58} + 0.676 \overline{TRS}_{58}/\overline{DPI}_{58}$$
$$(53.682) \qquad\quad (0.025) \qquad\qquad\qquad (0.137)$$
$$R^2 = .25$$
$$D\text{-}W = 1.39 \qquad \text{s.e.} = 0.0090$$
(A5.10)

$$\bar{C}_{58}/\overline{DPI}_{58} = 165.04/\overline{DPI}_{58} + 0.632 \overline{PERM}_{58}/\overline{DPI}_{58} + 0.733 \overline{TRS}_{58}/\overline{DPI}_{58}$$
$$(75.01) \qquad\quad (0.108) \qquad\qquad\qquad (0.110)$$
$$+ 0.057 Y90_{58}/\overline{DPI}_{58}$$
$$(0.020)$$
$$R^2 = .56$$
$$D\text{-}W = 2.40 \qquad \text{s.e.} = 0.0071$$
(A5.11)

[3]Lester C. Thurow, "Policy Planning Model of the American Economy"
(unpublished manuscript, 1967), uses the same specification with the addition
of lagged disposable income, but the coefficient on variables other than current
disposable income are statistically significant only when prewar observations are
added to the sample. Lagged variables do tend to be significant in a quarterly
specification.

$$\bar{C}_{58}/\overline{DPI}_{58} = 137.84/\overline{DPI}_{58} + 0.664 + 0.052Y90_{58}/\overline{DPI}_{58}$$
$$ (37.18) (0.065) (0.012)$$

$$ \text{(A5.12)}$$

$$R^2 = .56 F(2,\ 16) = 10.2$$
$$D\text{-}W = 2.25 \text{s.e.} = 0.0069$$

C_{58}	= Total annual consumption expenditures (billions of dollars, 1958 prices) (OBE)
DPI_{58}	= Disposable personal income (billions of dollars) deflated by implicit price index for personal consumption expenditures
$PERM_{58}$	= Estimated "permanent" income (billions of dollars, 1958 prices),

$$= \sum_{i=0}^{2} (DPI_{58})_{t-i}/3$$

TRS_{58}	$= DPI_{58} - PERM_{58}$
$Y90_{58}$	$= Y90$ deflated by implicit price index for personal consumption expenditures

Ordinary least squares; coefficient standard errors in parentheses. A bar appearing over a variable (e.g., $\bar{C}_{58}$) indicates that the variable is a mean value to be read as dollars per member of the population aged 14+, formed by dividing the affected variable by population aged 14+ measured in billions of persons (Table B-20, *Economic Report of the President*, 1967). [See note to Equations (A5.1)–(A5.7) for definitions of all distributional variables.]

If the cross-sectional marginal propensity to consume falls as income rises, an improvement in the upper tail of the distribution relative to the mean (at a given mean income) would shift income toward families having a low m.p.c.; consequently the aggregate marginal propensity to consume should decline. Conversely, a relative improvement in the lower tail of the distribution would imply a shifting of income to families with a higher than average m.p.c. Given this argument, we would expect the coefficients of the distributional variables in equation (A5.9) to be positive for the lower tail and negative for the upper tail.

The anticipated result does not occur. The inclusion of distributional variables does produce a 20 percent reduction of the standard error of estimate, but the upper tail coefficient is positive rather than negative, and highly significant. At face value, equation (A5.9) suggests an increasing m.p.c. across the upper portion of the distribution.

Objections can be registered against this initial conclusion for a variety of reasons. First, the above argument concerns changes in the tails of the distribution relative to the *mean*, not the median as specified in equation (A5.9). Given the complex relationship between the mean and the median, changing the specification of the distributional variables might alter the result.

Second, the upper tail of the distribution improves relative to the median during periods of recession. Thus we can assert that the m.p.c. increases during such periods, quite consistently with a permanent income hypothesis or with a declining average or marginal propensity to consume.[4]

Given these objections, the distributional variables were redefined relative to the mean, and separate provisions were made for changes in the marginal propensity to consume (m.p.c.) due to "transitory" income flows. In addition, a per capita specification was introduced to simplify the relationship of distributional variables to mean levels of income.

Equations (A5.10)–(A5.12) are based upon a specification of the form

$$\bar{C}_{58} = \alpha_0 + \alpha_1 \overline{PERM}_{58} + \alpha_2 \overline{TRS}_{58} + \alpha_3 \frac{Y10_{58}}{\overline{DPI}_{58}} \cdot \overline{DPI}_{58}$$

$$+ \alpha_4 \frac{MFAM_{58}}{\overline{DPI}_{58}} \cdot \overline{DPI}_{58} + \alpha_5 \frac{Y90}{\overline{DPI}_{58}} \cdot \overline{DPI}_{58},$$

where disposable personal income is split into crudely defined permanent and transitory components, while the positions of three distributional quantiles relative to the mean are permitted to affect the m.p.c. out of total disposable income. While the specification constrains distributional effects on the m.p.c. to apply equally to permanent and transitory income components,[5] variations from this theme yield only marginal differences in results. Lagged consumption continues to have no significant influence and is omitted from the specification.

Because of high collinearity among the right-hand variables and the possibility of correlation between the size of the standard error of estimate and the mean income level, the specification was renormalized to minimize the error in predicting the average propensity to consume, by deflating both sides of the equation (including the intercept) by real mean disposable income.

In equation (A5.10), the distinction between permanent and transitory income accounts for 25 percent of the deviation from a constant average propensity to consume; the implied marginal propensities to consume out of the permanent and transitory components are 0.93 and

---

[4] That is, the cyclic relationship between the upper tail variable and income changes prevents us from effectively observing improvements in the upper tail given a fixed mean, despite the formal appearance of the specification.

[5] An alternative hypothesis that changes in quantiles relative to permanent mean income lead to changes in the m.p.c. out of permanent income leads to an identical specification for estimation purposes.

0.68 respectively.[6] When distributional variables are added to the specification, only the upper decile variable is statistically significant; the marginal propensities to consume out of permanent and transitory income are no longer significantly different from each other. Better results were obtained by aggregating the components of disposable income; in equation (A5.12), the intercept is interpretable as the coefficient on disposable personal income.

Our basic result has not changed: the higher the top decile income relative to the mean, the higher the marginal propensity to consume. In interpreting the positive coefficient, however, we must recognize that the absolute level of the upper quantile is stable relative to the cyclical variations in the mean and in the lower tail. Rather than observe movements in the upper tail relative to a fixed level of mean income, as the specification formally states, we observe movements in the mean relative to an approximately fixed upper tail. The premise upon which our initial expectations were based is therefore open to question, as is the proper interpretation of the results.

To shed further light (or confusion) on the above question, the compositional impact of distributional changes upon durable, nondurable, and services consumption expenditures was examined. Final estimates of the three components of consumption expenditures appear in equations (A5.13)–(A5.18), along with definitions of the stock of consumer durables and of "permanent" and "transitory" income.

EQUATIONS (A5.13)–(A5.18). FINAL ESTIMATES, PERSONAL CONSUMPTION EXPENDITURES, 1947–65

$$\overline{CD_{58}/DPI_{58}} = -546.7/\overline{DPI}_{58} + 0.689 - 0.301\overline{CDA_{58}/DPI_{58}}$$
$$\qquad\qquad (84.1) \qquad\qquad (0.103) \;\; (0.067)$$

$$\qquad - 0.1505Y10_{58}/\overline{DPI}_{58} - 0.0397Y90_{58}/\overline{DPI}_{58} \qquad\qquad (A5.13)$$
$$\qquad\quad (0.0651) \qquad\qquad\quad (0.0159)$$

$$R^2 = .844 \qquad F(4, 14) = 18.95$$
$$D\text{-}W = 2.38 \qquad \text{s.e.} = 0.0050$$

$$CN_{58}/DPI_{58} = 27.32/DPI_{58} + 0.324PERM_{58}/DPI_{58} + 0.126TRS_{58}/DPI_{58}$$
$$\qquad\qquad (1.89) \qquad\quad (0.033) \qquad\qquad\quad (0.037)$$

$$\qquad + 0.00964Y90_{58}/\overline{DPI}_{58} \qquad\qquad\qquad\qquad (A5.14)$$
$$\qquad\quad (0.00682)$$

$$R^2 = .989 \qquad F(3, 15) = 451$$
$$D\text{-}W = 2.54 \qquad \text{s.e.} = 0.0023$$

---

[6]When the same regression is run without the deflation by DPI_{58}, the R^2 rises to .998.

$$\overline{CS_{58}}/\overline{DPI_{58}} = -113.1/\overline{DPI_{58}} + 0.1605 + 0.0152 Y90_{58}/\overline{DPI_{58}}$$
$$\quad\quad (13.8) \quad\quad\quad (0.0205) \quad (0.0049)$$

$$\quad\quad - 0.0341 MFAM_{58}/\overline{DPI_{58}} + 0.7123\overline{CS}_{58_{t-1}}/\overline{DPI_{58}}$$
$$\quad\quad\quad (0.0142) \quad\quad\quad\quad\quad (0.0755) \quad\quad\quad\quad\quad\quad\quad (A5.15)$$

$$R^2 = .991 \quad\quad F(4,\ 14) = 395$$
$$D\text{-}W = 2.49 \quad\quad \text{s.e.} = 0.0012$$

$$CDA_{58} = \sum_{i=1}^{3} (CD_{58})_{t-i} \quad\quad\quad\quad\quad\quad\quad\quad\quad\quad (A5.16)$$

$$PERM_{58} = \sum_{i=0}^{2} (DPI_{58})_{t-i}/3 \quad\quad\quad\quad\quad\quad\quad\quad (A5.17)$$

$$TRS_{58} = DPI_{58} - PERM_{58} \quad\quad\quad\quad\quad\quad\quad\quad (A5.18)$$

CD_{58} = Annual personal consumption expenditures on durable goods (billions of dollars, 1958 prices) (OBE)

CN_{58} = Annual personal consumption expenditures on nondurable goods (billions of dollars, 1958 prices) (OBE)

CS_{58} = Annual personal consumption expenditures on services (billions of dollars, 1958 prices) (OBE)

DPI_{58} = Disposable personal income (billions of dollars) deflated by implicit price index for personal consumption expenditures

$PERM_{58}$ = Estimated "permanent" income (billions of dollars, 1958 prices) defined by equation (A5.17)

TRS_{58} = Estimated "transitory" income, defined by equation (A5.18)

CDA_{58} = Estimated stock of consumer durables (billions of dollars, 1958 prices) defined by equation (A5.16)

$Y10_{58}, Y90_{58}, MFAM_{58}$ = decile and median income levels for total families (see Table 4.1 for definitions) deflated by the implicit price index for consumer expenditures

Two-stage least squares; coefficient standard errors in parentheses. A bar appearing over a variable (e.g., $\overline{CD}_{58}$) indicates a mean value per capita (14+), as defined in equations (A5.8)–(A5.12).

Durable consumption expenditures were expressed as a function of disposable personal income and of the stock of durable goods,[7] with distributional variables influencing the marginal propensity to consume out of disposable income. While an initial specification distinguished permanent from transitory income and permitted distributional variables to act separately on the two components, it absorbed valuable degrees of

[7]The stock of durable goods is defined to be the sum of the previous three years' durable expenditures, expressed in 1958 dollars.

freedom while not performing significantly better than the simpler equation (A5.13).[8]

Equation (A5.13) accounts for over 84 percent of the deviation from a constant average propensity to purchase durables. The higher the existing stock of durable, the lower the current level of durable expenditures. Improvements in either tail of the distribution, relative to the mean, lower the marginal propensity to consume.

Nondurable consumption does not depend as critically upon distributional changes as do the durable and services consumption. The best results are obtained when disposable income is split into permanent and transitory components, and when a per capita specification is not used. When specification (A5.14) is estimated by ordinary least squares, the coefficient on the upper tail variable is significantly positive, this significance is lost in a two-stage estimation procedure.

In equation (A5.14), there is a lower marginal propensity to consume out of transitory than out of permanent income. While the coefficient on the upper decile variable is positive, the apparent effect of distributional changes upon nondurable consumption is sensitive to the precise specification chosen.

In equation (A5.15), lagged services consumption has a dominating significance; given the lagged variable and distributional variables, results are not improved by recognizing a distinction between permanent and transitory income.

The positive effect of relative increases in upper decile income on total consumption reappears in the services equation. In addition, concentrations of income at the center of the distribution reduce the marginal propensity to consume services.

In summary, the shape of the income distribution appears to play a significant role in determining the composition and level of consumption expenditures. If the implicit cross-sectional marginal propensity to consume is plotted against income, we find a U-shaped function for services

---

[8] If durable consumption expenditures are specified as a function of "permanent" and "transitory" income, the following result is obtained:

$$CD_{58}/DPI_{58} = -153.1/DPI_{58} + 0.217 PERM_{58}/DPI_{58}$$
$$\quad\quad (41.3) \quad\quad\quad (0.028)$$

$$+ 4.604 TRS_{58}/DPI_{58} - 0.110 CDA_{58}/DPI_{58}$$
$$\quad (0.096) \quad\quad\quad\quad (0.044)$$

$$R^2 = .786$$
$$D\text{-}W = 2.24 \quad\quad \text{s.e.} = 0.0056$$
$$\text{Ordinary least squares}$$

and an "inverted U" for durable purchases. No strong pattern emerges for nondurable goods. These results are not inconsistent with a superficial examination of cross-sectional consumption data.

Gross Private Domestic Investment

Equations (A5.19)–(A5.23) report the three stochastic equations and two identities of the investment sector; separate equations determine the net change in business inventories, gross private fixed nonresidential investment, and gross private residential investment.

EQUATIONS (A5.19)–(A5.23).   FINAL ESTIMATES, INVESTMENT SECTOR, 1947–65

$$\Delta INV_{58} = -61.98 + 0.185(GNP_{58} - \Delta INV_{58}) - 0.776(INV_{58})_{t-1}$$
$$(10.13)(0.028)(0.134)$$

$$+0.306(WPI_t/WPI_{t-1}) + 0.147\Delta DEF_{58}$$
$$(0.112)(0.052)$$
$$\text{(A5.19)}$$

$$R^2 = .901 \qquad F(4,\ 13) = 29.7$$
$$D\text{-}W = 2.20 \qquad \text{s.e.} = 1.39$$
$$1948\text{–}65$$

$$INR_{58} = 13.24 + 0.149GPP_{58} - 0.044(KAP_{58})_{t-1} + 0.397(RET_{58})_{t-1}$$
$$(2.10)(0.025)(0.010)(0.109)$$
$$\text{(A5.20)}$$

$$R^2 = .974 \qquad F(3,\ 15) = 186$$
$$D\text{-}W = 1.32 \qquad \text{s.e.} = 1.36$$

$$IRS_{58} = -11.16 + 0.091GPP_{58} - 0.116(GPP_{58})_{t-1} - 5.05D_{47}$$
$$(21.39)(0.044)(0.044)(1.75)$$

$$-1.265I_{35} + 1.059POPF - 3.15DK_{51}$$
$$(0.999)(0.678)(1.22)$$
$$\text{(A5.21)}$$

$$R^2 = .883 \qquad F(6,\ 12) = 15.1$$
$$D\text{-}W = 2.18 \qquad \text{s.e.} = 1.18$$

$$INV_{58} = \Delta INV_{58} + (INV_{58})_{t-1} \qquad\qquad\qquad \text{(A5.22)}$$

$$KAP_{58} = (KAP_{58})_{t-1} + INR_{58} + IRS_{58} - (CCCA + NCCA)/PIFX \qquad \text{(A5.23)}$$

ΔINV_{58} = change in business inventories (billions of 1958 dollars) (OBE)

INV_{58} = $\sum\limits_{i=1935}^{t} (\Delta INV_{58})_i$ = total inventory stock from 1935 origin (billions of 1958 dollars)

INR_{58} = gross private fixed nonresidential investment (billions of 1958 dollars) (OBE)

IRS_{58} = gross private investment in residential structures (billions of 1958 dollars) (OBE)

GNP_{58} = gross national product (billions of 1958 dollars) (OBE)

WPI = Wholesale price index

DEF_{58} = federal government expenditures for defense, deflated by implicit price index for federal expenditures (billions of 1958 dollars)

GPP_{58} = gross private product (billions of 1958 dollars)

KAP_{58} = net capital stock (billions of 1958 dollars) = $\sum\limits_{i=1946}^{t} [INR_{58} + IRS_{58} -$

$$(CCCA + NCCA)/PIFX]_i + \frac{98.7}{0.381} + \frac{42.5}{0.446} + \frac{105.8}{0.357},$$

where 98.7, 42.5, and 105.8 are estimates of the 1945 domestic capital stock in nonresidential structures, equipment, and residential structures, respectively, in billions of 1929 dollars. [Source: J. W. Kendrick, *Productivity Trends in the United States* (Princeton, N.J.: Princeton University Press, 1961), p. 320.]

RET_{58} = Retained corporate "earnings" (billions of 1958 dollars),
= Corporate profits after income taxes plus corporate capital consumption allowances minus dividend payments, deflated by the implicit price index for gross private fixed domestic investment

D_{47} = Dummy variable = 1, 1947–50; = 0, other years

I_{35} = Interest rate on three-five year bonds starting in 1951
= 0 prior to 1951 (Source: Lester C. Thurow, "Policy Planning Model of the American Economy," 1967)

$POPF$ = Millions of United States families (CPS data)

DK_{51} = Korean war dummy = 1, 1951–53; 0, other years

$CCCA$ = Corporate capital consumption allowances (billions of dollars) (OBE)

$NCCA$ = Noncorporate capital consumption allowances (billions of dollars) (OBE)

$PIFX$ = Implicit price deflator for gross private fixed domestic investment

Two-stage least squares; coefficient standard errors in parentheses

The inventory investment equation (A5.19) began as an annual condensation of specifications in the Brookings model.[9] While the Brookings inventory functions are disaggregated, a typical specification expresses the change in inventories as a function of the change in unfilled orders, the level of unfilled orders, the ratio of the current to lagged wholesale prices, sales ($GNP_{58} - \Delta INV_{58}$), and the lagged inventory stock.[10] By substituting expressions for new and unfilled orders, a reduced form con-

[9] See Darling, Lovell, and Dutta, in J. S. Duesenberry et al., *The Brookings Quarterly Econometric Model of the United States* (Chicago: Rand McNally, 1965).
[10] Other variables were included in specific equations.

taining lagged unfilled orders plus the variables included in equation (A5.19) could be derived.[11] Unfilled orders were removed from the model after the coefficient proved to be only marginally significant, and after unsuccessful attempts to determine unfilled orders endogenously in the model.

Gross private fixed nonresidential investment equation (A5.20) is a function of real gross private product, the lagged capital stock, and lagged retained corporate earnings. The residential investment equation is quite unsatisfactory but could not be improved without a substantial diversion of attention from the primary objectives of this study.[12]

The expenditure sector is closed by two identities for the real levels of gross national product and gross private product:[13]

$$GNP_{58} = CD_{58} + CN_{58} + CS_{58} + \Delta INV_{58} + INR_{58} \atop + IRS_{58} + EXIM_{58} + GOV_{58} \qquad \text{(A5.24)}$$

$$GPP_{58} = GNP_{58} - GGP_{58} \qquad \text{(A5.25)}$$

Within the expenditure sector, changes in the distribution of income have a substantial impact on the consumer behavior. The investment equations are rather makeshift and have not received much attention in this study. The net export balance, government purchases of goods and services, and gross government product are assumed to be exogenous.

---

[11] An estimated form of this equation is:

$$\Delta INV_{58} = -68.93 + 0.198(GNP_{58} - \Delta INV_{58}) - 0.844(INV_{58})_{t-1}$$
$$\phantom{\Delta INV_{58} =} (9.64) \quad (0.044) \phantom{(GNP_{58} - \Delta INV_{58})} (0.212)$$

$$\phantom{\Delta INV_{58} =} + 0.331(WPI_t/WPI_{t-1}) + 0.138\Delta DEF_{58} + 0.054OU_{t-1}$$
$$\phantom{\Delta INV_{58} =} (0.111) \phantom{(WPI_t/WPI_{t-1})} (0.047) \phantom{+ 0.138\Delta DEF_{58}} (0.034)$$

$$R^2 = .928 \qquad F(5, 12) = 31.2$$
$$D\text{-}W = 2.69 \qquad \text{s.e.} = 1.23$$
$$2SLS \qquad 1948\text{--}65$$

[12] The initial intention was to use a residential investment specification used by Thurow, "Policy Planning Model." Thurow's equation (26), based on the years 1929–40 and 1946–65, has a corrected R^2 of 0.96 and a standard error of 1.56. He includes disposable personal income *per capita* to explain the *total* level of residential investment; when his equation is regressed over postwar data only, the personal income variable "bombs." While equation (5–13) has an un-corrected R^2 of only 0.883, the standard error of estimate is 1.18 compared to Thurow's 1.56 for the whole period. The high R^2 Thurow obtained by using pre-war data would therefore appear to be somewhat misleading.

[13] $EXIM_{58}$ equals the net export balance, GOV_{58} government purchases of goods and services, and GGP_{58} gross government product, all in billions of 1958 dollars.

THE INCOME SECTOR

The income sector covers all sources of personal income, tax equations, corporate profits, and capital consumption allowances. Distributional variables appear only in the personal income tax equations.

Sources of Personal Income

Equations (A5.26)–(A5.40) report estimates for all endogenous sources of personal income in the model. The level of private wage disbursements,[14] the largest individual income source, is defined as the product of an annual wage rate and private wage and salary employment. Although wage rates are usually defined on a man-hour basis, an annual wage per employee is used here. This formulation prevents the need for an endogenous determination of an hours-worked variable in the model; preliminary attempts to predict an annual average work week were unsuccessful.[15]

EQUATIONS (A5.26)–(A5.40).   ESTIMATES, SOURCES OF PERSONAL INCOME, 1947–65

A. Wage and Entrepreneurial Income

$$W_{58} = 1152.5 + 0.168\Delta X_{58} + 0.307(X_{58})_{t-1} + 0.056(K_{58})_{t-1}$$
$$\quad (57.5)\ (0.050)\qquad (0.029)\qquad\quad (0.014)$$

$$R^2 = .997 \qquad F(3, 14) = 1580$$
$$D\text{-}W = 2.32 \qquad \text{s.e.} = 25.2$$
$$1948\text{–}65$$

(A5.26)

$$\frac{\Delta W^*}{W^*_{t-1}} = -0.0142 + 0.544\,\frac{\Delta PCON}{PCON_{t-1}} + 0.286(PROF/GPP)$$
$$\qquad\quad (0.0125)\ (0.110)\qquad\qquad (0.105)$$

$$+\ 0.001622(LF/UN)_t$$
$$\quad (0.000369)$$

$$-\ 0.000722(LF/UN)_{t-1} - 0.195\,\frac{\Delta W_{t-1}}{W_{t-2}}$$
$$\quad (0.000321)\qquad\qquad\quad (0.094)$$

(A5.27)

$$R^2 = .945 \qquad \text{s.e.} = 0.00498$$
$$1948\text{–}65$$

[14]Government wage disbursements are assumed to be exogenous.

[15]Equation specifications which performed well on a quarterly basis did not translate well into annual specifications.

$$ENTR_{58} = 11.59 + 0.0396GPP_{58} - 0.0243(GPP_{58})_{t-1}$$
$$(4.60) \quad (0.0134) \qquad (0.0190)$$

$$+ 0.450(ENTR_{58})_{t-1}$$
$$(0.248)$$

(A5.28)

$$R^2 = .953 \qquad F(3, 14) = 95.2$$
$$D\text{-}W = 2.03 \qquad \text{s.e.} = 0.598$$
$$1948\text{--}65$$

$$WP = W^* \cdot [(EWS + EAWS)/1000]$$

(A5.29)

W^*	= Private annual wage disbursements per wage and salary employee (current dollars) $= WP/[(EWS + EAWS)/1000]$
W_{58}	$= W^*$ divided by implicit price deflator for GNP
EWS	= Private nonagricultural wage and salary employment (millions of persons), establishment data (Table B-25, *Economic Report of the President*, 1967)
$EAWS$	= Agricultural wage and salary employment (millions of persons) (Table A-9, *Manpower Report of the President*, 1966)
WP	= Private wage disbursements (billions of dollars) (OBE)
GPP	= Gross private product (billions of dollars)
EMP	= Total civilian employment (millions of persons) survey data (Table B-20, *Economic Report of the President*, 1967)
EG	= Total government employment (millions of persons), establishment data (Table B-25, *Economic Report of the President*, 1967)
X_{58}	= Gross private product per private employee (1958 dollars) $= GPP_{58}/[(EMP - EG)/1000]$
K_{58}	= Real capital stock per private employee $= KAP_{58}/[EMP - EG)/1000]$ [KAP_{58} defined in notes to equations (A5.19)–(A5.23)]
$PCON$	= Implicit price deflator for personal consumption expenditures
$PROF$	= Corporate profits before taxes (billions of dollars) (OBE)
$ENTR_{58}$	= Business and professional proprietors' income (billions of dollars) deflated by the implicit price index for GNP
LF	= Civilian labor force aged 14+ (millions of persons)
UN	$= LF - EMP =$ civilian unemployment (millions of persons)

B. Interest and Dividend Income

$$IPC = -4.77 + 0.0329(C_{58} \cdot PCON) + 0.0303(CD_{58} \cdot PCD)_{t-1}$$
$$(0.12) \quad (0.0020) \qquad\qquad (0.0140)$$

(A5.30)

$$R^2 = .998 \qquad F(2, 16) = 4288$$
$$D\text{-}W = 1.83 \qquad \text{s.e.} = 0.137$$

$$IPF = 0.461 + 0.0018913DF + 0.805IPF_{t-1}$$
$$(0.293) \quad (0.00046) \qquad (0.080)$$

$$R^2 = .977 \qquad F(2, 16) = 345$$
$$D\text{-}W = 2.54 \qquad \text{s.e.} = 0.227$$
Ordinary least squares

(A5.31)

$$IPT = IPC + IPF + IPS + IPNI \tag{A5.32}$$

$$DIV = 0.936 + 0.199(PROF + CCCA - TCP) + 0.1385DIV_{t-1}$$
$$\quad (0.237) \quad (0.013) \qquad\qquad\qquad\qquad (0.0512)$$
$$\tag{A5.33}$$

$$R^2 = .9915 \qquad F(2, 16) = 941$$
$$D\text{-}W = 2.04 \qquad \text{s.e.} = 0.357$$

IPC = Consumer interest payments (billions of dollars) (OBE)

IPF = Net federal interest payments (billions of dollars) (OBE)

$IPNI$ = Interest income included in national income (billions of dollars)

IPS = Net state and local interest payments (billions of dollars)

IPT = Personal interest income (billions of dollars)

DIV = Corporate dividends (billions of dollars)

PCD = Implicit price deflator for consumer durables (OBE)

$I3DF$ = Interest rate on three-month bills multiplied by publicly held federal debt (billions of dollars) (Thurow, "Policy Planning Model")

TCP = Corporate profit tax liabilities (billions of dollars) (OBE)

C. Transfer Payments and Social Insurance Contributions

$$OAS = -0.955 + 1.856BPIA \cdot (PP65/1000) + 0.866(OAS)_{t-1}$$
$$\quad\; (0.347) \quad (0.403) \qquad\qquad\qquad\qquad (0.046)$$
$$\tag{A5.34}$$

$$R^2 = .998 \qquad F(2, 15) = 3169$$
$$D\text{-}W = 227 \qquad \text{s.e.} = 0.303$$
Ordinary least squares
1948–65

$$UB = 0.804 + 0.191UN - 0.353UN_{t-1} + 3.275U26 + 0.015T \cdot UN$$
$$\quad (0.498) \quad (0.195) \qquad (0.093) \qquad (0.983) \qquad (0.004)$$
$$\tag{A5.35}$$

$$R^2 = .966 \qquad F(4, 13) = 91.4$$
$$D\text{-}W = 2.01 \qquad \text{s.e.} = 0.208$$
1949–65

$$TRAG = OAS + UB + TRO \tag{A5.36}$$

$$SICT = 1.328 + 0.958(TROA \cdot OASC \cdot OASW) \cdot (WP + WG)/MFAM$$
$$\qquad (0.281) \quad (0.175)$$
$$\qquad\; + 0.273TRU \cdot (WP + WG) + 0.380SICT_{t-1}$$
$$\qquad\quad (0.212) \qquad\qquad\qquad (0.150)$$
$$\tag{A5.37}$$

$$R^2 = .997 \qquad F(3, 14) = 1665$$
$$D\text{-}W = 1.89 \qquad \text{s.e.} = 0.466$$
1948–65

$$SICE = 0.123 + 0.5472SICT$$
$$\quad\; (0.111) \quad (0.0067)$$
$$\tag{A5.38}$$

$$R^2 = .997 \qquad F(1, 17) = 6774$$
$$D\text{-}W = 0.79 \qquad \text{s.e.} = 0.23$$

$$SICP = SICT - SICE \tag{A5.39}$$

$$PI = WP + WG + OLI + ENTR + ENTF + RIP + DIV + IPT$$
$$+ TRAG + TRB - SICP \qquad \text{(A5.40)}$$

OAS = OASDI benefits (billions of dollars) (OBE)

$BPIA$ = Maximum principle insurance amount for OASDI benefits (dollars)

$PP65$ = Population aged 65+ (millions of persons)

UB = State unemployment insurance benefits (billions of dollars) (OBE)

$TRAG$ = Total government transfers to persons (billions of dollars)

TRO = $TRAG - OAS - UB$ = "other" government transfers to persons (billions of dollars)

$SICT$ = Total social insurance contributions (billions of dollars)

$SICE$ = Employer social insurance contributions (billions of dollars)

$SICP$ = Personal contributions for social insurance (billions of dollars) (OBE)

$TROA$ = OASDI total contribution tax rate

$OASC$ = OASDI coverage rate (Thurow, "Policy Planning Model")

$OASW$ = OASDI wage base (dollars)

TRU = Contribution rate for unemployment insurance (Thurow, "Policy Planning Model")

WG = Government wage disbursements (billions of dollars)

PI = Total personal income (billions of dollars)

OLI = Other labor income (billions of dollars)

$ENTF$ = Farm proprietors' income (billions of dollars)

RIP = Rental income of persons (billions of dollars)

TRB = Net business transfers to persons (billions of dollars)

$U26$ = Millions of persons unemployed 26 weeks or longer

T = Time trend; 1947 = 1, 1948 = 2, etc.

Two-stage least squares; coefficient standard errors in parentheses.

The initial model utilized specification (A5.26), which predicts the real wage rate as a function of current and lagged real gross private product per private employee and of the private capital-labor ratio. In equation (A5.26), the wage payment out of changes in GPP is smaller than the long-run wage payment; thus, the wage share of GPP falls during rapid changes in output.[16] The higher the capital labor ratio, the higher the wage payment out of GPP.

In the model used for this study, a specification determining the rate of change of the current dollar wage rate was substituted for a real wage equation. Patterned after the specifications used by Schultze and Tryon in the Brookings model,[17] equation (A5.27) states the rate of change in

---

[16] The offsetting increase goes to the corporate sector, not to other sources of personal income.

[17] See Duesenberry et al., *Brookings Quarterly Econometric Model*, pp. 707 ff.

wages to be a function of the rate of change in consumer prices, the share of corporate profits in gross private product, the current and the lagged inverse of the unemployment rate,[18] and the lagged rate of change in wages. The standard error of estimate of 0.005 in the rate of change variable represents a dollar change roughly comparable to the standard error of equation (A5.26).

Business and professional proprietors' income (A5.28) is expressed in real terms as a function of current and lagged real gross private product and of lagged proprietors' income. The income share of proprietors rises during periods of rapidly changing gross private product. Equation (A5.29) defines total private wage disbursements.

Equations (A5.30) and (A5.31) predict the levels of consumer interest payments to persons and of net federal interest payments to persons. Consumer interest payments are a function of current consumption expenditures and lagged durable expenditures. The specification for federal interest payments, drawn directly from Thurow,[19] includes the product of the three-month bill rate and the publicly held federal debt, as well as lagged federal interest payments.

The corporate dividend equation follows the Lintner[20] tradition, except that corporate capital consumption allowances were included in the corporate profit term.[21] The use of a gross flow of funds term, rather than corporate profits, substantially improves the empirical results.

Equations (A5.34) and (A5.35) estimate OASDI benefits and state unemployment insurance benefits. Neither equation reflects the full intricacies of the legislation governing transfer payments; each approximates a more complex structural relationship. The level of OASDI benefits is a function of lagged OASDI benefits and of the product of the maximum principle insurance amounts applicable to beneficiaries and the population over age 65. The level of unemployment benefits is a function of current and lagged unemployment and of long-term (twenty-six weeks or more) unemployment. A time trend attached to the level of unemployment reflects increasing benefit schedules over time. According to equa-

---

[18] The explanatory power of the equation is improved by inverting the unemployment rate.

[19] See Thurow, "Policy Planning Model." He specifies consumer interest payments to be a bivariate function of personal income. The specification used in (5–23) provides a far better goodness of fit. Thurow's federal interest specification was left unchanged.

[20] John Lintner, "Distribution of Incomes of Corporations among Dividends, Retained Earnings, and Taxes," *American Economic Review* 46 (May 1956), 97–113.

[21] Kuh also includes capital consumption allowances in the Brookings model dividend equation.

tion (A5.35), unemployment benefits are high when long-term unemployment is high, despite the loss of payment eligibility suffered by such individuals. The positive coefficient on $U26$ implies a higher general level of payments rather than payments specifically to the long-term unemployed.

Two stochastic equations and an identity determine the level and allocation of social insurance contributions. Equation (A5.37) determines total social insurance contributions as a function of three variables. The first right-hand variable is a product of the total OASDI contribution rate ($TROA$), the OASDI coverage rate ($OASC$), the ratio of the OASDI wage base ($OASW$) to median family income, and total wage disbursements. The second term is the product of the average unemployment insurance tax rate (TRU) and total wage disbursements. The third term is lagged social insurance contributions. The equation is patterned after a disaggregated set of contribution equations used by Thurow. Equation (A5.38) is a bivariate relationship between employer and total insurance contributions. Identity (A5.40) closes the set of equations determining the sources of personal income.

Tax Equations

The tax block contains two personal income tax equations, two indirect business tax equations, and a corporate income tax equation. Equations (A5.41)–(A5.48) report these estimates in addition to the disposable personal income identity and alternative forms of the federal personal tax equation.

EQUATIONS (A5.41)–(A5.48). ESTIMATES, TAX EQUATIONS, 1947–65

A. Federal Personal Taxes

$$\overline{TFP} = -46.2 + 0.0648\overline{PI} + 0.318TXPM \cdot \overline{PI}$$
$$\quad (9.6) \quad (0.0100) \qquad (0.052)$$

$$R^2 = .977 \qquad F(2,\ 16) = 347$$
$$D\text{-}W = 1.37 \qquad \text{s.e.} = 8.22$$

(A5.41)

$$\overline{TFP} = 20.45 + 0.0549\overline{A} + 0.467TXPM \cdot \overline{A}$$
$$\quad (5.82) \quad (0.0119) \qquad (0.064)$$

$$R^2 = .985 \qquad F(2,\ 16) = 530$$
$$D\text{-}W = 1.64 \qquad \text{s.e.} = 6.68$$

(A5.42)

$$\overline{TFP} = 67.85 + 1.298TXPM \cdot \overline{A} + 0.081H_1 \cdot TXPM \cdot \overline{A} - 0.287TXPM \cdot MFAM$$
$$\quad (9.86) \quad (0.324) \qquad\qquad (0.030) \qquad\qquad\qquad (0.162)$$

$$+ 0.024TXPM \cdot Y90 \qquad\qquad\qquad\qquad\qquad\qquad\qquad \text{(A5.43)}$$
$$\quad (0.055)$$

$$R^2 = .991 \qquad F(4, 14) = 391$$
$$D\text{-}W = 1.88 \qquad \text{s.e.} = 5.52$$

Bars over variables indicate a mean value formed by dividing the appropriate variable by *total population* (*Economic Report of the President*, 1968, Table B-21); mean values expressed in dollars.

TFP = Federal personal tax and nontax receipts (billions of dollars)

$TXPM$ = Effective average tax rate on taxable income at median family income for a family of four (CPS median)

$\bar{A}$ = Estimated mean taxable income = $\overline{PI} - \overline{TRAG}$ − standard exemption level per capita ($600)

H_1 = Income at lower decile cutoff ($Y10$, total families) divided by average nontaxable income ($\overline{TRAG}$ + exemption level per capita)

B. Other Tax Equations

$$\overline{TSLP} = -29.3 + 0.0323\overline{PI} + 0.0042H_1\overline{PI} - 0.0296MFAM + 0.0127Y90$$
$$\quad\;\; (9.9) \;\;\; (0.0167) \quad\;\; (0.0019) \qquad\;\;\, (0.0093) \qquad\;\; (0.0032)$$

$$R^2 = .990 \qquad F(4, 14) = 343 \qquad\qquad \text{(A5.44)}$$
$$D\text{-}W = 1.87 \qquad \text{s.e.} = 1.68$$

$$IBTF = 3.18 + 0.0181GPP + 0.0090TGMF + 0.575DK_{51}$$
$$\quad\;\; (0.40) \;\; (0.0021) \qquad (0.0030) \qquad\;\; (0.186)$$
$$\qquad\qquad\qquad\qquad\qquad\qquad\qquad\qquad\qquad \text{(A5.45)}$$

$$R^2 = .992 \qquad F(3, 15) = 649$$
$$D\text{-}W = 2.30 \qquad \text{s.e.} = 0.27$$

$$IBTS = 10.71 + 0.0925GPP$$
$$\quad\;\; (0.93) \;\; (0.0023)$$
$$\qquad\qquad\qquad\qquad\qquad\qquad\qquad\qquad\qquad \text{(A5.46)}$$

$$R^2 = .989 \qquad F(1, 17) = 1608$$
$$D\text{-}W = 0.88 \qquad \text{s.e.} = 1.13$$

$$TCP = 1.704 + 0.801TXCP \cdot PROF + 0.093TXCP \cdot PROF \cdot D_{EPT}$$
$$\quad\;\; (0.350) \;\; (0.014) \qquad\qquad\;\; (0.011)$$
$$\qquad\qquad\qquad\qquad\qquad\qquad\qquad\qquad\qquad \text{(A5.47)}$$

$$R^2 = .995 \qquad F(2, 16) = 1722$$
$$D\text{-}W = 1.75 \qquad \text{s.e.} = 0.39$$

$$DPI = PI - TFP - TSLP \qquad\qquad\qquad\qquad\qquad\qquad \text{(A5.48)}$$

See Part A of this table for a definition of mean variables appearing with a bar superscript.

$TSLP$ = State and local personal tax and nontax receipts (billions of dollars)

$IBTF$ = Federal indirect business taxes (billions of dollars)

$IBTS$ = State and local indirect business taxes (billions of dollars)

DK_{51} = Korean war dummy = 1, 1951–53; = 0, other years

$TGMF$ = Tax rate on gasoline x motor fuel usage (see Thurow, "Policy Planning Model")

TCP = Corporate profit tax liabilities (billions of dollars)
$PROF$ = Corporate profits before taxes (billions of dollars)
$TXCP$ = Marginal corporate income tax rate
D_{EPT} = Excess profits tax dummy = 1, 1951–53; = 0, other years

Two-stage least squares; coefficient standard errors in parentheses

Changes in the size distribution of income can be expected to influence the level of personal tax payments. While an annual federal personal tax equation must remain fairly simple, the introduction of distributional variables produces substantially improved results.

Equation (A5.41) provides a convenient starting point for our examination of federal personal taxes. Mean tax payments are a function of mean personal median income. Since the effective tax rate rises with median income (given the tax structure), progressivity is built into the system.[22] The estimate is improved by using a crude estimate of mean taxable income in place of mean personal income; this substitution is made in equation (A5.42).

If the population were distributed into equal size family units, if income were equally distributed, and if consistent data sources were used, we would simply have $TFP = TXPM \cdot \bar{A}$. While variations in the size of income units will not be dealt with, the deviations from this identity brought about by distributional changes can be investigated.

Since the tax rate on taxable income at the median was the base tax rate for the years 1947–63, relative changes in the lower tail of the distribution would only affect the proportion of income units which pay taxes, not the level of receipts out of taxable income. Specifically, it is assumed here that the proportion of persons paying taxes increases linearly with H_1, the ratio of income at the bottom decile to the average level of *nontaxable* personal income.

Because of the progressivity of the tax structure, tax receipts out of taxable income should be higher than the median tax rate indicates as the median becomes lower relative to the mean. Furthermore, the effective tax rate should increase with the ratio of the upper decile to the mean or median.

Given these assumptions, we can express average federal tax payments as a product of the proportion of persons paying taxes and the average level of payments per taxpayer, or

---

[22] Thurow, "Policy Planning Model," adopts a similar federal personal tax equation, except that his tax rate is not precisely the same, and the specification is in total, not per capita, terms. See his equation (24).

$$TFP = a_0 + (a_1 + a_2 H_1) \cdot \{[a_3 + a_4(MFAM/\bar{A}) + a_5(Y90/\bar{A})]$$
$$\cdot \ TXPM \cdot \bar{A}\}, \text{ where } a_2, a_3, a_5 > 0 \text{ and } a < 0.$$

The specification was simplified by placing the H_1 term in the right-hand bracket, making the form to be estimated

$$TFP = a_0 + [a_3 + a_2 H_1 + a_4(MFAM/\bar{A}) + a_5(Y90/\bar{A})] \cdot TXPM \cdot \bar{A}.$$

While not all coefficients in equation (A5.43) are significant, the signs are consistent with prior expectations; the addition of distributional variables reduces the standard error of estimate by over 17 percent.

The pattern of distributional effects on income tax receipts is corroborated by equation (A5.44) for state and local taxes. In the latter case, no tax rate is used and personal income is not adjusted to a taxable basis; all distribution coefficients are significant. Both equations make effective use of distributional variables to indicate the progressivity of the income tax structure and constitute significant improvements in goodness of fit over specifications which do not utilize the shape of the income distribution.

Equation specifications for indirect business taxes are identical to those proposed by Thurow.[23] Corporate income tax liabilities are expressed as a product of corporate profits and the marginal corporate tax rate, with a coefficient dummy in effect for the excess profits tax levied during the Korean war.

Corporate Profits and Capital Consumption Equations

In addition to corporate dividend and tax equations presented above, the corporate block includes a simple gross flow of funds equation and two capital consumption equations. A GNP identity closes the income sector of the model. The indicated estimates appear in equations (A5.49)–(A5.52).

EQUATIONS (A5.49)–(A5.52). ESTIMATES, CORPORATE PROFITS AND CAPITAL CONSUMPTION ALLOWANCES, 1947–65

$$PROF + CCCA = -2.895 + 0.397GPP - 0.232GPP_{t-1}$$
$$(1.898) \quad (0.048) \qquad (0.050)$$

$$\text{(A5.49)}$$

$$R^2 = .989 \qquad F(2, 16) = 732$$
$$D\text{-}W = 1.17 \qquad \text{s.e.} = 2.29$$

[23] *Ibid.*, equations (11) and (12).

$$(CCCA/PIFX) = -13.40 + 0.0231(KAP_{58})_{t-1} + 0.0025D_{54_t} \cdot (KAP_{58})_{t-1}$$
$$ (1.09) \quad (0.0055) \qquad\qquad (0.0004)$$

$$+ \ 0.0024D_{62_t} \cdot (KAP_{58})_{t-1} + 0.0218GPP_{58}$$
$$(0.0004) \qquad\qquad\qquad (0.0120) \qquad\qquad\qquad \text{(A5.50)}$$

$$R^2 = .999 \qquad F(4, 114) = 2705$$
$$D\text{-}W = 2.36 \qquad \text{s.e.} = 0.314$$

$$(NCCA/PIFX) = -11.37 + 0.0226(KAP_{58})_{t-1} - 0.00030T \cdot (KAP_{58})_{t-1}$$
$$ (1.99) \quad (0.0022) \qquad\qquad (0.00007)$$

$$+ \ 0.0214GPP_{58}$$
$$(0.0049) \qquad\qquad\qquad\qquad\qquad\qquad\qquad \text{(A5.51)}$$

$$R^2 = .996 \qquad F(3, 15) = 1156$$
$$D\text{-}W = 2.12 \qquad \text{s.e.} = 0.244$$

$$GNP = PI + PROF + IVA + SICT - TRAG - IPC - IPE - IPS$$
$$- DIV - SUB + IBTF + IBTS + STAT + NCCA + CCCA \qquad \text{(A5.52)}$$

$CCCA$ = Corporate capital consumption allowances (billions of dollars)

$PIFX$ = Implicit price deflator for gross private fixed domestic investment

D_{54} = Capital consumption dummy = 1, 1954 and later years; = 0, earlier years

D_{62} = Capital consumption dummy = 1, 1962 and later years; = 0, earlier years

$NCCA$ = Noncorporate capital consumption allowances (billions of dollars)

IVA = Corporate inventory valuation adjustment (billions of dollars)

SUB = Subsidies less current surplus of government enterprises (billions of current dollars)

$STAT$ = Statistical discrepancy (billions of dollars)

Two-stage least squares; coefficient standard errors in parentheses. See equation (A5.33) for corporate dividend payments. See equation (A5.47) for corporate income taxes.

The gross flow of corporate funds is a function only of current and lagged gross private product; the assorted capacity utilization variables often used in such specifications are avoided.

Corporate capital consumption allowances are a function of lagged capital stock, with coefficient dummies beginning in 1954 and 1962 to reflect changes in the depreciation laws. In addition, capital consumption allowances tend to be higher during periods of high output.[24] Non-corporate capital consumption allowances are also a function of lagged capital stock, except that a negative time trend appears on the capital

---

[24]This may be because of initial year depreciation taken on current investment, not yet included in the capital stock.

stock coefficient. Noncorporate allowances are also higher during periods of high current output.

EQUATIONS (A5.53)–(A5.60).   ESTIMATES, EMPLOYMENT-LABOR FORCE SECTOR, 1947–65

$EWS = 4.319 + 0.0746GPP_{58} - 0.0570(GPP_{58})_{t-1} - 0.00635(KAP_{58})_{t-1}$
(10.940) (0.0269)   (0.0426)   (0.00635)

$+ 0.872EWS_{t-1}$
(0.421)   (A5.53)

$R^2 = .97$ $F(4, 13) = 103$
$D\text{-}W = 1.75$ s.e. $= 0.672$
1948–65

$EMP = EWS + EAWS + EG + EAO + ESEL + ERES$ (A5.54)

$(LFM/PP14_M) = 0.994 + 0.171(EMP/PP14) - 1.217(P19_M/PP14_M)$
(0.047) (0.087)   (0.080)

$- 0.881(P65_M/PP14_M) - 0.947(ARMY/PP14_M)$
(0.087)   (0.051)

$- 0.0586(Y10P/MMWP)$ (A5.55)
(0.0433)

$R^2 = .997$ $F(5, 13) = 954$
$D\text{-}W = 2.11$ s.e. $= 0.0015$

$(LFF/PP14_F) = 0.281 + 0.274(EMP/PP14) - 0.714(P19_F/PP14_F)$
(0.099) (0.120)   (0.204)

$- 0.704(P65_F/PP14_F) - 0.444(ARMY/PP14) + 0.00624T$
(0.488)   (0.45)   (0.00152)

$+ 0.128(Y10P/MMWP)$ (A5.56)
(0.079)

$R^2 = .992$ $F(6, 10) = 200$
$D\text{-}W = 2.02$ s.e. $= 0.00195$
1949–65

$PAR2 = 0.682 - 2.278(P19_F/PP14_F) + 0.300HFEM - 0.063JFEM + 0.00334T$
(0.094) (0.536)   (0.125)   (0.036)   (0.00064)
                                                                   (A5.57)

$R^2 = .636$ $F(4, 14) = 6.11$
$D\text{-}W = 2.44$ s.e. $= 0.0079$

$LF = LFM + LFF$ (A5.58)

$UN = LF - EMP$ (A5.59)

$U26 = -0.459 + 0.192UN + 0.056UN_{t-1}$
(0.064) (0.021)   (0.020)

$$R^2 = .926 \qquad F(2, 15) = 94.3 \qquad \text{(A5.60)}$$
$$D\text{-}W = 1.83 \qquad \text{s.e.} = 60.9$$
$$1948\text{–}65$$

EWS = Private nonagricultural wage and salary employment (millions of persons), establishment data [*Economic Report of the President (ERP)* Table B-25, 1967]

EMP = Total civilian employment (millions of persons), survey data *ERP*, Table B-20, 1967

EAWS = Agricultural wage and salary employment (millions of persons) [*Manpower Report of the President (MRP)* Table A-9, 1966]

EAO = Other agricultural employment (millions of persons) (*MRP*, Table A-9, 1966)

EG = Total government employment (millions of persons), establishment data (ERP, Table B-25, 1967)

ESEL = Nonagricultural self-employed (millions of persons) (*MRP*, Table A-9, March 1966)

ERES = Residual employment ($= EMP - EWS - EAWS - EG - EAO - ESEL$) (millions of persons), includes unpaid nonfarm family workers and discrepancy between "survey" and "establishment" data

LFF = Female civilian labor force aged 14+ (millions of persons)

LFM = Male civilian labor force aged 14+ (millions of persons)

PP14 = Population aged 14+ (millions of persons) (*ERP*, Table B-20, 1967)

P19 = Civilian population aged 14–19 (millions of persons)

P65 = Population aged 65+ (millions of persons)

ARMY = Armed forces population (millions of persons) (*ERP*, Table B-20, 1967)

PAR2 = Labor force participation rate, females, "other" marital status, data first quarter of year $t + 1$ [Bureau of Labor Statistics (BLS)]

UN = Unemployment (millions of persons)

U26 = Unemployment, 26 weeks or more (millions of persons)

Two-stage least squares; coefficient standard errors in parentheses. The subscripts *M* and *F* refer to male and female.

THE EMPLOYMENT-LABOR FORCE SECTOR

Equations (A5.53)–(A5.60) report estimates for the employment-labor force sector. The employment equation is one of the weakest links in the model. Specifications drawn from quarterly models could not be adapted successfully to an annual format. This lack of success was apparent in efforts to estimate both disaggregated components of wage and salary employment and a single wage and salary employment equation. Since disaggregation did not improve matters, a single employment equation was used. Sources of employment other than private nonfarm wage and salary were held exogenous.

Two equations estimate labor force participation by sex. A limited attempt was made to relate distributional variables to the participation rates. The labor force participation rate of "females, other marital status," is estimated for use in the female head block of the distribution sector. Estimation of this equation was hindered by the small size of the group and because the data were based on a March observation rather than upon annual averages.

An identity determines the unemployment level, while long term unemployment is a function of current and lagged total unemployment. The primary difficulty with the employment equation (A5.53) is the size of the standard error; when the unemployment estimate is defined by an identity, a standard error of 672,000 persons is excessive. Disaggregation did not reduce the size of the standard error. Identity (A5.54) defines total employment by incorporating the remaining exogenous components of employment.

The male labor force participation rate is expressed as a function of the fraction of the noninstitutional population employed, the proportion of males between 14 and 19 years of age, the proportion over 65, and the proportion of men in the armed forces. The relative position of the lower decile for families with a male head, wife present, was included to determine whether the male labor force responds to distributional changes.

According to equation (A5.55), a 1 percent increase in the employment rate (out of total noninstitutional population) produces a 0.17 percent increase in the male labor force participation rate. The participation rate is negatively related to the proportion of the male population under 20 or over 65 years of age. Increases in the armed forces withdraw men from the civilian labor force on virtually a one-for-one-basis. The negative coefficient on the distributional variable[25] suggests that male labor force participation rises slightly when low income families are doing poorly relative to the median; this lends marginal support to the notion that secondary workers enter the labor force when primary earners are unable to keep their jobs. In equation (A5.56), this notion is rejected for the case of women.

Female labor force participation responded more strongly to increases in employment than did male participation. A 1 percent increase in the employment rate leads to a 0.27 percent increase in the female

---

[25]The coefficient is statistically significant in a least squares version of the paper.

EQUATIONS (A5.61)–(A5.66). ESTIMATES, PRICE SECTOR

$$\frac{\Delta PGNP}{PGNP_{t-1}} = -0.00148 + 0.840 \frac{\Delta W^*}{W^*_{t-1}} - 0.392 \frac{\Delta X_{58}}{X_{58_{t-1}}} + 0.0212 Dp_1$$
$$(0.00437) \quad (0.099) \qquad (0.101) \qquad\qquad (0.0057) \qquad\qquad\qquad \text{(A5.61)}$$

$$R^2 = .900 \qquad \text{s.e.} = 0.00653$$
$$1948\text{–}65$$

$$\frac{\Delta PGPP}{PGPP_{t-1}} = -0.00586 + 0.896 \frac{\Delta W^*}{W^*_{t-1}} - 0.402 \frac{\Delta X_{58}}{X_{58_{t-1}}} + 0.0264 Dp_1$$
$$(0.00466) \quad (0.105) \qquad (0.108) \qquad\qquad (0.0061) \qquad\qquad\qquad \text{(A5.62)}$$

$$R^2 = .907 \qquad \text{s.e.} = 0.00697$$
$$1948\text{–}65$$

$$\frac{\Delta PCON}{PCON_{t-1}} = -0.00686 + 0.819 \frac{\Delta W^*}{W^*_{t-1}} - 0.303 \frac{\Delta X_{58}}{X_{58_{t-1}}} + 0.0203 Dp_1$$
$$(0.00436) \quad (0.099) \qquad (0.101) \qquad\qquad (0.0057) \qquad\qquad\qquad \text{(A5.63)}$$

$$R^2 = .892 \qquad \text{s.e.} = 0.00653$$
$$1948\text{–}65$$

$$\frac{\Delta PIFX}{PIFX_{t-1}} = -0.01235 + 0.992 \frac{\Delta W^*}{W^*_{t-1}} - 0.251 \frac{\Delta X_{58}}{X_{58_{t-1}}} + 0.153 \frac{\Delta PIFX_{t-1}}{PIFX_{t-2}}$$
$$(0.00669) \quad (0.144) \qquad (0.135) \qquad\qquad (0.084)$$
$$+ 0.0146 Dp_2 \qquad\qquad\qquad\qquad\qquad\qquad\qquad\qquad\qquad \text{(A5.64)}$$
$$(0.0050)$$

$$R^2 = .861 \qquad \text{s.e.} = 0.00836$$
$$1949\text{–}65$$

$$\frac{\Delta PCD}{PCD_{t-1}} = -0.02046 + 0.898 \frac{\Delta W^*}{W^*_{t-1}} - 0.332 \frac{\Delta X_{58}}{X_{58_{t-1}}} + 0.411 \frac{\Delta PCD_{t-1}}{PCD_{t-2}}$$
$$(0.00490) \quad (0.126) \qquad (0.114) \qquad\qquad (0.087)$$
$$+ 0.0318 Dp_1 \qquad\qquad\qquad\qquad\qquad\qquad\qquad\qquad\qquad \text{(A5.65)}$$
$$(0.0047)$$

$$R^2 = .922 \qquad \text{s.e.} = 0.00717$$
$$1949\text{–}65$$

$$\frac{\Delta WPI}{WPI_{t-1}} = -0.0327 + 1.032 \frac{\Delta W^*}{W^*_{t-1}} - 0.261 \frac{\Delta WPI_{t-1}}{WPI_{t-2}} + 0.0666 Dp_1$$
$$(0.0089) \quad (0.206) \qquad (0.080) \qquad\qquad (0.0114) \qquad\qquad\qquad \text{(A5.66)}$$

$$R^2 = .893 \qquad \text{s.e.} = 0.0128$$
$$1949\text{–}65$$

Dp_1 = Korean war dummy allowing for speculative price increase in 1951; = 1, 1951; = −½, 1952 and 1953; zero other years

Dp_2 = Alternative Korean war dummy; = 1, 1951; = −1, 1952 and 1953; zero other years

WPI = Wholesale price index, 1957–59 = 1.000

Implicit price deflators in national income accounts, 1958 = 1.000:

$PGNP$ Gross national product
$PGPP$ Gross private product
$PCON$ Total consumption expenditures
$PIFX$ Gross private fixed domestic investment
PCD Consumer durable expenditures

Two-stage least squares; coefficient standard errors in parentheses.
In simulation experiments a least squares estimate of (A5.61) was used; all coefficients were similar. See notes to equations (A5.26)–(A5.29) for definitions of W^* and X_{58}.

labor force participation rate. Equation (A5.56) shows the same negative response to increases in the proportion of persons (in this case women) under 20 and over 65. In addition, there exists a strong positive trend in female labor force participation. Unlike men, women tend to enter the labor force when the lower tail of the income distribution improves relative to the median. Both the distribution and the employment variables indicate that women are drawn into the labor force when employment opportunities are good, rather than when the heads of families are unemployed. A surprising feature of the equation is the decline of female labor force participation in the face of increased armed forces levels. One would expect a substitution of women for men in the civilian labor force under such circumstances.

The participation rate of "females, other marital status" (equation A5.57) has a positive time trend and is negatively related to the proportion of women who are under 20 years of age. It tends to increase when the lower tail of the FEM distribution improves relative to the median and to decline when the upper tail improves.[26] Long-term unemployment is a simple function of current and lagged total unemployment. Identities for the total labor force and for unemployment complete the employment-labor force sector.

THE PRICE SECTOR

Equations (A5.61)–(A5.66) provide estimates of rates of change for the six price levels appearing in the model. Each rate of price change is an increasing function of the rate of change of private wage disbursements

[26]Since the upper tail variable for the FEM group is not estimated in the model; its presence in (A5.57) is inconsequential for simulation uses of the model.

per employee and a decreasing function of the rate of change of real gross private product per private employee. In every case the coefficients are highly significant.[27]

The Korean war period was marked by a rapid increase in prices for 1951, beyond what would be predicted by wage and productivity changes alone. A large part of this increase can be attributed to speculative stockpiling of raw materials; the largest price increase occurred in the wholesale price index. The 1951 inflation was compensated by lower than normal price increases for 1952 and 1953, given the tightness of the economy.

A dummy variable was constructed to permit a concentration of the Korean war price effects in 1951. This was done by setting the dummy equal to 1 in 1951 and $-\frac{1}{2}$ in 1952 and 1953.[28] Such a variable provided better empirical results than a conventional dummy variable for 1951 or 1951–53.

Equations (A5.61)–(A5.63) report estimates for rates of change of the price deflators for GNP, GPP, and consumer expenditures. The three equations have similar coefficients and goodness of fit; in each case the standard error of estimate is less than 0.7 percent of the price level.

In the case of the price deflators of gross private fixed investment and consumer durable purchases, the lagged rate of price increase has a significant positive impact on the current rate of increase. One explanation of this might be that for investment and durable goods, order backlogs accumulate during periods of high demand and continue to exert pressure in the following year.[29] Changes in the wholesale price index, on the other hand, are negatively related to past changes. Speculative stockpiling could contribute to this pattern.

THE RESIDUAL

Because of the adding-up relationships which hold among income account components, we may not estimate each account item independently. To prevent the model from being overdetermined, one element of the income accounts must be defined by a residual identity.

---

[27] One exception is the coefficient on $\dfrac{\Delta X_{58}}{(X_{58})_{t-1}}$ in the PIFX equation, but even it is significant at a 5 percent one tail test level.

[28] An exception is equation (A5.64), where the sequence 1, -1, -1 yielded better results.

[29] Unfilled orders could have been included directly, but it was decided to omit unfilled orders entirely from the model rather than attempt to determine them endogenously. See the discussion of the inventory equation in chapter 5.

It must be recognized that the residual variable is endogenously determined by the specification of the model just as rigorously as if it had been directly estimated. In addition, it bears the cumulative impact of all errors generated elsewhere in the system. Thus, the residual item may have a more substantial error component than the directly estimated variables.

Given our declaration of endogenous variables, the residual must be chosen from the set of variables which would otherwise be exogenous. Our motivations behind declaring certain variables to be exogenous limit the choice considerably. If the initial intention was to use a variable as a policy instrument, this objective could not be fulfilled if the variable was determined residually. Similarly, if a variable is exogenous because it is a minor component which increases over time without cyclical fluctuation, the residual error should probably not be attributed to it.

Finally, a variable or sector may be exogenously set because it would require a major diversion of attention to explain its movement satisfactorily. Examples of this would be the net export balance or the price level. Before a decision was made to estimate price levels directly, consideration was given to the possibility of including an implicit model of price determination by treating the GNP price deflator as the residual variable.

Given the expenditure and income sectors of the model, the determination of a residual price level would be simple in principle. An expenditure identity defines real gross national product, while an income identity sets the current dollar level of GNP. A residual equation could define the GNP implicit price index as the ratio of current to real gross national product. In practice, the solution for the residual is complicated since price indices appear in the denominators of numerous expressions throughout the model. Other price levels could be defined relative to the GNP deflator.

Preliminary simulation experiments using a general price level as the residual led to unsatisfactory results: the model did not converge easily to a solution; once found, the solution values were highly unstable.

Far better results are obtained when the residual is defined as a simple statistical discrepancy between the income and expenditure sides of the model. Not only is the predictive power of the model considerably enhanced on both the income and the expenditure sides, but also the residual itself is held to a respectably low level. In simulations of a preliminary form of the model for the years 1960 through 1965, the statistical discrepancy between income and expenditure sides averaged less than $1.5 billion in absolute value. Given these results, the residual was left as a statistical discrepancy.

VALUES OF EXOGENOUS VARIABLES: 1968–72

In order to conduct simulation experiments, it was necessary to specify values through 1972 for all exogenous variables which appear in the model. The basic assumptions used are listed in Table A5.1, given a continuation of the war in Indochina. Deviations from these assumptions in specific simulations are noted in chapter 5.

TABLE A5.1. EXOGENOUS VARIABLES

Basic assumptions for 1968–72, given a continuation of the war in Indochina. Policy changes to be defined as explicit deviations from these assumptions.

Variable	Assumption
ARMY	Hold constant at 1968 level
BPIA	Continuance of amount specified in 1967 revised law
$DEFC_{58}$	Real defense expenditures held at 1968 levels, i.e., $DEFC_{58} = 0$ beginning in 1969
EAO	5.43 percent decline per year, 1968–72
EAWS	2.26 percent decline per year, 1968–72
EG	5.5 percent increase per year, 1969–72
ENTF	Hold at 16 billion, 1969–72
ERES	Zero, 1967–72
ESEL	Hold at 1962–66 average of 6,209, 1967–72
EXEM	Hold at $600
$EXIM_{58}$	Zero, 1969–72
GGP_{58}	4.8 percent increase per year, 1969–72
GOV_{58}	Nondefense portion 6.73 percent increase per year, average gain 1963–68
IPNI	10 percent increase per year, as in 1963–67
IPS	Constant at 0.3, 1968 value
IVA	Hold at −1.45, 1963–68 average
I3DF	Publicly held debt 1 percent increase per year; interest rate constant at 6.0 percent
I35	Constant at 6.0 percent
OASC	Increases 0.001 per year, 1966–72
OASW	1967 revised law remains in effect
OLI	9.4 percent increase per year, average for 1958–67
POP	Average of projections C, D in ERP,* Table B-21
POPF	Continues 1960–65 growth rate
PP14	Hold at 98.5 percent of ERP,* Table B-21, projection for 14 and over
PP65	Hold at 1965 level of 96 percent of ERP*, Table B-21, data and projection for 65 and over

TABLE A5.1. (cont.)

P14F	51.5 percent of *PP14*
P14M	48.5 percent of *PP14*
P19F	Hold at 48.8 percent of ERP,* Table B-21, projection for population aged 14–19
P19M	Hold at 47.85 percent of ERP,* Table B-21, projection for population aged 14–19
P65F	Hold at 56 percent of *PP65*
P65M	Hold at 44 percent of *PP65*
RIP	Increases total of 20.3 percent in 5 years, same as 1962–67
STAT	Set at zero, excluding residual discrepancy generated in model
SUB	Hold at 1.0 billion, all years
TGMF	Tax rate constant, motor fuel usage increases 5.1 percent per year
TRB	Increases 0.1 billion per year
TRO	8.7 percent increase per year
TROA	Revised 1967 law remains in force
TRU	Hold at 0.022 level
TXCP	Hold at 0.48 in absence of tax surcharge; increased 10 percent for surcharge, 1968 and subsequent years
TXPM	Hold nominal rate constant; assume 0.002 upward drift in effective rate, consistent with 6 percent annual rise in current dollar median income. Assigned values for 1966–72, respectively, are 0.157, 0.159, 0.161, 0.163, 0.165, 0.167, 0.169, in absence of tax surcharge; adjusted upward for surcharge, 7.5 percent in 1968, 10 percent in subsequent years.
WG	9.1 percent increase per year (current dollars)

Economic Report of the President. 1969.